BLACK PRINT WITH
A WHITE CARNATION

WOMEN IN THE WEST

SERIES EDITORS

Sarah J. Deutsch
Duke University

Margaret D. Jacobs
University of Nebraska, Lincoln

Charlene L. Porsild
University of New Mexico

Vicki L. Ruiz
University of California, Irvine

Elliott West
University of Arkansas

Black Print with a White Carnation

MILDRED BROWN AND THE OMAHA STAR NEWSPAPER, 1938–1989

Amy Helene Forss

UNIVERSITY OF NEBRASKA PRESS
LINCOLN AND LONDON

© 2013 by the Board of Regents of the University of Nebraska. Chapter 5 was previously published as "Mildred Brown and the De Porres Club: Collective Activism in Omaha, Nebraska's Near North Side, 1947–1960" in *Nebraska History* 91, nos. 3 and 4 (Fall/Winter 2010): 190–205. Used with permission. All rights reserved. Manufactured in the United States of America. ∞

Library of Congress Cataloging-in-Publication Data
Forss, Amy Helene.
Black print with a white carnation: Mildred Brown and the Omaha star newspaper, 1938–1989 / Amy Helene Forss.
pages cm—(Women in the West)
Includes bibliographical references and index.
ISBN 978-0-8032-4690-4 (pbk.: alk. paper)—ISBN 978-0-8032-4955-4 (epub)—ISBN 978-0-8032-4956-1 (mobi)—ISBN 978-0-8032-4954-7 (pdf) 1. Brown, Mildred Dee, 1905–1989. 2. African American women newspaper editors—Nebraska—Omaha—Biography. 3. Newspaper editors—Nebraska—Omaha—Biography. 4. African American newspapers—Nebraska—Omaha. 5. Omaha star. I. Title.
PN4874.B7815F67 2013
070.92—dc23   [B]   2013024669

Set in Garamond Premier Pro by Hannah Gokie.
Designed by A. Shahan.

I wish to dedicate this book to family: Reba Shelton, Mildred Brown's ninety-eight-year-old "country cousin" who othermothered me as a granddaughter, and to my husband, Dave, and my daughters, Leigh, Kim, Megan, and Samantha. Their willingness to listen to me talk endlessly about Mildred Brown and their continuous supply of positive energy made this project a reality.

Vi amo.

Contents

List of Illustrations	viii
List of Tables	viii
Preface	ix
Acknowledgments	xi
Introduction	1

PART 1. Laying the Foundation

   1. A Family of Fighters   21
   2. Involving the Community   43
   3. Politics of Respectability   59

PART 2. Ensuring Her Success

   4. Working within Her Space   83
   5. Collective Activism and the De Porres Club   101
   6. Restricted Housing and 'Rithmetic   123

PART 3. Transferring Ownership to the Community

   7. Changing Strategies for Changing Times   143
   8. The Death of an Icon   165

Notes	179
Bibliography	211
Index	233

Illustrations

Following page 114
1. Mildred Brown in front of the *Omaha Star* building
2. Mayor Mike Boyle presenting plaque to Mildred Brown
3. Somerville Courthouse, Somerville, Alabama
4. Louisville and Nashville Railroad Company train station
5. Miles Memorial College, Fairfield, Alabama
6. Malone AME Church, Sioux City, Iowa
7. Downtown Omaha, Nebraska, circa 1900
8. Lynching death of Will Brown
9. Intersection of Twenty-Fourth and Lake Streets
10. *Omaha Star* newspaper carriers
11. Mildred Brown's business card
12. Mildred Brown in her *Omaha Star* home
13. Mildred Brown in her *Omaha Star* office
14. Father Markoe and Mildred Brown
15. Jewell Building, northern Omaha
16. President Lyndon Baines Johnson and Mildred Brown
17. The Near North Side neighborhood burning
18. Littleton Alston's bust of Mildred Brown
19. Mildred Brown standing between images of her mother and father

Tables

1. Nonwhite-white segregation indices by year   160

Preface

Over the past two centuries several dozen black women have improved the newspaper business, but very few of their accomplishments reside in monographs. This book is a step toward rectifying their overlooked situation. It examines the historic life of Mildred Dee Brown, cofounder, owner, publisher, and editor of the *Omaha Star* newspaper, while telling the story of her times. Through the use of more than 150 oral histories, black weeklies and a few dailies, and documents from city, state, and federal levels of government, this book builds on and contributes to previous studies of African American and women's history. Brown's strong family background; deliberate involvement with the black community in Omaha, Nebraska; usage of the politics of respectability; knowledge through practical application and formal education; community collective activism; racial solidarity; and ability to change strategies ensured her status and her newspaper's longevity in the city's black enclave. During Brown's fifty-one-year tenure with the *Omaha Star*, she successfully challenged racial discrimination, unfair employment practices, restrictive housing covenants, the segregated public school system, and a freeway dividing the minority neighborhood. The Near North Side's matriarch, with her trademark white carnation corsage, was an iconic leader, and her legacy, the *Omaha Star*, continues as a source of racial uplift for Omaha's black community.

Acknowledgments

The adage it takes a village to raise a child is also true for a book. I started with Mildred Brown: I visited her grave, formally introduced myself, and asked for her permission to do this project. Then I contacted her relatives, who were scattered throughout the United States. They extended courtesies to me far surpassing Mildred's southern hospitality roots. I cannot say thank you enough to her great-nephews Andrew Battiste and William Brown; her nephew Bennie Drew Brown Jr.; her cousins David Winton, Druella Borders, and William Taylor Breeding for their mental and physical guided tours; her ex-husband's son, Shirl Edward Gilbert II, and daughter, Rosalyn Gilbert; her othermothered son, Marvin Kellogg Sr.; and grandsons, Marvin Kellogg Jr., Dale Kellogg, and Kenneth Kellogg; sister-in-laws Catherine Phillips and Harriet Hannah; and nieces Kathryn Battiste and Marguerita Washington. Their familial stories and reminiscences of Mildred gave me a fairly good idea of her.

But Mildred, also known as Miss Brown and to a special few as Millie, was a complicated woman. It took more than 150 interviews to reconstruct her. Many of the interviewees were in their seventies, eighties, and nineties, but they graciously spoke with me for hours at a time and shared their memories, photographs, diaries, and, of course, *Omaha Star* newspaper clippings. The North Omaha cooperation was substantial, and I need to thank several people individually, such as Rudy Smith, Matt Holland, Robert Armstrong, Archie Godfrey, Buddy Hogan, David Mason, Warren Taylor, Tommie Wilson, Mary Green Parks, La Veeda Banks, and Cathy Hughes, for consenting to multiple interviews; to give a heartfelt hug to Bertha Calloway,

Robert Samuels, Gwen Foxall, Royce Keller, Shirley Harrison, Katherine Fletcher, Bob Rodgers, and Korea Stowdarski for inviting me into their homes and lives; to acknowledge the factual and spiritual guidance from Reverends Reynolds, Vavrina, McSwain, McCaslin, McCullough, and Menyweather-Woods; and to offer an upward posthumous thanks to retired attorney Truman Clare for unraveling pages of Douglas County Courthouse legal jargon with me. I could not have accomplished this book without each named person and the trust and assistance of many others, such as academic mentors Drs. Margaret Jacobs and Harl Dalstrom; archivists John Allison, Joellen ElBashir, Gary Rosenberg, Gordon Rieber, and Les Valentine; Metropolitan Community College's Randy Schmailzl, Jane Franklin, Dennis Smith, Edie Sample, Jim Van Arsdall, Art Durand, Mary Lyons-Carmona, and Linda Milton; and University of Nebraska Press history acquisitions editor Bridget Barry for believing in my project, associate project editor Sara Springsteen for supervising it, and eagle-eyed copyeditor Susan Silver for making it a joy all over again. The community village was filled with numerous industrial and supportive residents.

BLACK PRINT WITH
A WHITE CARNATION

Introduction

On June 1, 1984, Mildred Brown slowly walked onto the stage dais of the Red Lion Inn, the finest downtown hotel in Omaha, Nebraska. She looked out at the multitude of white and black citizens facing her and said, "Am I dreaming?" Standing at the podium, serenaded by the sounds of the famous Preston Love Sr. Band, she looked radiant in her scarlet red gown and shimmering silver sequined evening jacket. Her trademark oversized white carnation corsage decorated her left shoulder. Brown, the cofounder, owner, publisher, and editor of the *Omaha Star* black newspaper, was the honored guest of 470 residents of the city of Omaha, most of whom were from northern Omaha, better known as the Near North Side. Harold Andersen, the white editor of the mainstream *Omaha World-Herald* newspaper, and Ben Gray, a local black television talk show host, served as the dinner's emcees. The men introduced each other to the interracial crowd. Gray incorrectly introduced Harold Andersen as Harold Washington, who at that time was Chicago's current and first black mayor. Andersen covered Gray's faux pas with a clever quip. He asked the television reporter if he wanted to meet his wife, Marian Andersen, as in Marian Anderson, the black operatic singer. The audience responded with a few nervous chuckles and laughs. Brown's former second husband, Noel Maximilian "Max" Brownell; her brother Bennie Brown Sr.; her nephew Bennie Brown Jr.; and her niece Marguerita Washington nodded approvingly at the head table. Ruth Harris Kellogg, Brown's beloved foster daughter, was not present; she had died seven months prior to the festive event. Her voice would not be among the videotaped speeches or thirty-five minutes of individual tributes to Brown.

Mayor Mike Boyle joined Brown at the podium and presented her with a "key to the city" plaque. The award added one more accolade to the 150 awards she had amassed during her lifetime. After the applause died down and the crowd started to disperse, Bennie Brown Jr. stood up from his chair and strode out of the hotel that Saturday evening, "impressed that his aunt was so highly thought of in Omaha."[1]

Brown was not just respected by the residents of Omaha; she was also the black matriarch of Omaha's Near North Side, the historically black part of town. She used her newspaper, the *Omaha Star*, as an activist tool to provide a voice for the black community and to conduct diplomatic forms of communication between the black and white residents of Omaha. For more than fifty years Brown and the *Star*, which most citizens of Omaha saw as synonymous, sought to uplift the black community with positive weekly news and successfully challenged racial discrimination, unfair employment practices in North Omaha, restrictive housing covenants, Omaha's public segregated school system, and the city's urban renewal. The iconoclastic female leader accomplished this impressive feat by nurturing, challenging, and speaking for her black readership from the moment she cofounded the *Omaha Star* on July 9, 1938, until the minute she died on November 2, 1989.

Posthumously, Mildred Brown holds the record for operating the longest running black newspaper founded by a black woman in the United States. This is an even more amazing feat when considering that all the other twentieth century's black women newspaper owners inherited their weeklies from their husbands. Today, what she referred to as "my paper" remains the only black newspaper in the state of Nebraska. Brown accomplished her lifetime feat as a result of a strong family foundation and through a variety of strategies: deliberately engaging with the black community, employing the politics of respectability, learning business through practical application and education, supporting community collective activism, encouraging racial solidarity, and changing strategies to fit the times. Her story illustrates a larger history dating from the nineteenth-century era of

Reconstruction and Jim Crow to the twentieth century's Great Migration, World Wars I and II, the Red Scare, the civil rights and black power movements, desegregation, and urban renewal. This project offers an examination of African American history during a century of political and social events and an overall view of the impact of the black press through a black newspaper woman's narrative.

Mildred Brown's story begins with her interracial common-law family in nineteenth-century Morgan County, Alabama. William and Sopharina Breeding, Mildred's great-grandparents, had witnessed the end of slavery, the reintegration of eleven former Confederate states into the Union, and the ratification of the Fourteenth and Fifteenth Amendments. But as an interracial couple, they knew that the federal guarantee of black citizenship and voting rights for black men did not permit them to marry in Alabama. While mixed "race" relationships were not uncommon in the South, many white Americans "believed that interracial marriage was unnatural" and "assumed that the marriage of one white man to one white woman was the only kind of marriage worthy of the name." Therefore, most white Americans did not question antimiscegenation laws banning interracial marriages between 1864 and 1967. But plenty of white men ran afoul of miscegenation laws. Their troubles did not happen while they were cohabitating with black women, but after they died. Most twentieth-century white Alabamans would have labeled Rev. Millard Breeding an "illegitimate Negro," but Brown's grandfather insisted in the successful 1899 *Breeding v. Breeding* court case that because he and his three brothers were the progeny of William Breeding, a white southern plantation owner, and Sopharina, an enslaved black woman, they were the rightful heirs to his property. The antimiscegenation laws that caused the trial became the core of Jim Crow, a center from which "a multitude of prohibitions and regulation radiated outward."[2]

State and local segregation statutes, also known as Jim Crow laws, encouraged racism by separating public transportation, churches, schools, housing, employment, and even cemeteries. Millard Breeding and his brothers, who inherited their father's property, became part of the black upper-middle class, but like every other person of color, they were forced to abide by segregation. These laws were not intended for the black person's protection and safeguarding but as a source of oppression and humiliation. The Thirteenth Amendment disallowed slavery, but post-Reconstruction segregation reinforced the daily reminder of strict containment and control of black Americans. Once the U.S. Supreme Court's *Plessy v. Ferguson* decision validated segregation's discriminatory practices as "separate but equal," it eroded the rights blacks gained during Reconstruction. Southern states exacerbated the inequality by devising a number of means to disenfranchise black people.[3]

Voiceless and disfranchised, black Americans, 90 percent of whom lived in the South in 1900, actively changed their lives by moving north during the Great Migration. According to the federal government statistic table in *Negroes in the United States*, the total number of black Americans living in the South was 1.9 million, and of this group approximately 1 million people migrated to the North and 300,000 relocated to the West. Between 1900 and 1930 this first wave of the Great Migration's rural families, including Mildred Brown and her family, migrated primarily for political equality and partially because of crop failures causing employment declines. By the time of the Great Depression, cotton crops were no longer yielding profits for two-thirds of the southern black farmers, cash tenants, and sharecroppers, which prompted another half a million southern migrants to move to the northern promised land of employment opportunities. The massive national movement was avidly supported by the black press. Urban black daily and weekly newspapers offered the key to relocation. The *Chicago Defender*, the *Baltimore Afro-American*, and the *Pittsburgh Courier* encouraged, cajoled, and demanded that their black southern readers go north and prosper. Black newspaper publishers were convinced that northern cities were the solution for the oppressed black citizen; the metropolis was the black person's land of opportunity.[4]

The northern black migrant worker replaced the previously unlimited supply of European immigrants working as unskilled and cheap laborers. The federal government's 1917 Immigration Act, enacted the same year as the Espionage Act, "safeguarded" the American population by curtailing much of European immigration with its literacy test and the exclusion of most Asians and Pacific Islanders. The older generation of naturalized Americans were now serving overseas as soldiers in World War I. Hundreds of northern factories, stockyards, and railroad companies dispatched agents to recruit black laborers from the South. In 1919, at the end of the Great War, Chicago's average black worker was earning forty-eight cents an hour. It was a wage unheard of in the Deep South. The passing of the 1924 National Origins Act established strict immigration quotas, which created another larger wave of the Great Migration. In the 1940s and extending to the end of the 1970s, a second Great Migration of almost 5 million blacks migrated from the South to the North. Approximately 1.5 million people left southern states for better employment during the World War II years, and another 3.5 million black Americans moved seeking political empowerment during the civil rights and black power movements and the urban renewal years of the 1960s and 1970s. The first and second Great Migrations resulted in the proletarianization and urbanization of black Americans.[5]

When Mildred Brown and Dr. Shirley Edward Gilbert, her first husband, relocated from Alabama to the Midwest, the regions had already witnessed the largest influx of southern migrants participating in the Great Migration. Brown, a certified teacher, and her PhD-educated, middle-class husband wanted more opportunities than were available to them in the South. Her husband was one of less than 1 percent of black doctors in the United States. The movement of rural black Americans into U.S. cities caused some of the country's worst outbreaks of violence. Black migrants living in Omaha, and most other black residents of large Midwest towns, were eyewitnesses to the backlash against the first wave of migrants. The nadir of violence against migrants occurred during the so-called Red Summer of 1919, aptly named by Harlem Renaissance "father" James Weldon Johnson to pertain to the multiple incidences of bloodshed in Washington DC, East St. Louis, Chicago, Knoxville, and Omaha and not to refer to the federal government's first Red Scare looking for black and white Americans joining the "red" communist Industrial Workers of the World.[6]

Twenty-six race riots occurred during the Red Summer's months of violence, and one of the worst was in Omaha. William Brown, a black meatpacking worker (who was no relation to Mildred Brown), became a lynching victim after he allegedly raped white nineteen-year-old Agnes Loebeck. Victor Rosewater, the white *Omaha Bee* editor and publisher, explained Brown's "crime" in an article titled "Black Beast First Sticks-Up Couple." City of Omaha readers learned how a crowd of angry white citizens surrounded the recently constructed two-million-dollar Douglas County courthouse where Brown was being held and forcibly removed him. During the fateful evening of September 28, 1919, William Brown died a brutal death. A skeleton crew of police officers attempted to stop his demise, and Maj. Gen. Leonard Wood, former commander of the Rough Riders and chief of staff of the U.S. Army, led a battalion of national guardsmen to Omaha, but they arrived too late. Riddled with more than a thousand bullets, Brown's corpse swung from a telephone pole at Eighteenth and Harney Streets. Hours later his murderers dragged his body through the city streets, burned his torso, and then, with cigars in hand, posed for pictures.[7] Lynching, by definition, is a hanging without a trial. Despite white rationales, lynching was not a random act of violence perpetrated by crazed vigilantes. Racist whites "homed in on [alleged] rape as the ultimate expression of the blacks' supposed incapacity for self-control." The barbaric, almost carnival-like ritual of lynching supplied sadistic whites with the necessary means of supposedly protecting white womanhood while instilling fear in the black community for threatening their white social, political, and economic manhood.[8]

Despite the fact that the *Omaha Monitor*, the city's sole black newspaper during this decade, denounced Will Brown's murder by printing the circumstances of the meat packer's demise and the destruction of the mob rioting, it only vaguely hinted at the involvement of Tom Dennison, Omaha's political boss. Orville Menard's *Political Bossism in Mid-America*, written in 1989, validated what the black and white population in Omaha had already known for years, even though few were bold enough to voice their opinions. It was not uncommon in postwar United States for conservative Democrats, like Dennison, to cause riots for political reasons, especially when it meant convincing an ignorant public to vote for machine candidates. The racist Jim Crow attitudes prevalent in the early twentieth century allowed Dennison, and men like him, to get away with orchestrated violence.

Major General Wood, whose soldiers stood on guard at Twenty-Fourth and Lake Streets following the riot, blamed Brown's grisly death on the communist elements of the "Industrial Workers of the World and its red flag," although the U.S. Army concluded that Brown's murder "was a lynching not a race riot." In the aftermath of Brown's demise, Omaha's black population relocated from the city's downtown and southern stockyard areas to the isolated, safer confines of the European Jewish neighborhood in North Omaha. The southern end of the Near North Side's Twenty-Fourth and Lake Streets became a thriving segregated community.[9]

Racial tensions continued to flare over employers hiring black men for menial labor jobs in the 1920s. Black men in Omaha gained employment with large industrial outfits, such as Union Pacific railroad yards, Philip D. Armour, Gustavus Swift, Michael Cudahy's meatpacking plants, and William Paxton and John A. Creighton's Union Stock Yard Company. Omaha's African Americans laborers, similar to minority workers in other urban cities, were "used as scabs, or strikebreakers, to force mostly [European] immigrant laborers to accept low wages and grueling working conditions." This volatile situation only increased the mounting racial tension. White workers living in the city of Omaha resented their fellow black workers, regardless if they were temporary or full-time. The upshot of the economically hostile situation was residential segregation.[10]

Housing became a chief means of "controlling black spatial mobility and fostering segregation as blacks migrated en masse to cities" during the World War I years. Home-owner covenants and the National

Introduction 7

Association of Real Estate Boards developed five patterns of residential segregation to ensure the races did not mix: all-white and all-black blocks, legalized housing segregation through city council districts, designated neighborhoods by the majority of residents, segregation by ownership rights, and occupancy through home-owner associations. The Federal Housing Administration forced subdivision contractors and home builders between 1935 to 1937 to comply with race-restrictive guidelines, thereby endorsing racist state actions. The practice of redlining, a banking practice in which loan officers denied individuals mortgage applications based on their skin color or the racial composition of the neighborhood in which they wished to buy a home, was prevalent in the neighborhoods surrounding the Near North Side of Omaha. This isolated urban black community needed a public champion and a voice to fight for its rights. A local black press would provide it.[11]

National black newspapers fought against racism and discrimination in the 1930s and 1940s with nationwide consumer campaigns, such as Ira Kemp's "Don't Buy Where You Can't Work" boycotts and "Spend Your Money Where You Can Work" campaigns. Through the coordination of the black press, minority communities realized their racial spending power in New York City and then in other participating cities, including Omaha. Buying power became black America's leverage for equality and inclusion. Selective-patronage campaigns forced white businesses to comply with fair employment practices. Mildred Brown understood the importance of these types of nonviolent economic strategies. Her uncle, Andrew Cato Brown, was the founder of the Colored Merchant's Association in Birmingham, Alabama. The association successfully established black grocery chain stores in Birmingham, Dallas, New York, Richmond, Detroit, Chicago, and Omaha from the 1920s to 1936. The key to these competitive stores was cooperative buying and group advertising. The Alabama-based association served as a model for potential black professional advancement in every neighborhood. White businesses began to see urban black consumers as financially noteworthy individuals. African

American city dwellers were no longer just considered poor migrants; they were the future black middle class. Collective spending, or lack of spending during a boycott, demonstrated the black community's regional and nationwide power.[12]

The *Pittsburgh Courier* started its successful Double V campaign on February 7, 1942. Brown, who always wanted the *Star* to be a maverick press like the *Pittsburgh Courier*, joined other black weeklies and her competitor, the *Omaha Guide*, in the campaign. World War II's Double V campaign created an instance of national black solidarity through the black press. Angered by the simultaneous hypocrisy of fighting fascism abroad while fighting racism at home, James G. Thompson, a black cafeteria employee in Wichita, Kansas, wrote a letter titled "Should I Sacrifice to Live Half American" to the *Pittsburgh Courier* newspaper. It became the most famous black editorial of the twentieth century. Thompson challenged other *Pittsburgh Courier* readers to accept Roosevelt's Double V campaign, but instead of the double Vs the president alluded to, as in victory in war and victory in the 1944 election, Thompson suggested his double Vs stand for "victory over our enemies abroad . . . and victory over our enemies from within." Each edition of Brown's newspaper carried the Double V emblem in the top right-hand corner of the front page. While black communities throughout the United States applauded the newspaper campaign against military subjugation, the loyalty of Brown and other black participants in the "crusading" or "fighting" press, as the minority dailies and weeklies became known during this time, concerned the government.[13]

The U.S. Justice Department, led by FBI director John Edgar Hoover, responded to the Double V campaign. Thomas Borstelmann's *The Cold War and the Color Line* describes Hoover as "a fierce anti-Communist and a segregationist of well-known racial prejudice." Hoover deliberately launched a nationwide investigation of black press editors, such as the *Pittsburgh Courier*'s Percival Prattis, the *Chicago Defender*'s John Sengstacke, and the *Omaha Star*'s Mildred Brown. Her FBI file, like those of her journalist contemporaries, numbered in the thousands of pages, but she ignored the federal agents watching her business and continued running the *Star* in a professional manner. Eight government agencies routinely investigated rumors of subversive black newspapers: the Federal Bureau of Investigation, Justice Department, Post Office, Office of Facts and Figures, Office of Censorship, Office of War Information, U.S. Army, and the War Production Board. The government agencies threatened the freedom of the black press by indicting several smaller black newspapers for war violations and revoking their second-class postage permits, which were necessary for sending newspapers through the country's mail. Hoover's sting operation involved almost every black newspaper, including the *Omaha Guide* and *Omaha Star* weeklies. Using words such as espionage, sedition, and suppression, agents reported any inconsistencies in the newspapers or possible affiliations with the American Communist Party. Black nationalist leaders, including W. E. B. Du Bois, encouraged the wartime Double V effort and did not demand the black press issue a "close ranks" retraction like he did during World War I. In the FBI Hoover soon realized he could push the matter only so far, especially since thirteen million people of color might turn against the U.S. war efforts abroad. It was not until after World War II ended that the FBI director and the federal government realized the enormity of change possible. A new generation of blacks who were no longer willing to tolerate segregation, lack of voting rights, and other indignities would eventually desegregate the United States. However, the black press first became the target of anti-Communist reactionaries.[14]

During the Red Scare in the 1950s, the House Un-American Activities Committee worked hard to undermine and discredit integrationist associations by attempting to paint them "red." Hoover, the previous mastermind of the first Red Scare during and after World War I, again chose to monitor the black press. Whether or not the weeklies and dailies were considered radical "depended more on the fears, stereotypes, and prejudices of agents and bureaucrats" than the black press's editorial content. The American Communist Party did attract some black nationalist and desegregation activists because its antiracist agenda rejected gradualism and publicly fought for black equal rights. But few black leaders, such as socialist A. Philip Randolph, encouraged joining the Soviet-based political party; Randolph disagreed with the party's ideological conformity and strict discipline regime. Whatever their position on communism, every black leader agreed something had to be done on a nationwide level to uplift the American black community.[15]

The national black community was assisted by numerous northern Catholics in its fight against segregation in the late 1940s. The anti-Catholic prejudice, which had once fueled Ku Klux Klan membership rolls, had dissipated after World War II, and much like the Euro-American Jewish immigrant population, Euro-American Catholics had enough ethnic white privilege to challenge their segregation. Northern Catholic congregants had empathy for the black neighborhood because they had experienced xenophobic discrimination and limited opportunities of menial employment. These naturalized Catholics eventually assimilated, acculturated, bought homes in low-income and working-class parishes, and, according to church canon law, "served all souls living within its [parish] boundaries." Catholic home owners tended to permanently stay within their parishes, even with the encroachment of the black community. Interaction between the two minority communities was inevitable. It was not surprising that the Catholic archdiocese, which had an association with Brown, constructed Saint Benedict the Moor Parish and High School one block north of the *Omaha Star* office. The *Star* publisher's connection with Father Edward Flanagan's Catholic Boys Town home and school was established in the 1930s when she contacted the Jesuit priest about caring for several black Omaha youths. The new school building became necessary after the Near North Side's black Catholic students were denied membership in white Omaha parishes. The archdiocese viewed Saint Benedict's as only a "social segregation," a temporary situation in which the community's black Catholics were more comfortable in isolation but still regarded by the church as equals. It was not unusual for priests, such as Father James Groppi in Milwaukee and Father John

Markoe in Omaha, to align with local black leaders and fight against deliberate segregation. Markoe's interracial De Porres Club along with Brown's *Star* embarked on a grassroots movement for fair employment in Omaha's black neighborhood. The two entities staged successful boycotts, sit-ins, and picketing ten years before the national civil rights movement.[16]

The countrywide fight for civil rights was made easier after the Supreme Court ruled in 1954 that "separate but unequal" educational facilities were unconstitutional in the *Brown v. Board of Education, Topeka, Kansas* decision. Within one year, Dr. Martin Luther King Jr. and his wife, Coretta Scott King, who was a close friend of Brown's, were leading the Montgomery bus boycott in 1955. No documentation exists to show a possible connection between the Alabama protest and Brown's earlier successful 1952–54 bus boycott in Omaha, but her picketing rhetoric and organizational style were strikingly similar to those later used by the Kings. It would be hard not to recall the famous photograph of King and the white reverend Glenn Smiley being greeted by the white bus driver's "we are glad to have you" smile as they sat side by side on December 21, 1956. King's Southern Christian Leadership Conference and the Committee of Racial Equality, which Brown joined and became a prominent Omaha member, were already committed to civil rights several years prior to the southern black sit-ins of the early 1960s. From these associations came the roots of other activism, which resulted in the Civil Rights Act of 1957, the first piece of civil rights legislature passed since the Civil Rights Act of 1875. It supposedly protected the constitutional rights of voters, but violence caused by city and state police and the Ku Klux Klan, which had a solid history in twentieth-century Nebraska, kept most blacks from voting at the polls. Indeed, several black activists, including Medgar Evers, died trying to uphold the legislation.[17] Frustration with the national challenges of protecting bludgeoned freedom riders and the bloodied protestors at the Edmund Pettus Bridge outside of Selma, Alabama, led President Lyndon Baines Johnson to demand on national television that Congress pass a national voting rights act:

"We have already waited a hundred years and more since equality was promised . . . and the time for waiting is gone."[18] Johnson's attempt at staving off a militant civil rights confrontation was an excellent start, but it was inadequate.

The subsequent rise of the black power movement in the mid to late 1960s awakened the dormant ties of black radicalism and black separatism. Black power provided an outlet for the frustrated urban black American man through black masculine ideology. It did not promote black women's leadership. Mildred Brown's status in the Omaha black community was sorely tested during this time. Even Gloria Richardson, a longtime national African American civil rights protestor, "experienced the wrath of the new male activists" when she was labeled as a castrator of black men. Many Americans, black and white, agreed with Daniel Moynihan's sociological report, *The Negro Family*, which contended that black matriarchal women, like Brown, were responsible for the poverty experienced by the black community. These women supposedly marginalized black men. According to this theory, the black matriarch was responsible for the emasculated angry black man fighting for his civil rights. Huey Newton and Bobby Seale's Black Panther Party for Self-Defense encouraged the black male domination of civil rights by having members read Mao Tse-tung's *Little Red Book* and reciting the philosophies of Karl Marx, Frantz Fanon, Che Guevara, and Malcolm X, who originated in Omaha. The party emphasized "self-determination, community empowerment, and separatism," while rejecting the mainstream ideals of white middle-class society and the nonviolent strategies practiced by interracial civil rights organizations. Hoover labeled the organization and its philosophies "the greatest threat to the internal security of the country." His words proved prophetic, but not because of its militant stance.[19]

It was a case of frustrated and bitter black Americans reacting with violence to the slow pace of progress toward racial equality. Between 1965 and 1969 there were hundreds of disturbances and approximately 150 riots in cities throughout the United States. One of these race rebellions amounted to the worst destruction in black Omaha's history. It was the Red Summer of 1919 in reverse. Instead of white mobs attacking black businesses, black mobs ransacked white stores. "Pictures of flaming cities, looting and embattled mobs, and smoking ruins were regularly featured in newspapers and on television." The rioters in cities like Omaha were frustrated with pent-up desire for civil rights and the American Dream. Retail stores, the inescapable daily reminder of ghetto residents' economic deprivation, suffered a much greater proportion of damage. Looting and burning of white businesses operating in the black neighborhood gave rioters the chance to destroy credit ledgers as well. The National Negro Business League, which originally included one of Mildred Brown's relatives, absolved the rioters by saying it was "naive for anyone to expect the very poorest of the American poor to remain docile and content in their poverty." While Brown agreed with similar sentiments concerning residents of northern Omaha's minority population, she disagreed with the actions of the national black community and refused to print articles on civil disorder and destruction.[20] President Johnson, who visited with Mildred Brown four times at the White House during the turbulent 1960s, created the National Advisory Commission on Civil Disorders to answer three questions: "What happened? Why did it happen? What can be done to prevent it from happening again?"[21] The Kerner Report, published five months earlier than expected due to the urgency of the situation, concluded that the United States was dividing into two separate but unequal white and black societies because white racism had racially divided the country.[22]

Congress responded to the Kerner Report by passing the Fair Housing Act and the Housing and Urban Development Act of 1968. The latter act completed what the Housing Act of 1949 began by rehabilitating older housing and creating twenty-six million public housing units. The promise of new housing only partially alleviated the frustration of the black community. The Federal Housing Administration invested in black and racially mixed neighborhoods, but urban city developers still viewed the black population as a poor investment. The massive public housing projects created in every major city became Trojan gift horses by the 1960s. Omaha, with its dilapidated federal housing projects, was no exception. Years of discriminatory employment and restrictive covenants resulted in Near North Side black residents living in decaying communities. Brown referred to the projects as "the dagger in the heart of north Omaha." The U.S. Supreme Court's *Shelley v. Kraemer* previously decided restrictive covenants were illegal in 1948, but it seemed to make no difference. The Federal Housing Administration created a "hierarchy of neighborhoods" where many blacks hoped to buy homes, but few realized their dreams until the 1970s or 1980s.[23]

While the number of black suburbanites doubled during the 1970s and 1980s as minority residents moved into previously denied neighborhoods, segregation persisted in the schools. The city of Omaha, similar to most major cities in the United States, was still ignoring the federal desegregation mandate. After all, the 1954 *Brown* decision addressed only public school systems, and its "all deliberate speed" enforcement lacked the urgency of serious legislation. It was not until the Supreme Court's 1974 *Miliken v. Bradley* decision that the battle against educational segregation ended. The Omaha public school system, forced by legal mandate, desegregated schools, staff, and student body in 1976. Norbert Schuerman, head of the Omaha school desegregation task force, commended Brown and her *Star* for supporting him and thus streamlining the process for the black community. But as Michael Harrington concludes in *The Other America*, it was possible "to have a public policy for integrated schooling, but if the school districts [were] themselves a product of residential discrimination," the schools continued as Jim Crow constructions anyway, even when the federal government said otherwise.[24]

In the 1970s and 1980s federal construction projects, such as the national urban-redevelopment projects, nicknamed "Negro removal" by the black community, replaced slums and areas considered unfit for human habitation. But the newly created schools and expressways ultimately divided black neighborhoods because the primary concern in most larger mainstream cities was to rebuild, not to help unemployed black citizens. In the late 1970s employment plummeted in mass-production industries, such as the auto industry, the stockyards, and the railroads. The same western Sun Belt, northern Rust Belt, and midwestern Corn Belt employment opportunities that had enticed the participants of the Great Migration disappeared as factories moved away from urban central business districts and relocated in the suburbs of cities. The National Urban League's *The State of Black America*, an annual "state of the black union" address, pronounced 1989, the same year Mildred Brown died, as a challenging but surmountable year. It marked another year in the black community's constant struggle against racism and denied opportunities, but the black population was keeping its eye on the prize by seeking equality and inclusion in every sector of American life.²⁵

While Mildred Brown's great-grandparents lived through the late nineteenth century's Reconstruction and the beginning of the Jim Crow laws, she lived through the modern litany of twentieth-century markers from the Great Migration to urban renewal. The eight chapters of this monograph chronologically explore her role in these events while answering the question of how she maintained the success of her black newspaper, the *Omaha Star*, despite over half a century's worth of racial turbulence.

Chapter 1 examines Brown's ancestral family in Alabama. Because her nonconformist great-grandparents and activist grandfather achieved financial stability through Alabama's court system, their descendants, which included Brown's parents, siblings, and herself, benefited from class privileges and, in particular, the gift of higher education. Brown's marriage to Dr. Shirley Edward Gilbert, a black physician, solidified her middle-class status in the black community. Chapter 2 focuses on Mildred Brown Gilbert's successful participation in the Great Migration. She and her husband first migrated to Chicago, Des Moines, and Sioux City. While they resided in this latter northern Iowa city, the Gilberts created the *Silent Messenger* black newspaper for their fellow black congregants at the Malone African Methodist Episcopalian Church. From Sioux City the couple, with their informally adopted daughter, Ruth Harris, moved to Omaha in

1937. As a couple they founded the *Omaha Star* newspaper in 1938. The Gilberts' church, political, and community involvement connected them to the black neighborhood, which in turn boded well for the longevity of the *Star*. Chapter 3 provides an analysis of Mildred Brown through the positive persona of the black matriarch. As a newly divorced woman, Brown continued mothering her daughter and the office staff while acting as the protector of the black community. She built her gendered credibility through the politics of respectability, higher education, and networking with the black male leaders of the Near North Side and white administrators in the city of Omaha. Chapter 4 explores the origination of the national black press and the National Negro Press Association and recounts the history of Omaha's black newspapers and black male publishers. It discusses the role of gender and politics in the newspaper industry. Brown's usage of the *Star* as a tool of positive reporting and racially uplifting articles on the "awareness of self-presentation" provided black migrants and established residents with a sense of economic possibility and physical freedom. Deportment advice columns and excerpts from black etiquette manuals, which were a fairly standard feature in black newspapers, taught Brown's readers that their improved appearance would demonstrate self-respect while registering collective progress and expediting social acceptance in personal and professional situations.

Chapter 5 showcases Brown's involvement with the interracial nondenominational De Porres Club. The combination of the *Star* and the club proved beneficial for northern Omaha, as the two forces successfully combated unfair employment practices and discrimination against the black population of Omaha. This chapter illustrates the Catholic connection with the black community through the strategies created by Father Markoe and Mildred Brown. Chapter 6 explores the end of Omaha's restrictive covenant housing and the desegregation of the Omaha public school system. This chapter examines Brown's gradual political shift from activist to mediator between Omaha's white administration and the local black male dominated organizations in northern Omaha. Chapter 7 focuses on the psychology of Omaha's three race riots in 1966, 1967, and 1969. It demonstrates Brown's strategy adjustments as she worked with white and black administrators to promote a better life for black Omahans. She challenged the black stereotypical imagery created in the *Omaha World-Herald*, the city's sole mainstream daily newspaper, while maintaining the *Star*'s invaluable asset of positive news and informed communication during the open housing crisis and the expressway's division of the black community.[26] Chapter 8 concerns Brown's last years and her decision not to name her successor. It discusses her death and funeral and reflects on her local and political achievements as well as the continuation of her and her newspaper's legacy.

The *Omaha Star* remains Mildred Brown's legacy to the Near North Side of Omaha, Nebraska. It continues to uphold her personal motto: "Dedicated to the service of the people that NO good cause shall lack a champion and that evil shall not go unopposed."[27] As one of the few black newspaper women in the United States printing a black newspaper spanning a half century's worth of human events, Brown occupied a unique historical position. In the 1960s the Kerner Commission concluded that "the world that [mainstream] newspaper and television portray is almost totally white, in both appearance and attitude... as if Negroes do not read the newspapers or watch television, give birth, marry, die, and go to PTA meetings."[28] Mildred Brown, the stylish black activist who always wore a white carnation corsage, and her *Omaha Star* documented the life history of the Near North Side black residents and fought for their civil rights.

Part 1 Laying the Foundation

1

A Family of Fighters

The jury reached their decision. After nine hours of deliberation, Foreman C. T. Burt read the one-sentence verdict written on the torn scrap of lined legal paper: "We the jury find for the plaintiff and that the will is valid." The twelve white jurors concurred that William Breeding did indeed write his last will and testament while he was of sound mind and body and he was not affected by any "undue influence of his beneficiaries." The judge proceeded with the case and awarded William Breeding's estate to his four sons. For a long moment there was silence, and then the contestants' reactions were simultaneous. Amid shouts to burn down the Decatur courthouse building, James Breeding, his siblings, and other assorted relatives, including Sam M. Dunnaway, stormed out of the two-story brick building to file an appeal. Alabama's supreme court in Birmingham would spend several months during the winter of 1900 considering James Breeding's request for the verdict to be overturned, but before spring planting began in 1901, the higher court upheld the lower court's decision. Millard, William Taylor, Wilson, and Gus Breeding were officially and legally recognized as the four biracial heirs of William Breeding, their white plantation father.[1]

Mildred Dee Brown came from a long line of fighters who challenged white supremacy. William Breeding, Brown's white great-grandfather, and Sopharina Breeding, her black great-grandmother, lived and loved openly in Alabama during the Civil War and post–Civil War era but they were forbidden to marry by the state's miscegenation law. Existing as a common-law couple meant cohabiting as an unrecognized family unit. As historian Peggy Pascoe wrote in

What Comes Naturally, "When societies decide who can and who can't legally marry, they determine who is and isn't really part of the family."[2] But Brown's great-grandparents refused to accept this societal racial standard and bequeathed their property to their mixed-race sons. Brown's grandfather, Millard Breeding, son of William and Sopharina and eventually the coexecutor of his father's will, defended his and his brothers' inheritance and championed the legality of interracial unions in their court case, *Breeding v. Breeding*. The estate property they won changed their lives and the lives of their descendants. Along with her portion of the court-awarded land, Mildred Brown inherited the gumption of her great-grandparents and grandfather, which taught her to be a trailblazer in Nebraska, through the medium of her black newspaper, the *Omaha Star*.

Back in the late 1800s, while William and Sopharina Breeding were defying southern mores, one of their sons, Millard Breeding, refused to accept himself as a biracial other. Brown's ancestors were living during a time when mixed children did not inherit their white father's fortunes, especially when their plantation-owner father claimed their enslaved mother as a common-law partner. Interracial sex in the Deep South was common and often tolerated or ignored by the state and local authorities. As Pascoe writes, "The law was usually inclined to step in only when interracial couples began to claim the public respectability and the property and inheritance rights that went with marriage." Indeed, the largest number of court cases involving interracial common-law marriages pertained to inheritance struggles over the estates of white men after their demise. Millard Breeding fought for himself and his siblings, even though by asserting their legal rights, he created a potentially dangerous reaction. His college education, his spiritual standing in a predominantly white community, and his perceptive understanding of the law accomplished a rare David-against-Goliath outcome in Alabama's judicial system. The 1899–1901 probate trial of *Breeding v. Breeding* successfully passed through Alabama's supreme court system literally months before the ascension of Jim Crow laws in mid-1901.[3]

The Breedings' atypical victory began when William Breeding, a former Civil War private in the Confederate "Company E of the 11th Regiment of the 11th Alabama Calvary," met Sopharina. She was the love of Breeding's life and also the slave of William's pale-skinned Irish mother, Telitha Winton Breeding. When Telitha's husband, Samuel Breeding, died in 1852, Telitha inherited his plantation. It included the industrious twenty-one-year-old Sopharina, appraised at $900; her eleven-month-old son, Robert, worth $150 (she had him before she cohabited with William Breeding, and his fate remains unknown); and her thirty-seven-year-old mother, Aggy, who listed at the price of $500. When the Civil War ended in 1865, Sopharina and her mother were no longer enslaved women because of the passage of the Thirteenth Amendment.[4]

Aggy, a resolute woman and Mildred Brown's great-great-grandmother, decided she wanted to be legally married. Aggy became the first married emancipated black woman in Morgan County when she obtained a marriage license for herself and David, her betrothed. An indomitable Aggy must have waited in line for quite some time, since the first sentence on the first page of the Morgan County Colored Marriage License Ledger solemnized the "rites of matrimony between David Breeding (Freedman) and Aggy Breeding (Freedwoman) ... this 26th day of Nov., 1865," before any of the other marriages listed that day. Unfortunately, Sopharina, whom William nicknamed Sophy, was unable to obtain a marriage license. Her interracial relationship prevented legal marriage. Alabama's miscegenation law, which passed in 1852, forbid Sopharina and William from "living in adultery" or legally marrying. Interracial relationships were defined by the judgmental and pejorative term "miscegenation," which insinuated a societal "intrinsic horror of interracial mixing."[5]

When Telitha Breeding died in 1871, her Decatur property, which included her slaves and a large tract of land, transferred to her son. William, Mildred Brown's great-grandfather, inherited the family homestead in Morgan County. While he appreciated the property, the acreage had a sordid past. His father, Samuel Breeding, obtained

A Family of Fighters   23

sections of it by literally acting out the family's surname. According to David Winton, a white Breeding sixth cousin, their estate started out as a small piece of land, but during the antebellum era, the Breeding plantation owner accepted payments of property tracts from other slave owners for providing female "stud services": Breeding bred his neighbors' male slaves to his healthy female slaves at an annual spring sale. Since the U.S. Constitution banned the importation of slaves in 1808, some southern slave owners, like the elder Breeding, undermined the federal law and reverted to an old slavery statute. The *partus sequitur ventrem*'s law controlled the wombs of enslaved black women, meaning that "every black woman who was enslaved and gave birth did so to an enslaved child." It was more than possible for enslaved raped women, whose average fertile years ranged from eighteen to forty-five, to each conceive thirteen children. William Breeding heartily disliked his father's seasonal breeding transactions. He protected Sopharina from participation in the enforced mating, removing her far from the family "breeding" farm during these brutal months.[6]

Although the land's past carried an inhumane legacy, it offered William and Sopharina a fairly tolerant region in which they could live as common-law husband and wife. The town of Decatur was located within Morgan County's Tennessee Valley and Hill Countries, better known as Upcountry. These areas were renowned for anti-Democratic politics, and the residents considered themselves neither Democrats nor Republicans, even though Alabama was almost a thoroughly Democratic state. Upcountry residents may have owned numerous slaves, but they considered themselves Independents and therefore exempt from state or federal politics. They prided themselves on their spirit of rebellion and wholesome contempt for authority. Morgan County had already made a name for itself during the Civil War when it voted *against* secession, along with several other Hill Country regions. Almost three thousand men from the region served in the Union army. Their dislike of the Confederacy did not mean, however, that Upcountry men and women disagreed with the predominant racist attitudes of white Alabamians and, for that matter, most white Americans of any political persuasions. The people in Reconstruction Hill Country tolerated the Breedings, and some even liked the couple, as long as they lived within their social boundaries. William would tell their frequent visitors to make themselves comfortable when they visited the Breedings. Then he would yell, "Go whip up some biscuits, Soph, and I'll go rob the bees." In every sense, Sopharina was his spouse, although once a traveling fire-and-brimstone preacher almost succeeded in breaking up their happy union.[7] William and Sopharina attended one of the minister's sermons at the Center Spring United Methodist Church in Somerville. After listening to him preach against interracial couples living in sin, which was a favorite sermon subject during the Reconstruction years of 1865–77, Sopharina refused to sleep with William for a long time. Fortunately her love overcame her fear of damnation.

The U.S. government, though, did not recognize William and Sopharina as husband and wife or their four sons as legal offspring. In 1880 the appointed government census taker knew they lived together as an interracial couple, but he complied with the state's marriage ban and listed them as separate individuals, each head of his and her household, who resided at the same address. William's employment description was that of a farmer, while Sopharina operated her household as a cook living with four children: Millard William Breeding, born in 1855; William Taylor Breeding, born in 1865; Wilson Peter Breeding, born in 1873; and Gus Edward Breeding, born in 1878. The census taker listed her black children's employment as servants. By the rule of hypodescent, also known as the one-drop rule, the Breedings' racially mixed sons were also considered black. The federal and state authorities relied on supposedly scientific biological definitions of race rather than making a moral judgment on miscegenation.[8]

Cognizant of his sons' tenuous legal and social status, William Breeding directed his children's education by home-schooling them. Country schools in the area were plentiful for white youth, but education for antebellum or Reconstruction's biracial children did not exist. William was a nurturing educator. He possessed a warm, friendly nature and shared his love for nonfiction texts. The family's domicile was consistently cluttered with stacks of dusty law, history, and general-interest texts. The elder Breeding frequently visited the county seat courthouse; he enjoyed talking with the lawyers and judges trying cases in the nearby town of Somerville. William taught his progeny as much as he knew and then, accepting his limitations, he insisted his two older sons continue their schooling at institutes of higher education. By 1870 Reconstruction legislation had provided the beginning of Historical Black Colleges and Universities. Millard Breeding attended a Freedmen's Bureau school in Huntsville, Alabama, which later became Alabama Agricultural and Mechanical University. After graduation he became a pastor in the newly created Colored Methodist Episcopalian (CME) Church. William Taylor "W.T." Breeding initially matriculated at Alabama State University but completed his studies at Booker T. Washington's Tuskegee Institute, built in 1881. The second eldest Breeding son served as the superintendent of black schools in Montgomery, Alabama.[9]

To ensure all four of his sons' futures, William Breeding sought legal advice from Gen. Samuel M. Morrow, his mother's lawyer. Breeding brought his son Millard with him when he met with Morrow. The two older men knew each other professionally and personally, so it was a cordial, informal visit. Breeding trusted Morrow because he previously settled Telitha Breeding's estate and, like Breeding, Morrow was an ex-Confederate soldier. Morrow was aware of white men being prosecuted under the laws of miscegenation but also knew that "white men's sexual freedoms and civil rights, including the right to choose their own wives and control their own property," conflicted with the state ban on interracial marriage. Morrow discussed leaving land to his offspring, wills, and executors with Breeding while counseling him to name executors with firmness and nerve because his white siblings would try and run over his family. Breeding appreciated Morrow's legal knowledge and suggestions concerning his possible will. The plantation owner knew it would cause strife between his white family and him. But since his brothers and sisters charged William a considerable sum of money for farming and sharing rental profits from their mother's estate, he disregarded their potential hurt.[10]

William Breeding wrote his will three days after Sopharina Breeding died on September 5, 1887. Breeding took Morrow's advice and designated Millard and W.T., his two eldest sons, as coexecutors. He also followed his friend's instructions to mention the contents of the will only to them and the witnesses to the will. Within a few days Breeding filed his will at the Somerville courthouse in Morgan County. He had done as much as he legally could do to secure his sons' future. When he died on May 16, 1899, his white and black family was informed his last will and testament "disinherited his brothers and sisters" due to their earlier bad treatment toward him and left "his estate to his four black sons in equal portions to share and share alike." Breeding's large estate contained 1,916 acres of land, which meant each of the sons inherited 479 acres. The property value of the land was $1,650. Because the county seat changed in 1891 from Somerville to Decatur, Alabama, Millard Breeding, as coexecutor of his father's will, refiled it in Decatur two days after his father's funeral. A probate court battle between William's four beneficiaries and his white nuclear family ensued.[11]

James and John Breeding, brothers to the deceased William Breeding, contested the will on seven grounds of coercion and miscegenation. James, the senior contestant, argued as his sixth ground that since the "said beneficiaries are Negroes, incapable of inheriting the estate of said [William] Breeding except by will," if the court ruled in favor of the four sons, it would "make said device [will] against public policy." During the preliminary hearing on June 12, 1899, James insisted that William was under "undue influence from his black live-in Sophy and her mulatto sons." According to James, Sopharina assaulted an ill and feebly minded William with "a large stick or other weapon" and then she threatened "to kill him unless he made a promise to make a will bequeathing his estate to the four sons." He announced to the court, "The said instrument is not the last will and testament of William Breeding. William was of unsound mind and mentally incapacitated when the instrument was executed. William was unaware of the contents of the instrument when it was executed. The instrument was by the undue influence of its named benefactors. The instrument was

A Family of Fighters 27

procured by fraud by its named benefactors."[12] James claimed the will was an act of conspiracy and demanded an estate trial with the unusual request of a twelve-man jury. John Breeding, another one of William's brothers, filed for Special Letters of Administration to collect and preserve William's property until the trial convened. John maintained that since "said William Breeding left no children" and John was a "full brother," he qualified as the special administrator for the estate. The court approved his claim and several men, including S. M. Dunnaway, witnessed John purchasing a good faith security bond for $1,500.[13]

An outraged forty-two-year-old Millard Breeding contested his uncle John's right to act as the executive administrator of his father's will. In a statement beseeching Alabama's supreme court for assistance, he wrote, "I am a natural son of William Breeding, deceased. I propounded his will for probate, and am one of the persons referred to, in said will, as being one of the sons of the deceased, and a legatee therein named, and executor thereof.... My mother was a Negro woman." At the time of the court proceedings, the eldest son of William Breeding was a father to six children, ranging from twenty-three to seven, and well understood the financial importance of settling his father's will. Alabama's highest court denied his appeal and not only upheld John's appointment but also ordered Milliard to pay for his uncle's administrator court fees. William's property was assessed on August 3, 1899. The estate appraisal revealed a wide variety of items. The following list contained the contents of William's estate minus the acreage:

3	Head of black cows and a calf. One yearling bull.	$20.00
	Black smith tools, vise, anvil and buttress	5.15
22	Bee hives	22.00
9	Empty bee gums	.90
5	Augers	.60
1	Chisel	.10
2	Iron wagon axles	.75
4	Wagon tires	2.00
1	Cotton Seraper	.15
1	Plow	1.50

1	Sausage mill	.25
1	Handsaw	.25
2	Gallons of strained honey	2.40
2	Wagon wheels and bolsters	.50
1	Watch	1.50
1	Clock	1.00
1	Bureau	2.00
1	Single barrel shotgun	3.00
1	Infield rifle	1.00
5	Counter pains [sic]	.50
2	Under bed ticks	.50
1	Bed spread	.10
3	Quilts	2.00
3	Cover lids	6.00
2	Feather beds	14.62
2	Pillow cases	.90
2	Bedstands	1.50
1	Coat and vest	.75
1	Thread needle	.75
1	Pair of black shears	.25
	Confederate Money (face value of $2,043.75)	.50
4	Books	1.00
1	Bible	2.00
1	Syringe	.50
2	Trunks	.75
1	Saddle	.50
19	Pounds of twist tobacco	4.75
45	Pounds of hand tobacco	9.00
1	Spinning wheel	.75
2	Walking sticks	.10
3	Gees	.45
28	Mexican silver dollars	28.00
11	Dollars in ancient coins	11.00
4	Half dollars with holes in them	2.00
31	in United States money	31.00
		186.92[14]

While preparations for the trial slowly moved forward, the perishable estate goods, namely one cow, one calf, one bull, several hand

A Family of Fighters 29

and twist tobacco plaits, twenty-two bee hives, and several gallons of honey, were sold in October 1899 to William's white relatives. The forced sale totaled $41.75 dollars; it reflected discounted prices for each of the previously assessed items. Haggling over the estate continued throughout the holiday season until James's attorneys met in Montgomery on January 29, 1900. By now the probate case was in its seventh month. The elaborate process of subpoenaing witnesses and selecting a jury unrelated to either side of the white or black Breeding family would extend the court preliminaries an additional nine months. Finally, on October 16, 1900, the court case commenced.

Judge William E. Skeggs, a lifelong friend of William's, informed the selected twelve white jurors that they were to decide three questions during *Breeding v. Breeding*: (1) Was William Breeding's will authentic?, (2) Did he have testamentary capacity?, and (3) Was the will procured by undue influence? Judge Skeggs reminded the jury "that William had a sound mind if he recalled the property and to whom he wanted to give it and what consequences would result because of his actions. [Moreover,] numerous witnesses testified to his sanity prior to, at the time, and after the will." Skeggs concluded his ten-page judicial directive to the jury with a rarely given instruction for the times. He informed the jury "not to allow racial prejudices to influence their decision, which must be rendered in strict conformity with the evidence and the law." The jurors listened carefully to Judge Skeggs. After all, he was the great-grandson of John Hunt, namesake of Huntsville, and, like most other white professional men in Decatur, a member of the Democratic Party and the Masons. Skeggs was one of the most well liked and admired residents of Alabama's Hill Country.[15]

The judge's willingness to hold a fair trial, regardless of the color of the proponents, demonstrated that prejudice and discrimination was not monolithic in the Deep South and certainly not in Morgan County. Instances of miscegenation were not uncommon in Alabama Hill Country, but progeny demanding and winning their inheritance remained unheard of in the region. Millard's claim to his father's inheritance was ultimately decided after the testimony of James's star witness, whom court transcripts documented only as an elderly negro woman. Under oath she testified that "William was the father of the four black men listed in his will."[16] James, who knew the verity of her words, reminded the jury that his brother William and his former slave Sopharina had lived in "fornification" for approximately twenty years and therefore their offspring were inconsequential in the eyes of the law.

The jury ignored James's diatribe and decided *Breeding v. Breeding* in Millard Breeding's favor. Oceola Kyle, Millard's white lawyer, was delighted with the verdict in the "famous Breeding will case," especially since Morgan County residents "almost universally believed that the jury would render against the will." According to Kyle's great-grandson, Attorney J. Timothy Kyle, he had recently moved from Tuskegee, Alabama, and knew and respected its most famous citizen, Booker T. Washington. Several of Alabama's white newspapers, such as the *Montgomery Advertiser*, updated its readers about William Breeding's thousand-acre estate being awarded to his black offspring, while the local *New Decatur Advertiser* ended the media's interest in the court case with one last terse statement: "M.W. Breeding (colored) paid off all claims of the heirs and gets the property."[17]

The probate court case of *Breeding v. Breeding* was an anomaly because of its timing. It remains the first and only case tried in early twentieth-century Morgan County in which a black man legally and politically defeated a white man. *Breeding v. Breeding* occurred between 1890 and 1901, the short era between Reconstruction and the white supremacy revival. It was this transitional era in southern race relations that allowed Millard Breeding a brief moment of legal equality. If *Breeding v. Breeding* had taken place even one year later, it was questionable if the outcome would have been the same. Within months of the case's conclusion, the state legislators of Alabama reformatted their state constitution. The year 1901 marked the beginning of forty years of the most intense racism in the United States.[18]

Delegates from each of the state's counties convened at Alabama's Constitutional Convention, which ran from May to September in

1901–2. While the elected officials voted on several statewide initiatives, their goal was to encourage permanent white supremacy in Alabama. Morgan County delegates from the state's upper hill country, who were respectfully referred to as "hillbillies," disagreed with the new initiatives, especially the one excluding blacks from politics through disfranchisement. The Black Belters, wealthy planters from southern Alabama, held a majority of Alabama's political power and approved the disfranchisement measure to block the alliance of Populist lower-class whites and blacks. Alabama's lawmakers were following the path of every ex-Confederate state when they amended the state constitution. The approved amendments included a poll tax, which caused black registration to fall from 181,000 to 3,000 voters; jury selection limited to only male citizens reputed to be honest and intelligent (a code phrase for white); and adoption of a state-wide Democratic primary, which unified Alabama's Democrats and made Upcountry Republicans ineffective voters. The era of Jim Crow racial doctrines would promote and rationalize antimiscegenation laws, discrimination, racism, and national segregation.[19]

At the successful conclusion of *Breeding v. Breeding*, an elated Millard Breeding added two new members to his already large family. The Alabama court system ruled that Gus Breeding, his younger brother, was non compos mentis, or mentally disabled. Gus's share of their father's estate transferred to Millard, who became Gus's permanent guardian. Gus moved in with Millard and Mary Elizabeth Curry Jackson Breeding, his second wife, and their combined family. Millard, a widower, had remarried on Christmas Day during the early stages of the *Breeding v. Breeding* trial in 1899. Millard's second marriage to the widow Mary produced no additional children, but Tommie, her five-year-old daughter from her previous marriage, moved into the Breeding homestead as well. After the trial ended she joined Millard's biological children, twins Maggie and Henry, Robert, Ebb, Annie, and Millard Leander. Reba Shelton, Tommie's daughter, remembers her grandmother as a kind woman who never raised her voice, while Millard Breeding, who was already respected in the black community as a CME pastor, transformed from a free black man to a landowning resident in the community. Millard and Mary and their combined family of seven children thrived during their seven years of marital bliss.[20]

Their happiness was cut short by a racist tragedy that occurred in December 1907. It happened at the train station in Hartselle, a town located twelve miles south of Millard Breeding's home in Decatur. While waiting for his train to take him home, Breeding noticed a young black boy desperately trying to free his foot from the railroad tracks. He simultaneously observed an oncoming train heading into the station. Eyewitnesses later said Breeding rushed to the boy's side and managed to free his trapped foot. The CME minister pushed the youth away from the track just seconds before the train approached, but Breeding's brave action cost him his life. He died a hero's death as the train crushed his body. It was not until a few days later that Breeding's family found out the train engineer refused to apply the brakes once he realized the young boy and his rescuer were black.[21]

A strong-willed Mary Breeding sued the Louisville and Nashville Railroad Company for negligence. The railroad company settled out of court for $2,500, and she received the settlement on April 25, 1909. Since Millard Breeding died intestate, without a will, his wife and six biological children equally divided his estate. Millard's property included his and Gus's portion of his father William's estate and an additional three thousand acres of land he purchased between 1900 and 1907. Millard's eldest children, twins Maggie Dreweather Breeding and Henry Drew Breeding, were thirty years old at the time of their father's death, and they each inherited five hundred acres of land. Maggie's portion included the Breeding family homestead.[22]

Maggie Breeding followed her parents' footsteps. In the 1890s she attended Agricultural and Mechanical University in Normal, Alabama. It was the same Freedmen's Bureau school her father attended during Reconstruction. At sixteen years of age she graduated with a music teaching certificate. In 1901 the year of her father's historic probate victory, twenty-four-year-old Maggie married thirty-one-year-old CME reverend Benjamin Joshua Brown. Although minister of the gospel, V.

A Family of Fighters 33

L. Bailey performed their marital ceremony; the judge who issued their marriage license was none other than William E. Skeggs, the judge who presided over her grandfather's probate trial. Benjamin married Maggie in a civil ceremony. Morgan County's ledger documented them as "Mr. Benjamin J. Brown, Colored, and Miss Maggie D. Breeding, Colored," entering in matrimony on November 25, 1901. Maggie's father and stepmother, Mary, whom she called "mama," were the only set of parents aware of their marriage. Brown's mother had passed away in his youth, and he did not communicate with his father. His estrangement started years earlier when Brown, a courageous twelve-year-old, gathered his four younger siblings and they left their parent's common-law home. The five brothers walked twenty miles to distance themselves from their white father's abusive beatings. Brown later described his father as "tight with money, strict and domineering." Despite a rough upbringing, Benjamin Brown earned a degree in divinity from Lane College in Jackson, Tennessee.[23]

Reverend Brown gladly served as a CME traveling minister, and Maggie faithfully followed him to various towns in Alabama while they raised four children. Annie Lee arrived in 1902; Millie Dee was born on December 20, 1905; Bennie Drew came in 1908; and Willie Andrew completed the family of six in 1912. When Millie Dee was born her family resided in Bessemer, Alabama, but within a few years relocated to nearby Birmingham.[24]

Reverend Brown was highly respected by his revolving congregants but poorly paid by the CME Church. They always had plenty on hand, but Maggie, like many African American women, augmented her husband's fluctuating salary by selling cosmetics and toiletries. Her part-time employment did not denigrate her husband's social standing in the Birmingham community, and she taught her sales techniques to thirteen-year-old Millie, who often accompanied Maggie. Years later, Mildred Brown claimed that her lifelong enjoyment of selling things started with her mother's door-to-door entrepreneurship.[25]

Millie emulated her family's interests and characteristics throughout her teenage years and adulthood. Because Reverend Brown kept a small flower garden at their home and her uncle Andrew Cato Brown voluntarily tended the flowerbeds of Mount Zion African Methodist Episcopalian (AME) Church, Brown learned to appreciate flora as well, especially carnations. While her father taught her how to uplift his congregation, her mother, a kind, humble lady who spoke with a mellow voice, showed her how to lovingly raise children. Millie was similar to her mother in looks and attitude. Millie always had a smile, just like Maggie, and she followed her mom's advice: "Whatever a person tells you to do, do it. Do not put things off. Do not procrastinate." Maggie practiced what she preached to Millie. She demonstrated the importance of education by earning a second teaching certificate in elementary education from nearby AME Church–supported Miles Memorial College in Fairfield, Alabama.[26]

Millie's parents made religious education and the reading of black newspapers family priorities. Reba Shelton, Millie's first cousin, recalled Reverend Brown as a man who only occasionally communicated. He was usually busy sitting in his rocking chair reading the Bible. While none of the Brown children became ministers, they each valued the role of the church in their lives, especially Millie, who later worked with several ministerial alliances in various cities. The first time Millie ever really read a black newspaper, instead of just looking at the headlines, she was fifteen years of age. She recalled, "I had seen them, but they didn't interest me. I was more aware of the pretty pictures of women entertaining, of people who were getting married and of people taking trips." Her social interests corresponded with her publishing choices in her newspaper years later.[27]

On May 27, 1924, Millie graduated from Miles Memorial High School and College, her mother's second alma mater, with a prenormal teaching certificate for elementary and secondary instruction. The Progressive Era's standardization of education required that teachers attain the proper license or certification for each field of instruction. For some reason, Brown would claim that she was sixteen at the time of graduation, which made her first career seem more important at such a young age, but she was actually eighteen when she earned her high school diploma. Brown started her teaching career that fall at Charles F. Hard Elementary School in her hometown of Bessemer. During the next three school years, she taught second, third, fourth, fifth, and seventh grade; it was not unusual for teachers to instruct several grades at once.[28]

In August 1927 Reverend Brown died of a heart ailment, and a financially challenged Maggie moved the family to Fairfield. Maggie, now the head of the household, gained employment as a school matron at Carrie Ann Tuggle Elementary School. In 1903 Alabama's legislators, the same group who had disenfranchised black male voters by amending their state constitution, built the school in honor of Carrie Tuggle, the founder of the *Birmingham Truth* weekly and Alabama's first black newspaper woman. Millie would later earn the same achievement in Nebraska.[29]

On October 2, 1927, Millie Dee Brown started her own family when she married Shirley Edward Gilbert in Pulaski, Tennessee. Brown's relatives summarized that she most likely met Gilbert at one of the many meetings she regularly attended. Regardless, theirs was a quick courtship with a private wedding ceremony. Millie kept her marriage secret because she wanted to continue teaching. Social custom, starting in the 1850s and extending through the 1920s, dictated a married woman was no longer eligible to work as a teacher. The Gilberts married out of state, most likely because her husband's hometown was Culleoka, Tennessee. At the time of their marriage, he was twenty-five and in his final year at Howard University's pharmacology school. Shirley Edward returned to Washington DC shortly after the wedding and remained there until graduating with a doctorate of pharmacology on June 8, 1928. They promptly moved north.[30]

Maggie Breeding Brown died at the beginning of May in 1929. She used her last few days to speak with Annie, Millie, Bennie, and Willie, her adult children. She begged each of them to never sell their soon-to-be inheritance, her portion of the Breeding estate property. Maggie's white relatives, the Dunnaway family, descendants of S. M. Dunnaway, who fought against her father, Millard, during *Breeding v.*

Breeding, were currently living in the Breeding family home. Between the rent money the Dunnaways paid Maggie and the annual sale of the Breeding acres' trees to timber companies, the land generated enough revenue to each of her children without them having to sell it. After her death her four beneficiaries buried Maggie in Birmingham, and, as she requested, they divided their mother's land into four equal portions.[31]

Without any parental ties or responsibilities and a nest egg of Breeding property, Dr. and Mrs. Gilbert planned their permanent departure from Alabama. They rejoined the Great Migration from the South to the North, a mass black movement that signaled a collective disavowal of economic and racial oppression. W. E. B. Du Bois nicknamed it "Northern Fever" and applauded the migratory participants' expression of black autonomy and self-help. Between the years 1916 and 1921 more black Americans relocated to the North than the total number of previous migrants between 1870 and 1910. In the 1920s another million black citizens followed the previous wave of migrants and relocated to northern midwestern urban areas such as Chicago, Minneapolis, Cleveland, and Milwaukee. The Gilberts left the small southern town of Bessemer and migrated to the large northern city of Chicago for Shirley Edward to start his career and Mildred to pursue higher education. Shirley Edward found employment as the manager and pharmacist of the Pythian Temple Pharmacy in downtown Chicago. After almost two years of employment, he left Chicago, for unknown reasons, and relocated to Lawrence, Virginia, to serve as the chair of the Saint Paul Polytechnic Institute pharmacy department until May 1930. While her husband changed jobs, Mildred matriculated at Crane Junior College and the Chicago Normal School. She planned to augment her primary teaching certificate with a degree in education and then return to Bessemer and resume her career as an elementary teacher. But her husband was offered an excellent career job in Des Moines, Iowa.[32]

In June 1930 Mildred left Chicago and joined Shirley Edward in Des Moines on the second leg of their Great Migration journey. He was already working as a pharmacist at James W. Mitchell's Community Pharmacy, an upscale drugstore located at 1200 West Center Street, in the center of the city's black neighborhood of 5,428 black residents. Once again, Mildred pursued her dream of higher education and enrolled at Drake University. The couple joined the Saint Paul AME Church, the largest black church in the city. Shirley Edward was an active member, participating in the male church choir and once even delivered a homily titled "If He Should Come Again—Now." The *Des Moines Bystander* black newspaper praised his singing talents and encouraged the black community to attend his sermon. The reporter noted, "You have heard Doc Gilbert sing, you've heard him debate, now let's see if he can preach." Gilbert's editorial to the newspaper thanked the publisher for supporting him and the community. He wrote that "nothing is needed more [in Des Moines] than clean and sound newspaper organs, such as the *Bystander*, to guide the thought and minds of the general public." It was advice the Gilberts would put into practice in Nebraska several years later. The Gilberts' stay in Des Moines was longer than their time in Chicago, but after three years they continued their trek through the United States' Corn Belt and migrated west to northeastern Iowa.[33]

In 1933 the Gilberts migrated to the small midwestern town of Sioux City, Iowa, ostensibly to advance Shirley Edward's employment; in retrospect, it was the beginning of Mildred's newspaper career. Shirley Edward finally had what he wanted for his career goal. He was the chief pharmacist of his own pharmacy, and his drugstore represented a milestone for Sioux City's black community. It was the only black-owned pharmacy in a city with a population of 1,004 black residents. Mildred assisted her husband by working at the lunch counter making sandwiches, but the pastor's daughter and former school teacher in her produced a social worker's desire to do more with her days and uplift the community.[34]

Acting as a public servant and social housekeeper, she volunteered as the Sunday school superintendent of the Malone AME Church. La Veeda Banks, who was a member of Malone, fondly remembers the superintendent. "Everyone liked Mrs. Gilbert, even though she wore funny hats. She took us on church picnics at Riverside Park. She liked children even though she did not have children." But Malone Church, like most religious affiliations during the Great Depression, was unable to supply refreshments for Gilbert's Sunday school children. Undeterred, Gilbert made a decision that provided treats for the children and, more important, changed her ideas about her role in the black community. She decided to approach Sioux City's white businesses and ask them to make donations to her church. She was persuasive, insistent, and unwilling to take no for an answer. She collected enough funds to supply ice cream for every child for every Sunday of the year. Gilbert's success as her church's public servant expanded her desire to uplift the city's black community.[35]

Mildred and Shirley Edward founded the Booker T. Washington Club to assist migrants in Sioux City's black neighborhood. It was an active neighborhood organization promoting Washington's self-help philosophy through better community living and interracial understanding. Similar to the Urban League, the community-funded club assisted new residents with finding employment, housing, and church membership. Even more important, the club provided a place where the black community, which did not have a communal center, could regularly convene, whether for political purposes or milestone events. The club, which met in the upstairs room of Dr. and Mrs. Gilbert's drugstore, became an integral part of Mildred's mission to improve the future for black youth in the United States.[36]

Mildred took her role as the unpaid, unofficial social worker of Sioux City's black community one step further when she and her husband informally adopted Ruth Lee Harris in 1936. Congregant Banks was not surprised when she heard that David Harvey Harris, the Malone AME's traveling pastor, had called a private meeting with the Gilberts to discuss an urgent matter. Harris, a publicly stern pastor with a private easygoing nature, needed the couple's assistance with his daughter, Ruth. His wife, Roberta, died shortly before he and his daughter moved to Sioux City. Knowing that his church tenure amounted to possibly one to two years of future service in Sioux

City, he wanted stability for Ruth, his only child. She needed a healthy, regulated home life because her heart murmur required adequate rest and a daily dose of aspirin. The Gilberts agreed to raise Ruth, and the shy thirteen-year-old transferred her belongings to their house.[37]

Pastor Harris had one other important matter to discuss with the couple, a plan that would provide a black newspaper for the community. Years later Mildred Brown reminisced about their fortuitous meeting: "Reverend Harris suggested I start a newspaper. I laughed because it sounded like a fairy tale." Harris expected her reaction and showed the Gilberts an edition of the *Pittsburgh Courier*. He told them, "This is what the Negroes here should have." The Gilberts committed themselves to making a black newspaper in Sioux City a reality. Mrs. Gilbert visited with some of the same local businesses who helped her with the Sunday school donations and, much to her surprise, raised the necessary sales revenue. "Everyone I approached gave me an ad. That was the beginning of my newspaper career." The Gilberts named their one-to-two-page newspaper, which was really more of a newssheet, the *Silent Messenger* and weekly printed the local news as they saw it. Dr. Gilbert, still operating his pharmacy, acted as the part-time associate editor of the newspaper while his wife managed the advertising. Although they printed only limited copies of each *Silent Messenger* edition, most black residents could not afford it.[38]

By the end of 1936 the Gilberts were in financial difficulties, most likely because Shirley Edward no longer owned his drugstore and worked in it as a clerk. Mildred later insisted she was in favor of moving back to Chicago because if she had to lamppost it (declare bankruptcy), then she preferred to do it in her favorite city. Instead of moving, the Gilberts decided to stay in Sioux City but compromised by relocating to a smaller, more affordable home. During the holiday season of that year, the Gilberts received a serendipitous visit. Charles Chapman (C.C.) Galloway, the black founder and publisher of the *Omaha Guide* black newspaper, traveled the hundred-mile drive between Omaha and Sioux City to offer them a proposal. He wanted the couple to work for his *Guide*. The Gilberts considered his offer and, in view of their financial straits, accepted it. The small family of three packed their belongings and migrated to Omaha. The Gilberts' route was circuitous to Nebraska, but as the Federal Writers' Project's *Negroes of Nebraska* documents, as a rule, black migrants generally stopped in other states before settling in Nebraska. Omaha would become Mildred Brown Gilbert's second hometown. The great-granddaughter of William and Sopharina Breeding and the granddaughter of Mildred Breeding had learned the lessons her family of fighters had taught her. She would blaze a trail of her own, in Omaha, Nebraska.[39]

2

Involving the Community

On the morning of July 9, 1938, Near North Side black residents wishing to read about local and national news had the usual option of buying a copy of Charles Chapman Galloway's *Omaha Guide* black weekly or, for the first time, an edition of Dr. Shirley Edward and Mildred Brown Gilbert's *Omaha Star* newspaper. Those who chose the *Star* saw two large photographs beneath the newspaper's banner. The picture on the left depicted "S. Edward Gilbert, General Manager and Editor," and the image on the right showed "Mildred D. Gilbert, Financial Secretary and Advertising Manager." The photographs looked familiar to readers; they were the same portraits used in Galloway's *Omaha Guide* when he first introduced the Gilberts to Omahans in the spring of 1937. On the initial front page of the *Star*, the southern-born couple proclaimed their intention to unconditionally serve Omaha's black neighborhood while asking residents for local sponsorship of the *Star*.[1] Mildred Gilbert was confident that "every true Nebraska citizen" needed another, but more powerful voice to speak for the northern Omaha black community:

> To the Citizens of Omaha: It is with profound pleasure that the *Omaha Star Publishing Co.*, an organization of energetic, well trained journalistic minds, give to you this day a paper of the people, by the people and for the people. We here and now wish to have you know that the *Omaha Star* dedicates its existence to the task of serving the general public in every way humanly possible. It shall be our policy to move in an unerring path of duty on the behalf of Black America in Omaha, bringing to you the local

news of the city as we find it, as well as the national highlights. Promoting and backing for the welfare of the citizens of Omaha and Black America in general. . . . Give the *Omaha Star* a firm foundation by way of subscribing and reading support and we will assure you that we in turn will build an enterprise worthy of consideration, a mouthpiece and a force for the people of Omaha.[2]

When Dr. and Mrs. Gilbert and their foster daughter, Ruth Harris, arrived in Omaha in February 1937, it was the largest black community they had lived in since they migrated from Alabama. The midwestern city's black population had tripled during the years of the first Great Migration. While the predominantly white city of Omaha residents numbered 232,982 inhabitants, northern Omaha's black neighborhood totaled 13,166. Despite the Gilberts' temporary financial difficulties, they decided against renting an apartment and opted to sign a year's lease on a large home at 2423 Maple Street. Their two-story domicile represented their desire to continue their middle-class southern upbringing.[3]

Mrs. Gilbert did not attend church regularly, but she understood her new black community's hierarchy of religious membership. Elite black Omahans attended Saint Philips Protestant Episcopal Church and professional up-and-coming blacks attended Saint John AME Church, while working-class and lower-income blacks divided their church membership among Omaha's other twenty-nine houses of worship. The Gilberts joined Saint John AME, Omaha's oldest black institute. The AME churches generally appealed to the post–Great Migration black population striving for the middle class by conducting more decorous, dignified services than the CME churches that Mildred's father presided over in the early years of the twentieth century. As Joe William Trotter explains in *Black Milwaukee*, "Shouting, for instance, was condemned by congregants as ignorant behavior." The southern migrants in Omaha, and most black newcomers to other large cities, desired northern dignity in their religious worship services.[4]

The question of Ruth's educational instruction was an even more serious matter for Mildred. Coming from a long line of religious and secular educators, Mildred insisted that her foster daughter attend the best high school available to Omaha's black community. The Gilberts were aware that the majority of northern Omaha's youth enrolled at Omaha Technical High School, but the secondary school's focus on technical education and athletics instead of academics made it intellectually unacceptable for their daughter. The Gilberts chose to enroll fifteen-year-old Ruth at Central High School. Registering Ruth at Central confirmed and enforced what Mrs. Gilbert had already learned from her great-grandparents and parents: knowledge is power. Not only was Central the best public high school in Omaha, it also had the city's highest rate of student body integration, although that did not mean there were no instances of racism.[5]

Black students attending Omaha's Central High School encountered both covert and overt racism. Near North Side resident Wilda Stephenson, who attended Central, a large imposing 1912 stone structure, recalled how black students could belong to any of the school's academic organizations, but it was an unwritten rule that minority teenagers did not socialize with white teenagers outside of these activities. Resident Emmett Dennis also attended Central. Dennis was the first black quarterback on the school's football team. He explained this simply: he was the best athlete and therefore his teammates accepted him as the team's leader. The acceptance only went as far as the playing field during football games; however, his father told him to ignore any discrimination off the field and to focus instead on honoring his family name.[6]

Ruth Harris maintained a C-grade average, but her scores did not demonstrate her intelligence. She missed several days of school each month because of her heart murmur. She faced her most difficult health challenges during her senior year when she had twelve excused absences for medical reasons. But she managed to meet fellow student Marvin Kellogg. The handsome young man had her foster mother's approval before he even met Harris. Kellogg recalled his first meeting with Mrs. Gilbert. It occurred after he read a marketing announcement Mildred created to publicize a Thanksgiving Day food giveaway.

Involving the Community   45

Kellogg can still see her standing outside of Saint Benedict Catholic Church, taking care of the community while encouraging recipients to subscribe to the newspaper. Mrs. Gilbert gave him a box of graham crackers. She instantly liked Kellogg; she still approved of him when he started dating Ruth.[7]

Omaha, or as Mildred pronounced it, "O-mee-haw," consisted of two racially separated regions, the city of Omaha and northern Omaha, but it had not always been so narrowly segregated. In the early 1890s Omaha's black population of approximately five thousand residents peacefully coexisted in Omaha's downtown central business district and southern Omaha alongside other established ethnic enclaves. The peripheral sections of Omaha were enclaves for the Irish, Scandinavians, and Germans in the early 1800s and the Italians and Eastern European Jews in the 1880s and 1890s. Jewish immigrant shopkeepers operated stores like Mayfield's Deli, Glass's Butcher Shop, Hornstein's Grocery, Forbes' Bakery, and Epstein's BBQ and dominated businesses at the southern end of Twenty-Fourth Street. Until the lynching of 1919, the black population, which mainly resided at Twentieth and Harney Streets, was able to choose where they wished to live in Omaha.[8]

After the lynching of African American Will Brown on September 28, 1919, Omaha's black community relocated to northern Omaha for their own safety. Without a strong voice in either the black or white community to neutralize another possible planned racial disturbance, black business owners started moving their stores uptown. Because Omaha's downtown was becoming a vice-ridden area known as the city's red-light or tenderloin district, within a few years the remaining black entrepreneurs, like Jimmy Jewell, who owned Phannix's Billiard Hall, joined their fellow migrants and relocated their businesses at the northern end of Twenty-Fourth Street.[9]

Known as "Deuce-4" and "2-4," Twenty-Fourth Street became the heart of Omaha's black community. Resident Hattie Matlock Smith insisted, "24th from Cuming to Ohio Streets was to us what Rodeo Drive is to Hollywood where the stars hang out. And to be on 24th

Street in those days made you feel like a STAR." On a much smaller scale but similar to the scene in Chicago, the nation's jazz capital in 1920, the Dreamland Ballroom made Omaha the center of midwestern regional jazz. Located in Jimmy Jewell's newly constructed building at Twenty-Fourth and Grant Streets, the Dreamland offered the local musical talents of Preston Love Sr. and the International Sweethearts of Rhythm, and nationally known musicians, such as Duke Ellington, Count Basie, Earl Hines, and Louis Jordan. Martha Melton, a longtime resident of northern Omaha, recalled the famous showplace: "It was decorated so beautifully. It really was a dreamland." While regional and national entertainment burgeoned, housing segregation isolated the inhabitants of the black community.[10]

The national model of segregation was evident in Omaha. The Federal Housing Administration originally supported restrictive covenants. The legal stipulation provided the best protection against undesirable encroachment and assured property values would increase in white neighborhoods. Omaha's adoption of zoning ordinances and restrictive covenants stopping the outward expansion of blacks moving into white neighborhoods mirrored an already national phenomenon. Near North Side residents, like many other black residents in large cities, lived a marginal isolated existence. President Franklin Delano Roosevelt's administration attempted to solve this issue by creating the Housing Act of 1937. The act, also known as the Wagner Housing Act, provided the necessary government money for sheltering the nation's urban poor, a disproportionate number of whom were black citizens. Omaha's city government, like in other cities throughout the United States, benefited from the act with inexpensive urban federal housing that was supposed to alleviate overcrowding in black communities. The housing projects were the only modern housing open to black residents. Omaha's Logan Fontenelle Housing Project, originally named Northside Village, was a two-million-dollar Public Works Administration construction. The favorably viewed building took its name from Logan Fontenelle, the famous Native American leader. Omaha completed the federally constructed project in 1938.[11]

Although they themselves did not live in Logan Fontenelle, the Gilberts supported the public housing unit as a benefit for indigent and working-class Omahans. Dr. Gilbert worked part-time as an application clerk for the low-income apartment housing complex. Mrs. Gilbert applauded the government's efforts. She explained to her readers the New Deal benefits for the black community by stating, "Under the Works Progress [sic] Administration and the relief program, the Negro has received equal treatment with the white man. He senses that, at least he has been granted equal economic brotherhood, and that is a step forward." Historian Harvard Sitkoff's *A New Deal for Blacks* supports her assessment. For the first time in American history, Roosevelt's federal administrators were providing affordable, decent, segregated housing for indigent, working-class, and middle-class African Americans. About 41,000 of the 122,000 federal housing projects built between 1937 and 1942 were specifically for black Americans. By 1941 the Omaha Housing Authority (OHA) created an additional Logan Fontenelle extension consisting of another 272 units. In a few years three additional housing projects, Hilltop Homes, Spencer Homes, and Pleasantview Homes, offered more public units.[12]

There was plenty of housing for low-income black and white residents, but the housing projects clearly segregated occupants. The OHA followed the government and the real estate industry's discriminatory housing practices. Because the OHA separated the apartments into black and white units, it denied integrated housing and encouraged ghettoization. Resident Richard Artison correctly perceived that "wherever you lived is where you went to school." Omaha's solution to this problem was to have OHA manage the derelict housing on the Near North Side, but it was hopeless; the project units became institutional ghettos, basically a city within the city of Omaha. Like numerous other cities, Omaha was the beneficiary imposing apartment complexes, but within a decade the projects were filled with impoverished dwellers living in substandard housing tracts without running water. Unbelievably, the Federal Housing Administration deemed the housing units a success. After all, the FHA reasoned, homogeneous neighborhoods were a better investment. At the same time that low-income residents endured substandard housing, they also grappled with financial stability in northern Omaha.[13]

Employment opportunities in Omaha mirrored the nationwide job positions available to the black community. Black men and women experienced approximately 8 percent unemployment in Omaha and worked at menial, entry-level, low-paying, and occasionally dangerous and dirty jobs within a limited scope of occupational categories that had little job security. Survival necessitated either both parents working or taking in boarders. In Omaha most black men worked as domestics, waiters, janitors, and porters. These menial jobs paid about $14.00 to $22.00 a week, although porters averaged $7.00 to $18.00 a week. About one-third, or 1,800, of Omaha's Near North Side men worked at the meatpacking plants and another one-fourth at the railroad yards of the Midland Pacific, Union Pacific, or Burlington. Discriminatory employment practices meant black workers were the last hired and the first fired when the economy weakened, as it did during the Great Depression. Employment for black women was even more limited. Before 1920 black women worked primarily as servants because white family class status and tradition required it. By the 1930s and 1940s approximately 1,700 of the 1,800 black women living in Omaha were live-in domestics. Female citizens of the Near North Side who worked outside of someone else's home were punching timecards as hotel maids, charwomen, and elevator operators, the latter euphemistically known as "up and down" girls. These women, many of whom did not possess an education past high school, averaged a weekly pay of $7.00 to $10.00, $10.52, and $11.75, respectively. The newly arrived and teacher-certified Mildred Gilbert Brown was already promised employment at the *Omaha Guide*, the town's black weekly newspaper, when she moved to Omaha with her family.[14]

Shirley Edward and Mildred Gilbert worked for C.C. Galloway, a six-foot-three, gruff, domineering, lifelong bachelor. As the owner, editor, and publisher of the *Guide*, he chose to live in an apartment above the newspaper's office at 2420 Grant Street. The black weekly had a circulation of twenty-five thousand subscribers and provided local and national political news for its readers. Galloway prided himself on producing a progressive newspaper. On February 6, 1937, the *Guide*'s publisher introduced the Gilberts to his readers as the "New Addition to Staff of the *Omaha Guide*" and "New Advertising Department Head for the *Guide*," respectively. Galloway described Dr. and Mrs. Gilbert as enthusiastic and energetic newspaper people who were ready to increase the circulation growth of the *Guide*. While Mrs. Gilbert sold ads, her husband, who acknowledged his pharmacy doctorate in print but for some reason after this point chose to dismiss his medical degree in practice, wrote the first of his weekly activist columns, An Echo from My Den. Younger readers signed up for Gilbert's Guidite Club. The club encouraged children to write letters asking for advice from "Uncle Gil." He created a following of readers in the newspaper, while Mildred improved the profit of the *Guide* by selling advertising throughout northern Omaha and the city of Omaha.[15]

In 1938, after working at the *Guide* for eighteen months, the Gilberts decided to create their own northern Omaha newspaper because of creative differences with their employer. Julia Sanford Galloway, the *Guide*'s eighteen-year-old secretary, was not surprised. She remembered several spats between Galloway and the Gilberts. It was even rumored that Galloway had possible connections with the city's underworld, in particular with Tom Dennison, the deceased Omaha crime boss most likely responsible for the murder of Will Brown in 1919. The heated arguments between the Gilberts and C.C. usually revolved around new ideas for the newspaper and venues for weekly information. Galloway subscribed to the Crusader News Service, which was run by left-wing communist Cyril Valentine Briggs. The Gilberts, who were staunch Roosevelt Democrats, disapproved. Mildred and Galloway were at loggerheads most of her tenure and it was a constant battle to discern which of the two were more strong-minded. As Julia Galloway recalled, there was little room for compromise at the *Guide*; "You couldn't tell C.C. anything." Mildred, who liked her boss personally, was unable to continue working with him professionally. Years later she remembered the thought process that took place before she resigned from the *Guide*: "A group of us spent night after night discussing plans for another weekly and one night I decided it would be called the *Omaha Star*." Once they decided the name of the newspaper, the Gilberts were ready to start their own weekly.[16]

Although the couple possessed only two dollars to finance the *Omaha Star*, Mildred felt confident in their newspaper's future. She had "a million dollars worth of faith in its future," and she was rich in human resources to help her. Mildred and her husband worked with some of the best newspaper journalists at the *Omaha Guide*. They hired their former colleagues, with whom they had excellent relationships, as their new employees. Clemmie Reynolds, the *Omaha Guide*'s stenographer and bookkeeper literally overnight became the *Star*'s stenographer and bookkeeper, while Edward Lane, the *Guide*'s shop supervisor became the *Star*'s shop supervisor, and Russell Reese, the *Guide*'s former Los Angeles correspondent, became the *Star*'s news reporter. Charles Davis and Cecile Walls, two recent high school graduates, served as copywriters, and Mrs. Gilbert's youngest brother, William Brown, acted as a special representative news reporter. Mary Green Parks was the *Star*'s other stenographer during the newspaper's opening months.[17]

Parks, a recent graduate of Omaha Technical High School, was also the sole secretary at the *Omaha Star*. The Gilberts paid her weekly three-dollar salary in pennies. Parks, the first employee to arrive at the newspaper office, opened it at 8:00 a.m. every day except Sunday. The Gilberts, who resided on Maple Street, augmented their initial meager income by renting out two rooms and eventually moved into the *Star*'s back apartment in 1939. Mary's first order of business on Monday morning was to intercept the florist's delivery of Mrs. Gilbert's seven carnation corsages for the week. The flowers, which Parks assumed the local florist supplied in exchange for a newspaper ad, became Mildred's trademark. Parks enjoyed her few months working at the *Star* and liked observing the owners. They were a happy well-matched couple. Sometimes Mildred would stride into the back office and say to her husband, "Well, let me show you what I got today. I sold an ad." Gilbert, a fairly quiet man who enjoyed smoking cigars, would reply, "Now that's progress."[18]

The *Star* newspaper office building became an economic mainstay at 2216 North Twenty-Fourth Street. Geographically, the *Star* was at the center of the black community. Because of that, distribution of the newspaper proved fairly simple. Like a Roman general, Mildred divided northern Omaha into two districts and used groups of ten youths to deliver newspapers in each region. Mildred implored readers to support not only their newspaper but also their teenage employees: "These young men will have the chance to make from 50 cents to five dollars per Saturday if the people of Omaha will purchase from them a copy of the *Omaha Star*. Now this is your chance to help our young men make a job for themselves." Creating jobs for young black men and women remained a priority for her throughout her life.[19]

Besides earning the Gilberts a living, the *Omaha Star* served a function by calling attention to the black community's accomplishments and emphasizing positive news. Although the Gilberts printed the *Star* in the identical page layout of the *Omaha Guide*, their newspaper became more of a success because of its local coverage. Michael Adams, former director of Affirmative Action's Omaha chapter, enjoyed reading the *Guide* because it contained less gossip and social news and more business and educational commentary about issues outside of the community and the city of Omaha. However, he thought the *Guide* was less fun to read and had very little personality. Both newspapers reported national news by using what Mary Green Parks called late news, meaning articles previously printed in other newspapers. Charles Rucker, former *Star* employee, recalled clipping articles from other black newspaper sources such as the *St. Louis Argus* and the *Kansas City Call*; it was what made up the national part of the *Star*. Readers ignored this news tardiness because the *Star* focused primarily on the people of northern Omaha. Nationwide, black newspapers had the monopoly on the black community's daily events. The black newspaper was indispensable to blacks, primarily because mainstream newspapers generally ignored them. There was essentially no other place for the black Near North Side population to get news about themselves. The *Omaha Star* became a communal space; black neighbors rushed to its newspaper office to supply stories and breaking news. Resident Elaine Rigley vividly remembers the *Star* edition that featured a photograph of her family in the Family of the Week column. Today, more than fifty years later, she still cherishes a framed copy of it. The Gilberts assured their readers that their newspaper was "an enterprise worthy of consideration, a mouthpiece and a force for the people. The *Omaha Star* is here to stay!"[20] The Gilberts' business started to flourish in the Near North Side. Mildred, who Parks credited as "the brains behind the organization," wisely placated C.C. Galloway, her former employer and now her journalistic competitor.

The rivalry between the *Omaha Star* and the *Omaha Guide* newspapers appeared minimal because each of the newspaper owners generally maintained a professional relationship. Mildred claimed she remained the best of friends with Galloway, whose *Guide* office was only two blocks away from the *Star*: "We invited each other to dinner. And we were the funniest rivals you can imagine. Whenever I'd sell an ad for the *Star*, I'd try to sell one for Mr. Galloway—or I'd tell him where he could find a prospect." One of the few instances in which Shirley Edward rebuked Galloway occurred when the *Guide*, the older, more established weekly, informed its readers that S. E. Gilbert supported Nebraska governor Robert "Roy" Cochran in his Democratic bid for the U.S. Senate. In an article titled "The *Omaha Star* Editor Fully Able to Make His Own Endorsements," Gilbert let Galloway know he replaced the Crusader News Service with the more moderately political International Negro Press for the *Star*'s news service, but that Gilbert was quite capable of announcing his own candidate choices without his former employer's assistance.[21]

But the marketing savvy team of S. E. and Mildred Gilbert did expect the assistance of the black community. Mildred, who strongly believed in Booker T. Washington's doctrine of hard work and religious uplift, exhorted her readers: "You now have a new enterprise in your community. This increases jobs and gives to our youth a respectable and legitimate livelihood. What will you do toward the building of a monument for your race, your city and your nation?" "Uncle Gil," better known as S. E. Gilbert, encouraged additional involvement from the youth.

> Don't forget
> If you have a bit of news
> Give it to the Omaha Star
> Or a joke that will amuse
> Tell it to the Omaha Star[22]

The *Star*'s Starite Club column, an obvious reincarnation of the *Guide*'s Guidite Club column, promised its younger readers a picnic to celebrate the founding of the black newspaper. Never one to miss a selling opportunity, Mildred offered a special Picnic Day annual subscription rate of $1.50 instead of the usual $2.00. Mayor Dan Butler, a portly, former football player and coach at Omaha's Creighton University, offered to give the welcoming speech at the picnic. For weeks the Gilberts teased readers with magnanimous offers of free ice cream and root beer floats on Picnic Day. When the *Star* owners finally selected September 10, 1938, as the chosen date, they exaggerated the guest list: "All the Midwest will be asked to participate in the *Omaha Star*'s mammouth [*sic*] Afro-American day.... The crowd should easily reach the 10,000 mark." While only a thousand participated, the newspaper's hopelessly false attendance projection indicated the Gilberts' desire to successfully market their newspaper while encouraging community unification.[23]

From its inception Mildred used the *Star* to unify the black neighborhood in a fight against unfair discrimination practices in Omaha. It was the type of 1940s American city "where you could sit anywhere on the bus" but "people would not sit near you." Mary Parks, the *Star* secretary, remembers visiting Mr. C's, a northern Omaha restaurant. Knowing she would be refused in-house restaurant service, she ordered items from the menu and picked up her meal at the drive-up window.

Parks, like many other black patrons in various cities throughout the United States, accepted this type of discriminatory situation without rancor, although today, thinking back on it, she acknowledges that "the thought of buying items from a place you could not work at was an injustice." Before the Gilberts arrived in Omaha, C.C. Galloway's way of solving public discrimination involved other Near North Side leaders, such as Arthur McCaw, Nebraska's first black state treasurer, and John Adams, the state's first black senator, walking into segregated restaurants. They had their wives, who were very fair skinned, book a table. If their wives were mistakenly seated because they "passed" as white, their husbands followed them into the establishment. If the couples were refused service, the men sued the establishment. The Gilberts applauded Galloway's individual efforts, but they wanted to create a grassroots community protest.[24]

Acting in concert with the 1930s national movement, Mildred deliberately engaged her newly adopted neighborhood in the Don't Buy Where You Can't Work and Shopper's Guide campaigns, which individually listed white northern Omaha businesses with black personnel. Drawing on nationwide boycott campaigns, Mildred and her husband instructed their readers to make every dollar count by joining their *Star* Don't Buy Where You Can't Work campaign. The Don't Buy national campaigns were usually led by individual leaders in black communities, although both the NAACP and the Communist Party offered their support. Chain stores in the inner cities, such as Walgreens Drug and Sears and Roebuck quickly revised their hiring policies and placed "We Employ Colored Salesmen" signs in store windows. The New York City campaign alone created seventy-five thousand new jobs for urban black workers during the Great Depression. Demanding the same from her readers, Mildred protested for a similar outcome in Omaha. She informed her predominantly minority audience, "It is your hard-earned dollar. Make it count by spending it with merchants and firms who show willingness, not by words but by action, to give employment to all Americans, regardless of race." By joining the *Star*'s local campaign, the black community created a better eco-

Involving the Community 55

nomic situation for everyone. As a newspaper owner, Mildred understood the power of consumer strategy boycotts and how a peaceful demonstration could effectively increase economic empowerment and black employment. Inner-city street-corner orator Ira Kemp's Don't Buy Where You Can't Work campaigns successfully targeted discriminating white store owners who operated businesses in the black belts of New York City, Chicago, Cleveland, and Detroit. Cheryl Lynn Greenberg's examination in *Or Does It Explode? Black Harlem in the Great Depression* of how black picketers would beg would-be shoppers to be self-respecting citizens and take their business elsewhere illustrates a situation S. E. Gilbert discussed with readers: "I stood across the street in the vicinity of 24th and Lake Streets. I saw car after car stop, doors open and black Americans step out and into the [Reed's] ice cream shop, void of a singular Negro representative employee, to purchase a delicacy that a Negro gave to the world. After counting in sixty minutes, over one hundred such entrances, I said to myself, 'how long, oh, how long' will the Negro of Omaha continue to sleep on their economic rights, the right to make their money count by spending where Negroes are employed."[25] Even though the owner of Reed's ice cream shop supported the *Star* by buying an ad in the newspaper's first edition, Mildred and her husband risked losing him as a valued client by persisting with their campaign. Indeed, her newspaper's Shopper's Guide column encouraged white and black readers alike to do business only with cooperating equal opportunity merchants. The *Omaha Star*'s campaign became even more important of a key civil rights precedent after the Supreme Court ruled consumer boycotting was a legal form of protest, in its 1938 *Garment Workers' Union v. Donnelly Garment Company* ruling.[26]

City of Omaha and northern Omaha administrators noticed and appreciated the positive effects of the *Star*'s political activism. Francis P. Matthews, president of the mainstream Omaha Chamber of Commerce, patronizingly congratulated them for producing a newspaper "for the welfare and happiness of a very important group of Omaha's population." Millard T. Woods, executive secretary of the Urban

League, commended the owners in a more convincing tone. "Your newspaper is great. I can see no reason why this venture shouldn't be an unusually successful one. With two go-getters like Mrs. Gilbert and you at the helm, I can easily visualize the *Star* as the Midwest's leading paper in but a few short years." The Urban League director's words proved partially correct; within the year, the *Star* boasted five thousand subscribers. At five cents a paper, the black weekly sold at a reasonable price. Larger black journals, such as the *Chicago Defender* and the *Pittsburgh Courier* charged ten cents an edition. Dr. and Mrs. Gilbert were following a textbook example of Booker T. Washington's ideals of self-autonomy and self-reliance. The couple became pillars of the black community. S. E. Gilbert even attempted to pursue his part-time political aspirations. He unsuccessfully ran for state legislator in the fifth district in 1942.[27]

The *Star* provided what the Republican national news-oriented *Omaha Guide* weekly did not: positive local news about individuals, organizations, and neighborhood concerns. Mildred's connection with national black issues and national black movements started the process of unifying the Near North Side's minority residents. She and the *Star* spoke for the city's isolated black community during a time when the minority population was otherwise invisible outside of its center at Twenty-Fourth and Lake Streets. While the *Star*'s version of Don't Buy campaigns succeeded in creating jobs, it did not solve the problem of unemployment in northern Omaha. But Mildred's contribution—the creation of new black businesses and an upsurge in selective black community spending—demonstrated the power of black consumerism and gained the attention of white and black leaders in Omaha.[28] As the daughter of a minister and as a former educator, Mildred Brown Gilbert's motherly figure would lead the community's transformation. It became her calling to teach black northern Omahans to demand a new level of respect while promoting an overall racial uplift of the Near North Side.

3

Politics of Respectability

"Wake up! Wake up! And give these future citizens an opportunity to develop into the kind of men and women to which you can point to with pride." Like a mother shaking her offspring, Mildred Brown Gilbert scolded her readers for not paying enough attention to themselves and their children. It was time to stop "expecting God and white folks" to do what the community could do by itself. If Omaha's largest minority, especially its black youth, only knew "what to wear, how to wear it, when to wear it and where to wear it," the mainstream population would take the black community more seriously. As the black matriarch of the neighborhood, Mildred insisted that the Near North Side could "wipeout mass ignorance" by learning proper etiquette. It was a common solution employed by black middle-class women associated with racial uplift organizations such as the Phyllis Wheatley Club and the Urban League. Like many other black American women in the twentieth century, Brown adhered to what Evelyn Brooks Higginbotham labeled as the politics of respectability.[1]

Higginbotham's *Righteous Discontent* explained how this middle-class phenomenon originated among black Baptist women at the 1900 Woman's Convention. By mirroring the white middle-class cult of true womanhood ideals, the politics of respectability supplied the foundation from which African American church women demanded complete equality with white America. Creating a mainstream respectability also refuted northern white misconceptions of southern black migrants. While the politics of respectability empowered women, it also created a counter middle-class image: "Their discursive contestation was not directed solely at white Americans; the black Baptist women condemned what they perceived to be negative practices and attitudes among their own people."² Using the example of assimilation equaling empowerment, these ladies insisted that the black minority must conform to the white majority's societal standard of manners and morals. The respectability gained by mimicking the dominant culture defined black women outside the parameters of the prevailing racist discourse.

As the female leader of the Near North Side, Mildred modeled the politics of respectability on a daily basis, whether it was redefining the meaning of black matriarchy; educating, raising, and uplifting Omaha's black youth for future advancement; establishing herself as a credible, respectable member of the Omaha community; or using her *Star* newspaper as a vehicle to instruct subscribers and refute racial stereotypes. Like many black women activists, Brown believed that her "moral standing was a steady rock upon which the race could lean" and that it was her womanly duty to provide maternal leadership for the black neighborhood.³

While Mildred Brown Gilbert fashioned a strong public motherly foundation for the community, her private maternal role fluctuated in her household. She had little control over the dynamics of the Gilbert family in the early 1940s. The United States' entry into World War II reinstated the Selective Service Act. Twenty-four-year-old resident Marvin Kellogg, who was engaged to Mildred's twenty-two-year-old foster daughter, Ruth, received his draft notice on February 24, 1942. Between Marvin's basic training and shipping overseas, the couple hurriedly married in March 1942. African Methodist Episcopalian pastor David Harris, the bride's father, arrived in time to witness their wedding but not officiate at it. Rev. Boyd Johnson conducted the ceremony at the home of Marvin's mother, Anna Kellogg. Mildred, whom Ruth referred to as Millie, attended the wedding alone. She acted as the mother of the bride at the private nuptial. Days later Technical Sergeant Kellogg rejoined the Army's Quartermaster Corp. Ruth became accustomed to living by herself in their new house. At the end of World War II in 1945, Kellogg returned to Omaha. With two of their three sons already born, he went to work for his mother-in-law as a part-time salesperson at the *Star*. She paid him straight commission on the ads he sold each week. Working also as the first black full-time truck driver for Robert's Dairy, Kellogg continued his part-time employment at the *Omaha Star* for the next twenty years. The permanency in Ruth Harris Kellogg's household eluded the residents of the Gilbert home.[4]

The Gilberts' marital discord started with a *Star* newspaper interview. A question-and-answer dialogue between Shirley Edward Gilbert and Virginia Cheeks of the Women's Army Auxiliary Corps (WAAC) in early April 1943 sparked romantic interests. Gilbert revisited with Cheeks at the Fort Des Moines training facility in Iowa the following week. Cheeks, a beautiful and intelligent lieutenant, was one of only forty black WAAC officers in the Midwest and only one of the four thousand black women serving nationwide. By the middle of April, she opened a temporary ten-day Omaha recruiting station at 2213 Lake Street; it was adjacent to the *Star*. To promote Cheeks's volunteer efforts, Dr. Gilbert created WAAC-tivities, an armed forces column dedicated to the newly renamed Women's Army Corps. Apparently Cheeks recruited more than women WAACs. In July 1943 *Star* readers opening the fifth-anniversary edition of the *Star* noticed a large prominent front-page article naming Mildred Gilbert as the "sole General Manager and Owner of the newspaper."[5]

After sixteen years the Gilberts' marriage ended in divorce on August 20, 1943. Divorce was not uncommon in the black community at this time, but three-quarters of divorced black couples were childless. Court papers listed Millie D. Brown Gilbert as the plaintiff and Shirley Edward Gilbert as the defendant. The Douglas County Divorce Court ruling "found the plaintiff conducted herself as a faithful and dutiful wife and fully performed all of her duties as wife of the defendant." Notwithstanding this conduct on the part of this plaintiff, the defendant "has been guilty of extreme cruelty." Mildred chose marital misconduct as the basis for the granting of their divorce. In the early to mid-twentieth century, a plaintiff wishing to divorce needed to present just cause for the dissolution of marriage. No-fault divorces did not exist until the 1970s. Mildred Gilbert asked the court for restoration of her former name and for the *Omaha Star* to remain hers. Shirley Edward Gilbert, who publicly agreed to both requests, privately insisted on an agreement between him and his soon to be ex-wife. An addendum to their divorce included a notarized paper stating that if S. E. remarried and had children, his children had the right to own the newspaper. It was a right his future offspring considered but rejected years later. Freed of his marital commitment, Gilbert joined the army's Medical Corp. Cheeks, the new recruiting officer of the Seventh Service Command in Kansas City, was his fiancée. Gilbert married the Charleston, West Virginia, native the following year. In 1945 he and his new wife had a son, Shirl Edward Gilbert Jr., and in 1947 the couple's daughter, Rosalyn Gilbert, arrived. Brown remained close friends with Gilbert. Several times she stayed at her former husband's home when attending newspaper conventions in Missouri. Dr. Shirl Edward Gilbert II fondly remembers the *Star* publisher visiting with his parents at their dinner table. He explained the underlying reason for his father's divorce pertained to children; apparently, Brown, the matriarch of the Near North Side, did not want children. Perhaps she realized she could devote more time to raising children in the community if she did not biologically have any of her own.[6]

As the owner, publisher, and editor, Brown had complete control of the *Omaha Star* newspaper. She paid off the property's final loan balance of $2,100 and purchased it from the Trebor Realty Company. The "East One Hundred Ten (E 110) feet of lot Three (3) in Block Seven (7) in Patrick's Second Addition to the city of Omaha," better known as the *Omaha Star*, was her sole property. Brown thanked the black community for its confidence in the *Omaha Star*, which she labeled as "the most Progressive Weekly in the State of Nebraska." Brown managed to increase the number of pages in the newspaper despite a small staff of seven. A society page and a children's page allowed more promotion of Near North Side residents, which increased sales of her black weekly.[7]

Financial stability enabled Brown to take a vacation at the end of 1946. She accompanied her brother Bennie and his wife, Lila Pryor Brown, on their annual holiday to Jamaica. Bennie earned a sizable salary as a United Service Organization coordinator. Between leisure activities with her brother and sister-in-law, Brown met Jamaican native Noel Maximilian "Max" Brownell. She was forty-two and he was nineteen years old. Brown was smitten with the attractive younger man. This may partially explain why Brown, like many ladies of her generation, did not readily disclose her age for the rest of her life. Even her personal physician, Dr. Laurence Zacharia, did not know her correct birth date. When someone asked her age, she responded, "Old enough to keep to it myself." Regardless of Brown's issue with age, Brownell accompanied her on the return flight to the United States. Within months of their return, Bertha Calloway, Brown's secretary, noted in her diary, "Miss Brown and her West Injun friend" were frequent guests at northern Omaha social gatherings. Brownell became a fixture in Brown's home while working as the *Star*'s office manager. Their relationship spanned the rest of Brown's life, and with Brownell by her side, she scolded, challenged, and protected the black residents of northern Omaha.[8]

According to Deborah Gray White's *Ar'n't I a Woman?*, three main stereotypes have plagued black women throughout American history: Jezebel, Mammy, and Sapphire. This trio of erroneous categorizations supplied false representation of black women. Prior to the Civil War the prejudiced image of Jezebel, the scandalous slave-rooted woman who "had never been able to close [her] legs to a white man," prevailed. Jezebel was the counterideal of the nineteenth century's version of white Victorian womanhood. This lascivious black woman originated as a rationale for white owners and slavers who were raping her as she toiled in the fields. Dominating the post–Civil War years was the figure of Mammy, Jezebel's opposite. Mammy was the postbellum black woman, reconstructed from Jezebel's framework but redemptive of the previous slave owner–black woman relationship. Mammy imbued white supremacy's patriarchal slavery nostalgia. She was a super nursemaid who could accomplish anything and everything. She was the surrogate mother to white children and white owners, manager of the house servants, and an expert in domestic matters. By the post–World War II years, though, characteristics of the first two mythical women reconfigured into Sapphire, the overbearing black woman who consumed men and refused "the black man to be a man in his own house." This updated twentieth-century stereotypical version, the black domineering matriarch, emerged as one of the leading characters on the popular *Amos 'n' Andy* radio show. The show's broadcast aired on a weekly basis starting in the mid-1940s. Millions of listeners heard the racist fabrication of a black married couple: muddled husband, Kingfish, and his overbearing emasculating wife, Sapphire. This fictional woman was no jewel, but ignorant mainstream audiences accepted her and even enjoyed her demeaning monologues. Sapphire represented a construction of what bell hooks calls the "anti-blackwoman." Her weekly portrayal contributed to the twentieth century's inaccurate belief that black women caused the downfall of black families and communities, a belief that later gained wider credence with the publication of the Moynihan Report in 1965. Supposedly, the black matriarch "transformed social relations into cultural preference, constructing matrifocality as an attribute of personality." Placing the blame on nature instead of history "obscured the role of unemployment, racism and state policies in undermining the African-American family."[9] Although Mildred Brown was alternately seen as a combination of Jezebel, Mammy, and Sapphire, she infused a positive sense of achievement into the negative mold of black matriarchy mythology.

Brown's maternal influence in the black community created an improved image of black matriarchy. She adhered to and advocated the African mindset of children needing more than one woman raising them. It was an old cultural tradition created in response to European colonialism and transatlantic slavery. Historically, black women raised other women's children when the parent or parents were absent, sometimes in a long-term arrangement, such as an informal adoption. Accepting this responsibility allowed any black woman "to treat biologically unrelated children as if they were members of their own families." Brown, whose role demonstrated a component unique to black American womanhood, acted as an "othermother," a modern term coined by Patricia Hill Collins. Brown served as fictive kin to all of Omaha's black community. She foster mothered Ruth Harris Kellogg and treated Ruth's sons, Marvin, Kenneth, and Dale, as her grandchildren. Brown repeated this maternal connection with her newspaper carriers.[10]

Despite the fact that Brown bore no biological children, she instinctively mothered and provided employment for many of northern Omaha's black youth from the 1940s through the 1960s. Selling newspapers was almost a rite of passage; Brown taught northern Omaha's youth about work, money, and accountability. Resident Michael Adams took pride in selling the *Star*. Brown taught him more than selling newspapers; she gave him the important sense of being appreciated through her demanding kind of way. She insisted carriers present themselves neatly with tucked-in shirts. Insubordination led to unemployment. Bill Parr admitted he did not deliver his newspapers in his youth. Max Brownell fired him, but first he spoke with Parr. In his Jamaican bass voice he said, "Now Billie, you are a Catholic. This is not the right thing to do." As a child Everett Reynolds depended on his salary as a *Star* newspaper carrier: "Two cents for each paper sold was a help to my family." Rodney Wead earned double that amount by selling papers for the *Omaha Star* and the *Omaha Guide*. But he liked payday better at the *Star*: "I can still see Miss Brown. She served us hot chocolate and cookies. She did not eat with us, but she enjoyed our company." When Rudy Smith turned twelve, he visited the newspaper's office to ask for a job. Wearing a housecoat and holding a cup of coffee, Brown gently smiled at him. After carefully writing down his name in her ledger, she said, "Here's twenty-five papers. Sell them."[11]

Brown's meticulous counting and distributing her weekly newspaper was a well-organized routine for her *Star* newspaper carriers. When the newspaper arrived from the printers in one big bundle, the carriers had to untangle it and count the papers; Brown wanted to make sure the printer was not cheating her. Newspaper carrier and office staffer Cathy Hughes recalled that the children folded the papers manually. There was no delivery through the mail, so the boys and girls packed them. Newspaper carrier Debra Bunting remembered Brown during this procedure. She was "larger than life, always impeccably dressed, hair down to the last detail, her corsage in place. She asked the carriers about their families and would always leave them with something positive, like 'study hard, honey.'" Brown's common-law husband, "Uncle Max," was in charge of distribution. The minute the bundling ended, no matter what Brown was doing, she would take a pile of newspapers and put them in her car. Max would shout, "Millie, you can't come in here and grab them off the stack." Millie just ignored him and repeated her action the next week. Twelve-year-old Hughes would try to stop her: "Miss Brown, here are your papers. They are counted." Brown replied, "No thanks," and took her own copies. "They were her papers!"[12]

As much as the *Star* was her business, Brown viewed raising the newspaper carriers as her maternal responsibility. Newspaper carrier Michael Adams saw Omaha's Near North Side as a village, and "Mrs. Brown was the village queen. We behaved as if we were her children and she behaved as if she had parental duties." During the two years Rudy Smith worked for Brown, she always took five minutes to talk to him. She tried to promote honesty and integrity by sharing her philosophy. She told him, "We try to help people at the *Omaha Star*. People want to read this paper. People are waiting for the paper. Be back here by noon. I'll be waiting for you." Between selling his copies, Smith read the *Omaha Star*. It was his first exposure to a black weekly publication and opened his eyes to the social life of the black community. Smith realized the people living in the northern Omaha neighborhood were intelligent and well read. Carrier Bob Partridge, who appreciated the hardworking and seemingly tireless Brown and her career philosophy, realized she was right: "She could do more with a smile than a lot of people did with a lot of effort." Brown was similar to Mary McLeod Bethune, who served as the Negro Affairs director for the National Youth Administration while she was a member of President Franklin Roosevelt's Black Cabinet, and Dorothy Height, who led Bethune's National Council for Negro Women for forty years, because they all insisted on involving the black community in their maternal efforts to effectively raise up "the race."[13]

As a black woman, Brown was culturally accountable for all of the community's children, in particular, the female children. It became an integral part of othermothering to offer individual "support for the task of teaching girls to resist white perceptions of black womanhood while appearing to conform to them." As a childless woman in a highly visible career, Brown had the maternal authority to preach and model the value of educating girls in the minority community. Aunt Millie took her family matriarchal duties just as seriously as her commitment to Omaha's black community. She paid for a large portion of her niece Marguerita Washington's college schooling. Her strong community bond resulted in maternal social activism. After all, motherhood was a sanctified role, a selfless life of sacrifice. Brown regularly published articles of great importance to her female readers, in which black women leaders, such as Nannie Burroughs, educated the Near North Side's population on how to "do for themselves." As a gendered and racialized strategy, maternalism and social housekeeping was as acceptable to white and black society as apple pie. As a community othermother, Brown created racial uplift, by focusing on the politics of respectability.[14]

Appearance was paramount to Brown's philosophy of personal, community, and corporate uplift. Her middle-class sensibility influenced Brown to embrace the opportunity to shape new urban communities by reforming migrants' dress, demeanor, and deportment. Brown had the time, the means, and, most important, the *Star*, to socially educate the various economic classes in the black community. Unlike black elitist educator Margaret Murray Washington, Booker T. Washington's third wife, who saw women's meetings as a way for the superior class of black women to teach domesticity to the African American masses, Brown, a former teacher herself, instructed her audience in social subjects not offered in the public segregated schools; her readership encompassed a larger classroom with a much more important agenda. Similar to the *Chicago Defender* informing newcomers what to wear and how to act properly in the city, the *Star* taught readers the correct mainstream way to present themselves. Female middle-class migrants did not necessarily accept white values, but they understood that respectability was the quickest route to social mobility. The *Star* weekly featured two favorite columns, Do's and Don'ts, a guideline for proper etiquette, and Christine Althouse's Beauty Culture, a commentary on the latest majority fashions. Brown informed her youthful readers, "It is your duty as young citizens to do your part in having that group who do not care how they look, act, or say to realize that society more often judges a district group by its worst than by its best." If astute readers ignored her advice, then "such conclusion will keep that portion of black America in Omaha who cares for his personal appearance from winning the place in society which they crave."[15]

By following white mannerisms, black women refuted stereotypes such as the Mammy and the Jezebel and lifted themselves into a space of superiority above noncompliant blacks and the working classes. They valued hard work, thrift, piety, and sexual restraint. These core ideals were values that were, theoretically, accessible to all classes and races and therefore routes of social climbing. Emulating this type of respectability distanced the "rough" working class from the "respectable" working and middle classes. The upwardly mobile black women embraced the Protestant work ethic, cleanliness, and temperance while warning against "gum chewing, gaudy colors, the nickelodeon, jazz, littered yards and a host of other perceived improprieties." Adhering to the politics of respectability not only enhanced Brown's image but also ensured her social mobility in the Omaha community. The conversion from southern rural disorder to northern urban order through migrant self-presentation and respectable behavior was a successful reform strategy. Brown worked tremendously hard to ensure that the words "backward" and "primitive" would not be used to describe her, her family, or her community.[16]

Mildred Brown became the model of a middle-class black woman. As the daughter of an impoverished but respected reverend, she understood the importance of social class. She recreated herself after she and her husband established the *Omaha Star*. As Victoria Wolcott writes in *Remaking Respectability: African American Women in Interwar Detroit*, "Middle-class blacks and members of the elite were keen to distance themselves from the dress and the demeanor of ordinary African Americans." Wolcott documented that practicing respectability involved observing set mainstream ideals, emulating society's normative values, and creating new African American versions of women's political, social, and cultural context. Brown stylishly dressed herself in classic designs; however, she was true to herself by insisting on flamboyant fabrics.[17]

Shocking pink, silver lamé, and beautiful scarlet red gowns hung from just a few of the dozens of hangers in Brown's closet. Near North Side resident Wilda Stephenson revealed Brown's fashion savvy secret. Because the *Star*'s owner was a little on the heavy side, she employed a seamstress. Between 1970 and 1989 Margaret Wright created classical outfits suited to Brown's personality and designed them specifically for her unique frame. Fittings at Wright's home were an event. Brown would always be late, stopping in just when she could. Before a fitting she would run through the house in her slip. Dress hems had to be longer in the back because Brown hunched slightly at the shoulders and tended to lean forward as she walked. Peggy Wright Daniels, Wright's daughter, recalled a particularly funny image: "Mom would sit on the front step, quibbling over the hem with Miss Brown. The *Star* owner would not stand up straight. Mom had to be a magician to make those hems work." The arguing was worth it. Brown walked with confidence, and she paid Wright an additional amount to create matching jackets for each of her dresses. The publisher separately bought the matching jewelry, gloves, hats, and shoes for every outfit. Daniels was in awe of Brown's finery. To her, the newspaper publisher was bigger than life.[18]

Very few of the more than 150 people interviewed for this book failed to comment on Brown's favorite matching accessory, her self-invented trademark, a large white corsage. Brown started her tradition of wearing a corsage when she cofounded the *Star*. After 1938 nothing she wore, whether it was a ball gown or a housecoat, was professionally appropriate unless it included a brace of flowers on her left shoulder. If a fresh corsage was unavailable, she would wait. She did not appear in public without one. Brown favored white flowers, usually carnations, but occasionally wore gardenias or roses. She said the blooms reminded her of her late father's small flower garden adjacent to their Alabama home. The flowers designated her as a middle-class woman, a special person, an honorary mother. Wearing a large corsage, similar to those floral badges worn by mothers throughout the United States on Mother's Day, provided Brown with matriarchal credibility. Brown enjoyed providing classy corsages for her niece Kathy Brown Battiste, and her sister-in-law Lila Brown, especially on the maternal May holiday. Brown also occasionally treated Kathy to a day at the beauty salon. Spending the afternoon having her hair done was one of Brown's favorite pastimes.[19]

Straight hair, also known as "good hair," became the respectable ideal of black womanhood. Women of color started making the weekly trip to the beauty parlor shortly after straightened hair became popular in the early 1900s. Cosmetologist Madame C. J. Walker, the country's first female millionaire, understood that a woman's hair was an integral part of black beauty culture and that the American standard of beauty used white women's hair as its guideline. Since the first years of the twentieth century, straightened black hair was an essential portion of proper grooming and the respectable appearance for modern black women. Hair relaxers, Walker's best-selling product, enabled mainstream styles. Beauty standards linked the hardworking religious black woman with the modern mainstream sense of femininity. Having straight locks became the standard of femininity for generations of black women. Cosmetics and straightened hair were no longer the realm of the 1920s flapper but the objective of proper women following the politics of respectability. Walker's ads deliberately featured minister's wives as models to counteract the church's stance against makeup and hair straightening as acts against the Lord. Brown, like her professional middle-class contemporaries, subscribed to this regimen of mainstream beauty because it was accepted by blacks and whites. Besides, her vanity prescribed it; she made sure her hair looked as good as her clothes. Charlie May Moore, whom everyone in northern Omaha called Sugar, except for Brown, who insisted on referring to her as Charlie, did the publisher's hair. Every week since Brown arrived in the Near North Side, she visited the Althouse Beauty Salon at Twenty-Fourth and Pratt Streets. The newspaper owner either had a facial or her hair done; her immaculate nails, manicured elsewhere, were always painted bright red. Charlie was Brown's confidant; Brown felt safe with her. Moore's beauty shop was a place Brown relaxed, insisting it was therapy. Kathy Peiss's *Hope in a Jar* explains that the beauty shop offered relaxation, sociability, and beauty. In particular, it was a nonthreatening space to decide which societal beauty standards the black woman wished to adopt while celebrating her sisterhood. Charlie's daughter, Lillian Burkhalter, loved Brown's snow-white hair, but the publisher did not. She had it dyed every week, even though she was allergic to the dye, which caused a reaction on her scalp. Annie, Brown's sister, pleaded with her to quit using the hair dye immediately. Brown ignored her elder sibling; she refused to be seen with white hair. It was unacceptable to her personal and professional image. Finally, Moore solved the problem by convincing Brown to do a rinse instead of a dye.[20]

The practical hairdresser attempted to persuade Brown to change her hairstyle as well, but that was not an option. In 1965 the Afro became a symbolic hairstyle. The natural hairdo represented resistance and pride to many African Americans. By refusing to use hair relaxers, black women demonstrated racial pride in their ancestral African heritage and a political ideology, especially for female nationalists and Black Panther Party members. Brown appreciated the hairstyle demonstrating that black people no longer needed to strive to act white, but the Afro was a generational hairdo that Brown saw as a hair don't. She wore her bouffant for more than fifty years.[21]

Observing mainstream hairstyles demonstrated a willingness to adhere, at least superficially, to white standards, whereas the issues of color gradation and passing were much more than skin deep. Skin color stratified the black population by creating a hierarchy observed by both the black and white community. Epidermis privileges began with white male sexual dominance over enslaved women. Gunnar Myrdal, a twentieth-century Swedish economist, called the attitude toward the children of such forced unions a "collective guilt on the part of white people for the large-scale miscegenation" they physically created. It brings to mind the sordid beginnings of the Breeding estate, the annual spring sale run by Mildred Brown's great-great-grandfather, Samuel Breeding, to breed women solely for the purpose of gaining new slaves. Myrdal, a fairly liberal man but still very much a product of his times, contended that "mulatto women have always been preferred to full-blooded Negroes as sex mates." As a contemporary of Brown's, Myrdal's dated thesis that the less socially handicapped mixed generations had a higher competitive value still bears some consideration. A majority of black nineteenth- and twentieth-century women leaders, like Brown, were light skinned or of mixed racial backgrounds and mixed parentage, like Mary Church Terrell and Anna Julia Cooper. These women had social opportunities because of the racist reasoning that their skin color was closer to white.[22]

During slavery, light-skinned African Americans received preferential treatment in work assignments, becoming household servants and sometimes receiving training in skilled trades. Because many were the offspring of plantation owners, they were more likely to be manumitted. After Emancipation these advantages gave them greater job security, independence, and influence. Straight hair and light skin affected everything from employment to club and church memberships. By the 1890s the "mulatto elite" were suspected of trying to become a separate caste or pass into white society.[23]

Because Brown's paternal and maternal great-grandfathers were white men, some of her racially mixed family had the choice of passing. Brown's mixed skin color was a shade of light brown. However, she was the darkest member of her immediate family. Her siblings' skin was lighter. Her brother, Bennie, was so fair skinned that with a hat on he easily passed for white. Charles Frank Robinson II's *Dangerous Liaisons: Sex and Love in the Segregated South* explains why many members of the black community regarded passing as a manipulative vulgar practice. A lighter complexion allowed black men and women social mobility in prejudiced mainstream society and the possibility of crossing class lines in the black community, but it often involved crossing cultural and racial lines. Passing enabled the Brown family to travel across the country. On family vacations Reverend Benjamin and Maggie Brown sent blue-eyed Bennie alone into hotels and gasoline stations. He paid for their middle-class lodgings and bought the necessary fuel. His parent's strategy sent a mixed message, no pun intended, to their children; it was a lesson each internalized. Brown refused to pass but she knew how to use her skin-color advantage. She regarded her lighter skin as a natural tool. Brown made her skin color more noticeable by wearing reds and pinks. Her brown skin was also a bankable asset. Historically, lighter-skinned black women were more likely to obtain jobs and earn higher wages, raises, and promotions. Light skin was associated with competence and whiteness. It was desirable by white employers and even employers of color who internalized white racial hierarchies. White employers preferred and black reformers desired to place the most respectable black women in public view.[24]

As the result of racist discourses and practices, the black male and female professionals with fairer complexions became the foundation of the brown middle class, and the darker-skinned blacks usually filled the black proletariat. It was not a prerequisite for middle-class or elite status, but lighter-skinned women, like National Association for Colored Women president Mary Church Terrell, who could and occasionally did pass for white, occupied leadership positions. Many middle-class blacks possessed an elitist mindset of color snobbery. Joining a black sorority might entail passing the brown paper bag test. Possessing skin at least as light as a bag meant one passed the test of sorority membership.[25]

Brown, who always referred to herself as a black woman in fifty years worth of *Omaha Star* editions despite her biracial lighter complexion, refused to accept a superior skin-color attitude, but she emulated middle-class ideals when establishing her credibility as a female publisher. The *Chicago Defender*'s founder, Robert S. Abbott, owned a Rolls-Royce; Brown's chauffeurs drove her Fleetwood Cadillac. Like the highly successful woman she was in the community, wherever she traveled she brought along an entourage of friends, family, and usually her accountant. Nephew William Andrew Brown confirmed that no matter how long Brown planned to visit him, she packed multiple suitcases. She had a separate suitcase for her hats while another piece of luggage was solely for her corsages. Dressing for outings took time. Niece Kathy Battiste remembers how much Aunt Millie liked public appearances, especially at mealtimes. Brown would place either her fur coat or mink stole over her stylish suits; then she would drag her fur behind her as the pair entered a restaurant. It was part of Brown's glamorous image of middle-class perfection. Catherine Phillips remembers her late sister-in-law best by her perfume. It was heavenly. Even though Brown lavishly applied Estée Lauder's *White Linen*, she still smelled wonderful. It was fitting that self-made entrepreneur Brown could not only refute the widespread Jezebel stereotype that black women were unclean but also wear a scent created by another successful businesswoman.[26]

The politics of respectability was not foolproof. It ignored racism's power and how it could damage even the cleanest, best-dressed, and most well-behaved black woman. Timothy Tyson's *Radio Free Dixie* recounted the violent tale of U.S. senator Jesse Helms's father beating an innocent middle-class black woman. Police officer Jesse Alexander Helms Sr. accosted the lady as she simply walked past him on the street. His father flattened the woman with his massive fists and dragged her off, with her dress over her head, to the nearest jailhouse in the same manner a cave man clubbed and dragged his sexual prey. Pulling up a woman's dress, especially a stylish garment, over her head was a cruel tactic used to degrade and demoralize a victimized black woman. When activist Fannie Lou Hamer was almost beaten to death by the police, she attempted to pull her clothing down, but she was stripped of her dignity anyway.[27]

Black women activists like Hamer and organizers such as Brown, usually started their leadership in marginalized spheres outside of traditional male leadership circles. Twentieth-century women of color excelled as community work strategists, negotiators, and organizers. According to Cheryl Townsend Gilkes, African American women bring three perspectives to community campaigns that make them politically assertive. First, their backgrounds are shaped by societal experiences, especially in the workforce. Second, they are privy to black men's suffering and feel it as well. Third, and perhaps the most integral source of discontent, is the effect of racial oppression on their children. Minimizing the damage done to their children and fashioning an inclusive future became a motivator for women's involvement. They construct group solidarity.[28] As a natural matriarch who subscribed to each of these three perspectives, Brown cared deeply about the future of Omaha's black youth. She committed herself to the survival and wholeness of the black community, and in typical maternalist fashion she focused on the most gendered essential relationship, that of a mother and her children. In Brown's case, that translated to her commitment to quality education: raising up black youth, one individual at a time.

Mildred firmly believed that education was the key to future empowerment. She subscribed to the same philosophy as her friend and contemporary, activist Dorothy Height: "The surest path to success is through education." Brown was aware of fellow educator Septima Clark, whose fifty years of teaching included the Highlander Folk School. Rosa Parks, the institute's most famous student, graphically demonstrated the power of education when she refused to give up her seat on a bus in Montgomery, Alabama. Institutes of higher education had always provided the means to escape from the working-class masses into the prominent middle class, regardless of one's skin color.[29]

Even as a middle-aged woman, Brown was a role model for northern Omaha's college-age students. She matriculated at the Municipal

University of Omaha between 1937 and 1966 and enrolled in forty courses. Her classes ran the gamut from Urban Sociology, Applied Psychology, and Practical Photography to Advertising, Newspaper Editing, Reporting and News Writing, Elementary Typing, and Speech for Business and Industry. Her transcripts showed many courses as Incomplete; Brown even repeated Principals of Economics five times. It did not matter. Regardless of whether she passed the class or not, she attended the course long enough to learn what she needed to know at that moment. Enrollment served her educational purpose to succeed in printing positive news to promote education and socially advance her black community. Completing the class was less of a goal.[30]

Brown offered her employees the opportunity to attend the university's classes and improve themselves through education as well. *Star* secretary Naomi Carter worked at the newspaper after she graduated from Omaha Technical High School in 1949. Brown paid her a hefty salary of eighteen dollars a week. For a young black girl in the 1950s, working at the *Star* was a chance at white-collar employment. Working as a secretary was an important job and being employed in an office was rarer than a minimum wage job with little advancement. Carter possessed no dreams of attending college since her large family had little extra money. But when Brown offered Carter and her other full-time office employees the opportunity to attend the Municipal University of Omaha, also known as Muni Uni, Carter accepted with pleasure. She registered for two classes, in which Brown also enrolled. The publisher's driver transported the two co-eds to and from campus. Carter, who still cherishes her class certificates to this day, earned an A in Psychology and a B in English, while Brown took Incompletes in both courses. Brown's matriarchal pride in Carter's educational achievement, despite the fact the newspaper owner's hectic schedule stopped her from finishing their classes, meant a lot to her young employee in the 1950s.[31]

Nationwide, though, community black matriarchs were deemed negative influences after assistant secretary of labor Daniel Moynihan blamed them for the impoverished state of black America in the 1960s.

The Department of Labor published Moynihan's historical, sociological, and statistical report, *The Negro Family: The Case for National Action*, better known as the *Moynihan Report of 1965*, and used it to explain the inferior status of black Americans. Moynihan concluded that African Americans existed in dire straits because black families were matriarchal constructions and therefore black men could not fulfill the role required of all men in an American patriarchal society. The federal government conceded that a black matriarchy, not a racist society, caused the deterioration of the black family. Furthermore, the black matriarchal system, which supposedly retarded the progress of black citizens as a whole, also imposed a crushing burden on black men and, consequently, on a great many black women as well. Moynihan excused American apartheid and instead claimed, "The problem with blacks was not so much white racism as it was an 'abnormal family structure.'" The working black mother became "the bad mother responsible for low educational attainment, crime, and delinquency." Moynihan embellished and damned the black Sapphire imagery even further when he stated, "A fundamental fact of Negro American family life is the often reversed roles of husband and wife." Whether or not Moynihan's now infamous report of 1965 intended to, it solidified the negative image of black womanhood. The double-pronged attack on black matriarchs for causing black male emasculation was complete. Even African American educator and historian John Hope Franklin bought into the report when he claimed, "The only way for our men to be more manly is for our women to be more womanly." His thoughts echoed Stokely Carmichael's, who allegedly stated, "The proper place of women in the Student Nonviolent Coordinating Committee [SNCC] is prone." His phrasing repeated a sentiment Brown's sister privately told her as well. According to Annie Washington, Brown's unhappiness in her first and possibly in her second marriage was because of the publisher's independent attitude. "You could find a nice man if you didn't try to dominate and boss every man.... A professional man isn't going to give up his business in another city to come to Omaha."[32]

The independent black woman, like her Euro-American counterpart, became unfeminine if she failed to display female subservience in a male-dominant society. Noncompliant businesswomen, such as Brown, who could hardly be classified as unfeminine, endured accusations of being too strong and of emasculating men. This false image, the black domineering Sapphire stereotype, still prevails in mainstream society. bell hooks's contention in *Ain't I a Woman* that Moynihan's report was yet another attempt by the white male power structure to cast the positive contributions of black women in a negative light remains irrefutable. The black matriarch label contains more negative stereotypes than any other derogatory myth characterizing black womanhood.[33]

Just as she challenged gender roles in public, Brown rewrote her definition of gender in her personal life. Max Brownell cooked for her while she ignored rudimentary housekeeping. Brown sporadically hired help to clean her home, and her grandson Marvin had a standing order to purchase Chinet paper plates from Kellogg's Market, the family's grocery store. Mildred did not wash dirty dishes. She was a busy two-career woman. Besides owning the *Star*, for a ten-year period she also owned the Carnation Ballroom, which she aptly named for her white corsage trademark. Brownell managed the Twenty-Fourth and Lake Streets nightclub with its jazz music and cocktail bar, which Brown assured the black community was policed during hours of business. Her venue provided younger residents with what she called a "place that is clean, well disciplined, and entertaining" and as "much of an asset as our church, our home, or our jobs." She booked several well-known artists like Chuck Berry, but usually had lesser-known musicians such as the Ravens and George Hudson and Orchestra; she occasionally gave the proceeds to the NAACP. Stars like Count Basie and Duke Ellington played at the Dreamland Ballroom, which was open only to adults of age. Brown used her ballroom mainly to hold wholesome nonalcoholic community events, like high school graduation dances, engagement parties, the Youth Amateur Show, the *Omaha Star* Home Appliance Show and Cooking School, talent shows, Dance Sundays, the Miss *Omaha Star* Annual Beauty Pageant, and the *Omaha Star*'s Christmas parties for news carriers. Mildred owned the establishment and booked its musical acts, but as the community's moral female leader, she was invisible to the primarily male customers except on special occasions like Valentine's Day, when she handed out long-stemmed carnations to her female clientele.[34]

As the owner of the Carnation Ballroom, matriarch of the Near North Side, and publisher of the *Omaha Star*, Brown firmly believed she had a maternal, moral, cultural, and economic obligation to the Near North Side. Brown was unable to protect herself from the personal pain of a divorce, but she used this life lesson to rededicate herself to the community and the *Star*. She took pride in modeling the politics of respectability through her dress and demeanor, and she taught these skills to the black residents, in particular the young men and women. It was one of the keys to the black neighborhood's future advancement and the basis of her credibility in the white and black communities of Omaha. As Brown created a lifetime career for herself, her staff, and her newspaper carriers, the *Star* produced new possibilities for the northern Omaha community.

Part 2 **Ensuring Her Success**

4

Working within Her Space

Mildred Brown saw her work at the *Omaha Star* as a ministry. She believed God had given her a calling, and being the publisher of the newspaper "gave her a pretty powerful calling card." Like other black female newspaper women, Brown saw journalism as a profession, but it was more of a community torch she took up specifically and explicitly as a black woman. African American female journalists initially started working in the newspaper business when white editor William Lloyd Garrison published Maria W. Stewart's antislavery speeches in his Boston abolitionist newspaper, the *Liberator*. Within months, Stewart was delivering heartfelt lectures throughout the city in 1833. "Unfriendly white doves . . . stole our fathers from their peaceful and quiet dwellings, and brought them hither and made bond men and bond women out of them. . . . African rights and liberty is a subject that ought to fire the breast of every free man of color in these United States." Inspired by Stewart's prose, *Liberator* staffer Mary Ann Shadd Cary and pastor Samuel Ward cofounded the *Provincial Freeman* in 1853. Thus, Cary became the United States' first black female editor of a black newspaper. Eighty-five years later Mildred Brown became Nebraska's first black woman editor of a black newspaper. Like her female predecessors, Brown became an impassioned advocate for her "race," gender, and profession.[1]

It had only twenty words on it, but her business card conveyed a great deal about her life and work: "Mildred D. Brown, editor and publisher of the *Omaha Star*, Nebraska's Only Black Newspaper Reaching a Multi-Million Dollar Market." Brown used her business acumen, practical sense, and college education to ensure the longevity of the *Star* and provide an alternative voice for the black neighborhood. The nationwide lifespan of minority weeklies averaged a mere nine years of operation, and of these 2,700 black newspapers published between 1827 and 1951, only 175 weeklies existed by the midcentury mark. Brown's organized marketing techniques and aggressive skills for selling ads, the financial lifeline of any newspaper, were the necessary ingredients keeping the *Star* in business and solvent. Her business sense was even more noteworthy when considering the *Star* had to compete against the *Omaha Guide*, northern Omaha's other black weekly, until the 1950s. Brown's *Star* followed a string of ten minority newspapers, each operated by religious or political black male leaders residing in either Lincoln or Omaha. She managed to outlast the other black weeklies because she was an excellent salesperson. She consistently promoted herself and the *Star* on local and national levels, while speaking out for the Near North Side community.[2]

She emulated her fellow black newspaper owners, men like Robert S. Abbott, founder of the *Chicago Defender*, and Robert Vann, creator of the *Pittsburgh Courier*, and especially women like her contemporary Charlotta Bass, who owned the *California Eagle*. Bass and Brown published their black weeklies from 1913 to 1951 and 1938 to 1989, respectively. While Brown retained the *Omaha Star* as part of her divorce settlement, Bass, who originally worked at the *California Eagle* as an advertising salesperson, purchased the rights to the black newspaper for fifty dollars at an auction. Marriage to her editor provided credibility for Bass, while divorce from her first husband convinced Brown to become an even more active participant in the *Star*. Brown lived with Max Brownell, her common-law second husband, whom she designated as the newspaper's office manager, whereas Charlotta Spears Bass hired Joseph Bass as an assistant and then married him. Kathleen A. Cairns's *Front-Page Women Journalists, 1920–1950* analyzed the Basses' office arrangement: Charlotta provided the editorial voice; Joseph kept the business solvent. But it was Rodger Streitmatter's *Raising Her Voice* that concluded how most newswomen became successful. They "achieved their journalistic successes while living independent lives." Bass's and Brown's state of childlessness, which relieved them of the

84 *Working within Her Space*

gendered expectations of their day, enabled them to travel throughout the United States. They attended NAACP and Urban League conventions and, most important, networked with other black publishers. Being black and middle-class, these two women had the desire and opportunity to operate Don't Buy Where You Can't Work and Double V campaigns to fight for civil rights in their communities. The *California Eagle* and the *Omaha Star* became the mouthpieces of their female owners, although Bass's newspaper eventually failed because she used it to preach the benefits of the communist-backed Progressive Party, while Brown kept her Democratic allegiance to herself.[3]

Brown dedicated herself to the Near North Side by making the *Star* speak for the black community. Nationwide, the black press was a key component for racial representation because the mainstream press predominantly printed news pertaining to the white community. It was the black weekly and the few black dailies, such as the *Chicago Defender*, that documented neighborhood events and provided national commentary concerning the black community. The black newspaper's function was to unify readers and "let white editors and citizens know that black citizens were humans who were being treated unjustly." In other words, the black press provided a much-needed voice. This was especially true in Nebraska.[4]

About thirty black newspapers appeared in Nebraska between statehood in 1867 and the founding of the *Omaha Star* in 1938. Unlike mainstream newspapers that relied on advertising dollars, black newspapers generally existed on the strength of circulation monies. The local black press obtained few ads beyond those infrequently sold to small black businesses. In 1876 Horace Newsom founded the *Western Post*, Nebraska's first black newspaper, in the small town of Hastings; it lasted only a few months. It conformed to the national pattern of black newspapers predominantly being newssheets.[5]

Nine Nebraska black newspapers, including the *Omaha Star*, gained enough local subscribers to become weeklies lasting longer than a year. Eight of these publications printed in Omaha and one newspaper was published in the state's capital city of Lincoln. Not surprisingly, these two cities, respectively, contained the largest and second-largest populations of black residents living in the midwestern state. In 1887 John B. Horton founded Omaha's first black newspaper, the *Omaha Chronicle*. Horton established it only two years after the creation of Omaha's leading mainstream newspaper, the *Omaha World-Herald*. The *Chronicle*, which published for only one year, did not enjoy the longevity of the *World-Herald*. Two years later, in 1889, the *Progress*, Omaha's second black newspaper, printed its first edition; eventually the circulation of the newspaper was five thousand readers out of a population of six thousand black Omaha residents. Its founder, Ferdinand L. Barnett, an Alabama migrant, published the *Progress* weekly until 1906. His newspaper's seventeen-year publication run was the longest in Omaha until the *Omaha Guide*. Four years after the creation of the *Progress*, two more black newspapers appeared in 1893. S. F. Franklin founded his pro-Republican *Enterprise* newspaper, while ex-slave Cyrus D. Bell created the pro-Democrat *Afro-American Sentinel*. The *Sentinel*, favoring the party of President Grover Cleveland, was a political anomaly in early twentieth-century black America but prefigured the black population's political switch from the party of Lincoln to the party of Roosevelt in the 1930s.[6]

Omaha's black press provided a space for its male publishers to debate political strategies for the city's fastest growing minority. Barnett, Franklin, and Bell became rivals. The three newspaper publishers of the *Progress*, *Enterprise*, and *Sentinel* jockeyed for leadership in Omaha. For example, Booker T. Washington's 1895 Atlanta Compromise speech earned positive and negative reviews, depending on the newspaper. Barnett's *Progress* doubted the benefits of accommodationism, while Franklin's *Enterprise* applauded Washington's leadership, and Bell's *Sentinel* endorsed Washington's "opposition to higher education for blacks" since "the race is in too big a hurry." The Democrat, Republican, or Popocrat (Populist and Democrat) political agenda of each publisher slanted their newspaper's viewpoint. Regardless, the three black political male leaders appealed to minority subscribers predominantly living in poor conditions.[7]

The city's black press motivated readers to join the Great Migration from the South to the North. In 1915, when African American reverend John Albert Williams created the *Omaha Monitor*, he encouraged participation in the mass movement by informing his black readers, "The *Monitor* will send out hundreds of transportation [vouchers] in the next two weeks in an effort to get as many applicants out of the South as possible." It remains difficult to ascertain how effectively Williams's incentive worked, but the black population in Omaha doubled by 1920. Responding to the first wave of migrants arriving in Omaha, Williams's business manager, George W. Parker, created a rival paper. Parker's *New Era* weekly printed from 1920 to 1926. After Parker's newspaper folded in 1927, Charles Chapman (C.C.) Galloway printed his Republican *Omaha Guide*. By the time the *Omaha Star*, a Roosevelt Democrat weekly, appeared in 1938, the *Guide* and the *Star* had a sizable pool of migrant readers in Omaha, but the weeklies were the only two black newspapers printed in Nebraska. The *Star*'s popularity over the *Guide* underscored the ingenuity of its cofounder and Nebraska's lone female newspaper publisher, Mildred Brown. The World War II era provided her weekly with the greatest opportunity for the black press since the Great Migration.[8]

Between 1939 and 1945 the black press reached its greatest level of influence and circulation in the United States. The nation's three largest black newspapers were thriving; the minority media could afford to keep the black community apprised of the fighting overseas and at home. John Sengstacke's *Chicago Defender* maintained 230,000 readers, while the *Pittsburgh Courier* had 350,000 subscribers, and the *Baltimore Afro-American* counted 170,000. These northern industrialized cities' circulation numbers increased as another wave of almost thirteen million black migrants left the South for northern employment; the greatest majority of travelers came from Mississippi and Alabama. Due to the shortage of white workers, most migrant black laborers obtained employment, but their positions were still menial and their housing segregated and limited. Emboldened by an expanding black population and a national platform through black New Dealer Mary

McLeod Bethune's National Youth Administration, blacks organized severe violent protests against this inequality, most notably during the 1943 riots in Detroit and Harlem. Francis Biddle, the United States attorney general, decided the answer to the bloodshed was reenforcing segregation abroad and at home.[9]

America's frustrated black communities responded with the nationwide Double Victory campaign, which the Federal Bureau of Investigation deemed subversive. The government surveillance during the Double V campaign almost compromised the black press during World War II. FBI agents would keenly read national newspapers, such as the *Pittsburgh Courier* and the *Chicago Defender*, and local race newspapers, including the *Guide* and the *Star*, avidly looking for seditious libel, especially after socialist A. Philip Randolph visited with Brown at the *Star*. But after monitoring Brown's newspaper for several years, the Justice Department agency decided the *Omaha Star* was a conservative weekly because Brown's former husband, Shirley Edward Gilbert, was no longer at the newspaper. The FBI had previously listed him as a "radical [editor] frequently writing rather irresponsible articles" that claimed the *Star* was "a militant organ, the true voice of the people." After all, during Gilbert's tenure at the *Star*, he had successfully sponsored Legislative Bill 263 on April 20, 1943: "It is unlawful for any person, firm, or corporation engaged, in Nebraska, in the production, manufacture, or distribution of any materials or national defense equipment for the State of Nebraska or the Government of the United States, to refuse to employ any person who is a citizen, in any capacity where said person is qualified, on account of color, race, creed, religion, or national origin of said person." FBI agents added an addendum in their report to director John Edgar Hoover that LB 263 was the first Omaha bill alleging employment discrimination. It was an issue Mildred Brown successfully addressed after the war ended; during the war she was too busy updating northern Omaha's citizens of Double V–rumored conspiracies.[10]

Brown kept her readers apprised of the anti-American rumor mill during the nationwide Double V fighting against fascism abroad and apartheid at home. Accusations against black communities throughout the United States were rife. An example of the typical types of rumors appeared in an agent's memo to Hoover. A white Omaha informant told an FBI agent that a particular teacher at the predominantly black Howard Kennedy Elementary School in northern Omaha allegedly overhead a pupil in her class say that "negroes" would "rather fight with people of our own color than with the white trash." The teacher wondered "if someone had been working among the negroes and inciting their dislike of the white people" and wanted to report the conversation to the federal agency, just in case it was true. In northern Omaha the rumors of residents being involved in subversive activities became so blatant the Urban League established a Rumor Control Center in Omaha. Run by an interracial group of Near North Side and city of Omaha residents, the center deflected random information concerning alleged incidents and supposed racial trouble caused by communist sympathizers. Brown's *Star* ignored this type of hearsay and continued displaying the Double V symbol on its newspaper cover. She urged her readers and "fellow American Negroes" to focus on "fighting against the Fascist doctrines abroad" but not to lose sight of the discrimination at home, "because the negroes have a stake in the American democracy" too.[11]

Eventually, President Franklin Roosevelt's administration decided to financially assist instead of politically hamstring black newspapers. Securing national advertisers for the black press was a difficult process until the government intervened in the 1940s. Prior to this time the Chicago-based advertising firm, W. B. Ziff Company; the Interstate United Newspapers; and Associated Publishers supplied national ads to black daily and weekly newspapers. Despite the best efforts of these three companies, it was not until Congress passed the excess profits tax of 1940, and its three subsequent statutes during World War II, that the sustainability of the black newspaper was assured. The 1940s taxes encouraged national corporations, predominantly owned by white businessmen, to advertise in black newspapers. It was not a case of big business supporting the black press, but rather the fact that these "businesses could avoid paying higher taxes on surplus cash by plowing the money back into the economy in new ways," such as advertising in black newspapers. Through this endeavor, national companies began realizing the value of the minority media as a conduit to the black community, which was an unexplored profitable new market. The resulting advertising windfall stabilized the black newspaper industry and solidified the power of the black press as a national institution.[12]

Mildred Brown was not among the original group of black newspaper publishers, editors, and executives who first met in Chicago to create the nationwide National Newspaper Publishers Association (NNPA) in 1940, but she explained to her readers the importance of the organization and how it would affect the continuation of the black press:

> The Negro Press, throughout its history, has been a medium of expression of causes potent to the Negro. First, for physical freedom; and now throughout America, the Negro press speaks out for the economic freedom of those it represents. On down through the ages, the Negro newspaper has served as eyes, ears and mouth of the group. For this reason it has become the most potent agency in Negro life in America, not only is it a great educator to Negroes, but also a great educator to white people, which is equally important. The Negro press is to be commended and should receive support of every Negro citizen in America, as well as in other lands. Therefore, it is with pleasure that the *Omaha Star* cast its lot with hundreds of other Negro publications, in an effort to impress its reading public with the past achievements in re-dedicating itself to the service of the people.[13]

The NNPA, whose two hundred newspapers had a circulation rise of 42 percent during World War II, was powerful enough to warrant the attention of presidents of the United States. Franklin D. Roosevelt first met with the NNPA in 1944 and promised to meet with the group annually, but the following May they met with Harry S. Truman, who assumed the presidency after Roosevelt's death. A few months later, in July 1945, Brown attended her first NNPA conference. Many other black newspaper publishers, including C.C. Galloway of the *Omaha Guide*, were in attendance. Undaunted by the dearth of male publishers, Brown eventually served as the NNPA membership chairperson and played a significant longtime role in the black organization.[14]

As Nebraska's only black female publisher, Mildred made a point to visit with as many of her fellow black publishers as possible when she attended the annual NNPA conferences between 1945 and 1989. At first, her colleagues equated Brown's appearance with her personality. Dorothy Leavell, publisher of the *Gary New Crusader* and *Chicago New Crusader* and current NNPA historian, distinctly remembers the first time she saw Mildred Brown at a conference in the 1970s. Brown arrived in a chauffeured station wagon. "You could hardly see in the windows because of the boxes. It had a hundred hatboxes and corsages she brought to the convention. The hotel put the flowers in their refrigerator. Miss Brown was so colorful." Garth Reeve Sr., publisher of the *Miami Times*, nicknamed Brown "the hat lady, since she never went anywhere without a hat." But after speaking with Brown, her constituents noticed more depth to her. Robert Vogel, publisher of the *Philadelphia Tribune*, observed that Brown "was not loud, very gracious and had a degree of elegance. She was a beautiful woman; every time you saw her. She represented an image; worldly, successful, distinguished, unique, someone who was respected, and success breeds attention." When John B. Smith Sr., the current president of the NNPA, met Brown in the 1960s, he was an impressionable twenty-five-year-old. "She stood out because she was one of the few women there." The northern Omaha publisher walked over to Smith and introduced herself. After a few minutes of conversation, she offered him some valuable advice. She told him to be true to his community in advocating power; it worked for her and the Near North Side. Smith continues to follow her advice to this day. As one of the few fellow black female newspaper owners, Leavell admired Brown's strength of character and conviction, especially concerning equality. "You did not want to ignore her. She felt strongly about inclusion and fair and equal treatment for all people. She would call you down. If you were rude to her, she would respond in kind." Leavell and the other black publishers decided Brown "put the *N* in nerve. She would talk with anyone in high places and made many friends that way. She had intestinal fortitude. Miss Brown lived in a man's world—if they said something, she gave it right back, and not with a dirty mouth." Always the southern-bred lady, Brown presented herself with decorum. Steve Davis, executive director of the NNPA, summarized one of Brown's best contributions to the black press organization: "Mildred does little things for little people to make them proud of what they have done. For the moment, that little person is big in the eyes of the community, and the community smiles upon them."[15]

The littlest people, the youth of northern Omaha, helped solve Mildred's most difficult task of assisting her limited full-time *Star* staff at the newspaper, or, as she referred to it, "The Store." Generally, the typical small black newspaper's office staff consisted of an editor and two reporters and one or two sales agents. Brown, like Robert Abbott, the *Chicago Defender*'s founder, cross-trained her salespeople as apprentice reporters. But she needed additional staff to provide news coverage she could not afford on a weekly basis. Brown's solution was to offer several northern Omaha youths unpaid positions at the *Star*. Joan McCaw Lincoln, daughter of Nebraska's first black state treasurer, wrote a weekly poetry column for the *Star* when she was eleven years old. Brown "paid" her only with pieces of fruit, but Lincoln never forgot the pleasure of seeing her poems printed each week. Bob Rodgers, a *Star* volunteer sportswriter in the 1940s, relished having Brown as a boss. Rodgers's *Star* sports column "was a fantasy; a kid of sixteen writing for a black newspaper, with work every week." In October 1946 one fantasy became a reality when Rodgers met Jackie Robinson. The famous athlete who broke baseball's color line stopped by the *Star* during a promotional tour in nearby Council Bluffs, Iowa. Near North Side resident Corrine White's writer aspirations came true when she served as an unpaid *Star* church reporter from 1944 to 1949. She recalled how the city's black churches had reporters writing weekly articles for the *Omaha Star*. While Brown updated the community with local church news, she received nominal church contributions, and residents purchased newspaper subscriptions. She even managed to increase the *Star*'s international coverage when Capt. Jim Cheeks, the personal black pilot of Ethiopian ruler Haile Salassie, was unable to secure a room at the Patton Hotel. Omaha's only hotel available to black customers was usually overbooked. Brown insisted the pilot stay in her second bedroom, and he in turn temporarily served as the *Star*'s world reporter. Brown took advantage of any situation to ensure the success of the *Star*.[16]

To keep her *Star* in business, Brown wrestled with the same dilemma that every black newspaper owner faced: securing ads. Like most minority newspaper publishers, Brown had to convince white advertisers to purchase ads by stressing the power of black consumerism. Her sales philosophy centered on understanding the community and her newspaper's role in it. "First, you must know your product and believe in it. You must believe in yourself. And in God. You can't fail if he is on your side, and you can't succeed if he isn't." It helped Brown that Galloway, her rival local black publisher, was no longer a vibrant participant in northern Omaha politics and that his newspaper, the *Omaha Guide*, was no longer a contender for Near North Side subscribers. Galloway attempted to sell his debt-ridden newspaper in the early 1950s, but no one in town wanted it. The *Guide* folded shortly after Galloway died in 1956. The demise of the other black weekly increased the *Star*'s advertising base because Brown no longer had to share ads or sales territory.[17]

Selling national and local ads for the *Star* was a challenge Mildred enjoyed immensely. Residents Tommie Davis and Darryl Eure remember listening to Brown discuss her favorite activity, what she called "the hot pursuit of ads." Brown's "eyes would light up when she talked about money. She would rub her hands together. She loved making money." Brown understood the publisher's need for advertisement. It was more important than news. She could not print a paper without money. Harold "Andy" Anderson, former *Omaha World-Herald* publisher, concurred with Brown's assessment of running a newspaper. "Revenue [must] exceed expenses or you can't be around to practice journalism too long." John Gottschalk, former *Omaha World-Herald* publisher, seconded their philosophies by remarking, "Selling was where it was at, since we in the advertising business sell distribution" first and news second. Brown, who considered herself a better salesperson than a journalist, had the right talent and priorities to ensure the longevity of the *Star*.[18]

She promoted the *Star* at public events and local community contests. To her, food fairs, baby contests, and fashion shows were venues to increase the newspaper's circulation. When Robert Vann's *Pittsburg Courier* promised a car to the employee selling the most subscriptions, Brown copied the Indiana black publisher and offered a new bike to the newspaper carrier with the highest number of subscriptions sold. Brown sold her *Star* so effectively, that unlike most weekly black newspapers that survived primarily through subscribers, she could boast, "I have never had to rely on circulation, I've always had a lot of advertising." Brown constantly practiced her successful mantra: "subscriptions do not keep the newspaper, ads do. Ads are the lifeline" and searched for salespeople to help her promote the *Star* even further.[19]

Brown changed Royce Keller's life when she hired him as a salesperson for the *Star* in the 1960s. Keller was a teenager working at the black-owned Texaco service station across from the *Star* building. He pumped gas and fixed flat tires five days a week. He had hoped to go to college, but his educated father could find work only as a janitor in Omaha. Keller's job was necessary to augment the family's finances. One afternoon Brown drove her Cadillac across the street for a wash and gas. Keller's coveralls were greasy and he was sweaty, but somehow she saw his potential. "She flat out offered me a job; there was no interview." Brown hired Keller as an advertising salesperson, even though he had not sold anything in the past. She thought he had the poise to do it. Keller learned the newspaper ad business by shadowing Brown on sales calls; sometimes he drove, sometimes she drove. It did not matter. Keller was an apt student, comprehending the business of sales.[20]

Brown also taught Keller the politics of respectability. She insisted that he wear a suit and tie that matched her professional dress. On a particularly difficult day, a white secretary refused Brown and Keller access to her supervisor. She treated them as if they were the stereotypical "uppity" black man and woman demanding equality. Being discriminated against while he was trying to learn a better living was traumatic for Keller. Discussing the experience with him afterward, Brown, forever the teacher, turned the upsetting situation into a golden teaching moment. She told Keller, "We were in there to speak with the manager and we dressed well and spoke well. Our presence was an affront." Noting his downtrodden expression, she soberly added, "Do not worry, whatever color we are, the color of money trumps the color of the person selling the product." Brown recognized the racial prejudice at work that afternoon, but she neither accepted it nor resigned herself to it. She and Keller were people of character first and people of color second. She refused to believe in the artificial categories of race. Brown shared this belief with her readers every week in the *Omaha Star* and practiced it in her newspaper business.[21]

Mildred possessed an assertive style for encouraging business owners to buy ads in the *Star*. Resident Archie Godfrey labeled it as "very aggressive with a feminine twist," while *Star* secretary Joyce Young appreciated Brown's no-nonsense approach in a more straightforward manner. "She would walk up to an owner and say, now you need to take an ad out in this paper, so here I am, so take this ad out." If the owner refused to buy an ad, Brown continued calling on him or her until they purchased one, and then Brown would say, "Now you need to do this every week." Ruth Thomas, YWCA director, remembered Brown selling ads in Omaha's downtown Brandeis department store, dime stores, and dress shops, although the clothing venues were a harder sell. Omaha's dress shops, like many white-owned urban stores during the 1940s and 1950s, allowed black customers to purchase items in their stores but forbid them from trying on merchandise. Despite this discriminatory practice, Brown seldom left these businesses without selling an ad. As Thomas fondly stated, "It was easier to buy one [an ad from Brown] than refuse it." She was almost a warrior; she was such a powerful presence. Indeed, she made it a point to know the city leaders of Omaha, people like Peter Kiewit and Warren Buffet, the local movers and shakers. That way, "Brown made her own footprint," with connections equal to the power of the city administrators. As the *Star* publisher, Brown had access to everyone. She knew everyone and everyone knew her.[22]

Brown used her ethnicity and gender to influence decision makers. Although it was not part of the politics of respectability, and it certainly did not fit with her desire to reconfigure Jezebel stereotyping, she used her blackness and gender as a subtle sexual enticement. Robert Armstrong, executive director of the Omaha Housing Authority, vividly remembers Brown telling him she never wore slacks when she was out selling ads. When she sat down in a male client's office, she would marginally hike up her skirt; that way a little bit of knee showed during her sales pitch. As a black woman living in Omaha, a city in which miscegenation laws forbid interracial marriages until 1963, Brown knew she presented a certain titillation. A well-dressed, attractive, biracial lady discussing serious business was a unique circumstance, especially when it meant one-on-one meetings with powerful white businessmen. She played on the age-old dominance of white plantation owners subjecting their black enslaved women, but Brown possessed the upper hand. While she flirted with these men, she had no intention of anything less than ladylike behavior throughout her business transactions. But she did intend to sell ads to keep the *Omaha Star* operating. Her sister-in-law, Catherine Phillips, still shakes her head in wonder at her tenacity. "Nothing got past her. She was a progressive woman." Brown used her assertive skills to the best of her advantage once she was inside a decision maker's office.[23]

"Hitting a client in the wallet" involved Brown's special technique of manipulating corporate administrators into buying *Star* advertisements. She would "rather hit a man in his pocketbook than in his stomach like he does you." Resident Paul Bryant recalled when Mutual of Omaha's CEO told her that buying an ad in the *Star* would not increase his business, Brown earned her ad by replying, "What if I write an article and repeat what you just said?" Brown refused to take no from her customers. During a particularly trying sales meeting, she and a corporate manager named Ed talked back and forth about buying an ad while *Star* salesperson Rudy Smith observed the successful session. "She never did play chess, but she always played verbal chess." The first move came when the client said no to the ad. Then Brown advanced by replying, "Yes, you are going to buy one." Otherwise, she would "run an old ad and next week people will be looking for your old merchandise. They will not like you. Plus, I am going to bill the national office for the old ad and tell them you sent the wrong ad in by mistake." Brown smiled at Ed. It was checkmate when she said, "Now, we do not want to upset the customer, do we?" Remembering another successful tenacious incident, Buddy Hogan, director of City Relations, laughed as he retold the story of a disgruntled white shoe-store owner calling his office. The man wished to file a complaint against a black woman threatening to harm his business if he did not advertise in her newspaper. Hogan knew the irate businessman was referring to the *Star* publisher, but he did not even bother informing Brown about the complaint. He knew what *Star* sportswriter, Bob Rodgers, discovered several years before him: "She ran the whole show. She ran it with an iron fist."[24]

Her hands-on fashion of operating the *Star* included personally visiting with each Omaha business client. She convinced local black store owner Floyd Westbrook to do business with her *Star*. His F&L grocery store existed during a time when "blacks did not have businesses"; he was the third black man in northern Omaha to own a store. Brown arrived at his business with an entourage, her driver, and a female friend and introduced herself to Westbrook. "I am Mildred Brown. I own the *Omaha Star*, and I think if you advertise through the paper I can help you." Westbrook told her he would consider buying an ad. A week later he visited the *Star*. The newspaper publisher called him by name and invited him into her back office to talk business. Brown chose an ad size that would work best for him. Westbrook ran it for a month and continued to buy an ad afterward. In between, Brown visited his establishment; she purchased homemade sausage and hamburger. After a few months the *Star* publisher noticed his store "had a lot of traffic" and asked about putting a newspaper stand by the front counter. Westbrook liked the fact that Brown was "straightforward, educated, had manners, and always asked him how his business was doing." He agreed to her proposal. "Every week twenty to twenty-five newspapers arrived; most weeks they all sold."[25]

While building relationships with local northern Omaha and city of Omaha customers, sometimes Brown became a client as well. After selling an ad to Louis Blumkin, son of Rose Blumkin, Nebraska Furniture Mart's founder, she walked back to the mart's accounting department. Truman Clare, a Creighton law student working part-time at the furniture store, handed her the store's check for purchasing an ad in the *Star*. After a number of these transactions, Clare and Brown became close friends, to the point that after he graduated from law school in 1951, she became one of his first clients. Brown also became a lifetime customer of the Nebraska Furniture Mart. Blumkin admired the owner of the *Star*. She was "smart, persistent, and followed everything up." He placed her in the same category as his successful mother. "They were both outstanding people, plus they were entrepreneurial in nature." As a successful black businesswoman, Brown was still an anomaly in Omaha, but as an American black female publisher living in the latter half of the twentieth century, she was starting to have plenty of company.[26]

By the early 1970s Brown was no longer one of the few black women publishing a black newspaper. In the Midwest Ada Franklin owned the *Kansas City Call*, and in the Southwest Eloise Banks controlled the *Phoenix Arizona Tribune*. Lenora Carter ran the *Houston Forward Times*, and Ophelia Mitchell operated the southern *Columbus, Georgia Times*. However, unlike Brown, none of these women founded their respective newspaper; each became the owner after her husband's death. Although older, contemporary black female newspaper editors, such as Ruth Washington at the *Los Angeles Sentinel*, E. P. Alexander at the *Los Angeles Herald-Dispatch*, and Lucile Bluford at the *Kansas City Call*, were born during Brown's era, she was unlike any of her contemporaries, because she controlled every process of the *Star*. She had the final say. She wrote, edited, and corrected copy; decided which stories ran; and picked photograph layout sizes to publish what she lovingly referred to as "my paper."[27]

Brown's dedication to the *Star* and her selling expertise kept her prominent in her field and in Omaha. Whether it was a posting of local church schedules, pictures of weddings, minutes from meetings, or job listings, Brown's newspaper covered it. As a Near North Side teenage newspaper carrier, Debra Bunting realized at a young age, "It was 'our news,' the social news that did not show up in the mainstream *Omaha World-Herald* newspaper. The *Star* was the go-to place for information; the paper presented a slice of life every day, a true story. It told you everything you needed to know." Brown's ministerial calling was to make the black community visible year after year, and she kept her *Star* financially solvent to reach her goal. Selling was her greatest business strength. Her clients wavered between pleasure and tolerance while she cajoled, convinced, manipulated, and made her gender work in her favor. She presented her *Star* as a vehicle benefiting her clients and ended her sales pitches by saying, "Do you want a page instead of a two column versus a three column?" Her regular clients, who knew her persistent methods, even joked with her, "How big an ad do you want this time?" Robert Armstrong stated what Omaha's white and black businessmen were beginning to understand: "If you were going to do anything in Omaha in those days, you would need to know Mildred Brown." Near North Side residents would soon discover the economic worth of Brown's valuable relationship with the black community during the late 1940s and 1950s.[28]

5

Collective Activism and the De Porres Club

Precisely at 10:00 a.m. on June 20, 1952, a stylishly dressed Mildred Brown urged Omaha's city council to "do all in their power to see that Negroes were hired as bus drivers and therefore end the lily-white hiring practices of the Omaha & Council Bluffs Streetcar Company." Speaking slowly, enunciating each word and standing at her tallest five feet and five inches, the publisher directed her comments to the council chair. "I say to you, your honor, the mayor, if the tram company will not hire Negroes as drivers we prevail on you to remove the franchise of the bus company." Straightening the carnation corsage fastened to her fuchsia suit jacket, she abruptly turned on her matching colored high heels. Approaching her chair, Brown looked over her shoulder at the row of white councilmen and said, "If our boys can drive jeeps, tanks and jet planes in Korea in the fight to save democracy, make democracy work at home."[1]

During the late 1940s and 1950s Brown committed herself to making democracy work in her community. Combining forces with white De Porres Club cofounders, reverend John Markoe and student Denny Holland, she led a collective activist campaign for black employment through the aegis of the *Omaha Star*. Brown, Max Brownell, her common-law second husband, and the interracial De Porres members tested racial employment policies and customer treatment among local businesses. If any of the club members were refused a job application or service, the store owners were quickly reminded of the law. If the owners still didn't comply, a warrant for their arrest was issued. The De Porres Club rarely lost a case. Brown's *Star* newspaper played a key role in challenging and changing unfair hiring practices and unequal customer treatment at several businesses on the Near North Side. Her newspaper kept readers informed of noncompliant businesses and printed flyers for community boycotts. Brown's local activism would later augment the national movement in the urban North.[2]

The newspaper owner started her grassroots movement against discriminatory hiring policies in February 1948. She requested a neighborhood meeting and instructed interested *Star* readers to meet her at the black Young Women's Christian Association (YWCA) building. Brown chose this location not only because she was a member of the organization but also because of the association's opposition to lynching, promotion of better race relations, and empowerment of women. At the appointed date and time about thirty-five people arrived at the YWCA. The interracial group listened to Brown expound on the unfairness of white business owners accepting the black community as customers but refusing to consider them as employees. Brown's staffers researched 534 available occupations listed in the 1940 census. They discovered Omaha's "negroes have no employment in as many as 96 occupations." Despite the fact that skilled black men and women applied for these positions, their applications met with rejection. On the day of Brown's meeting, about a thousand black citizens from the Near North Side were seeking work, while those employed were "at jobs far below their status, both in rank and pay." The Alabama native told members of her audience that they "must approach industry, commerce and big business with our problem and seek the opportunity to work and grow." She demanded those present to act quickly: "Let us resolve to be a people, and subsequently act in a way to show we appreciate employment of members of our group by patronizing all businesses where there can be found Negroes working." The racially mixed assembly agreed to convene again to outline a plan of action. They elected Brown as their chairperson. Brown's *Omaha Star* would become the key component of collective activism necessary to change discriminatory hiring practices in northern Omaha.[3]

Her newspaper campaign for equal opportunity employment gained momentum from the De Porres Club. Father John Markoe and six white Creighton University students founded the activist organization on November 3, 1947; additional branches appeared in Kansas City and Denver by the mid 1950s. The De Porres Club's first meeting in Omaha attracted an interracial crowd of forty-seven. Markoe, a tall, silver-haired former West Point graduate recently banished from Saint Louis University's Jesuit community, was looking forward to creating change in Omaha. He was already known for his eccentric habit of smoking old cigarette butts he found on the ground. Years earlier the priest took a vow against luxury, so he allowed himself used cigarettes only. Father Markoe already knew Arthur McCaw, Nebraska's black state treasurer and was good friends with Dwight D. Eisenhower, who had been McCaw's Sunday school teacher. At the meeting Markoe delivered the opening prayer. Afterward, he explained to those gathered that the organization borrowed its name from black Dominican friar Martin de Porres, a long deceased biracial monk, best known for his slave-ship ministry. Markoe informed the gathering that the club's goals were "better racial relations through constructive actions, to banish every form of compulsory segregation and abolish any and all forms of discrimination against individuals because of race, color or creed." Or, in the private words of the Jesuit priest, "to kick Jim Crow's ass out of Omaha." At the end of the initial meeting, members elected twenty-one-year-old Denny Holland as president of the club and *Omaha Star* reporter Harold Tibbs as the organization's vice president.[4]

The club demonstrated a national trend of the Catholic Church within impoverished black communities. Patrick Jones's *The Selma of the North* examines how Father Groppi and his congregation joined black urban residents in a church-approved fight against racism and discrimination in Milwaukee, Wisconsin. In a similar act of selflessness Father Markoe and his brother William promised "to give and dedicate our whole lives and all our energies, as far as we are able . . . for the work of the salvation of the Negroes in the United States."[5]

Some northern Omaha citizens incorrectly assumed that because the De Porres Club started as a Creighton University Catholic organization and became an independent interdenominational nonpartisan civic group, it was interested in helping only the black Catholic community. Indeed, residents interviewed for this project still believed this to be true, referring to the club as "that Catholic group" and saying that "it was Saint Benedict's" fighting against discrimination. In retrospect, there was some truth to residents' confusion. The black church's jurisdiction in Omaha's Second Ward partially connected it to the city's predominantly white thirty-three houses of Catholic worship. Stephen Szmrecsanyi noted in *History of the Catholic Church in Northeast Nebraska* that "no church in the [city of Omaha] archdiocese admitted blacks on a membership basis until the 1950s." Blacks who attempted to join segregated churches were "shown in a variety of ways that they were not welcome." But because of the success of the De Porres Club, Omaha's white archbishop Gerald Bergan committed mainstream city of Omaha Catholic parishioners to fighting against racial discrimination in northern Omaha.[6]

The De Porres Club taught its members to challenge discriminatory behaviors in the city of Omaha. African American Bertha Calloway and her husband, James, joined the club "because Omaha was a racist town; you couldn't eat downtown." She recalled the Jesuit priest encouraging members to fight against racism. "Father Markoe tried to keep quiet, but he talked about white people like you wouldn't *believe*, and then after he'd do his little talk, we would get together and have little meetings." Black De Porres member Dorothy Eure remembered these original breakout sessions. "Not only did we discuss the evils of racism, but we developed plans and strategy, maneuvering our small force to correcting the vicious acts." The city of Omaha, similar to other urban midwestern cities, reinforced southern de jure laws as accepted de facto segregation. An editorial in Iowa's mainstream newspaper, the *Des Moines Tribune*, indicated a common acceptance of Jim Crow laws among several prosegregation citizens living in one of Brown's former cities of residence. "Conditions are getting to be rather rotten in Des Moines, when Negroes are given the right by our damnable state law to enter the first class restaurants and be served food in the booths with white customers." Challenging and changing this same type of discriminatory viewpoint in Omaha was possible, but it would take the combined efforts of Brown, the *Star*, and the interracial De Porres Club.[7]

Mildred Brown and the De Porres Club first joined forces when Marvin Kellogg, Brown's adopted son-in-law, filed a discrimination suit against the downtown Greyhound bus station's Harkert Café. Kellogg and his interracial party of five, one of whom was Mildred, were refused service "because they were Negroes, . . . [but] if they wanted to take the food out," the owner might serve them. Brown's newspaper reported the incident as an opportunity of "civil rights guaranteed," since "those that were denied service immediately went to the necessary task of swearing out a warrant for the arrest of the manager of the eating establishment concerned." In an editorial the *Star*'s owner summed up the situation as one that would disappear soon. "Such law enforcement will soon rid our city of such degrading happenings if the citizens that are refused service will continue to have those concerned arrested. Not much trouble involved. It just takes a little time." The club hosted a "Marvin Kellogg Rally" to pay Kellogg's legal expenses, while the *Star* publicized the event. The response from Near North Side residents was overwhelming. Possibly intimidated, Frank Clay, the Harkert Café owner, failed to appear on his court date. Specifics of Kellogg's discrimination case might offer a better assessment of the city's latent racism, but records of Kellogg's suit and all other northern Omaha discriminatory grievances filed at Omaha's Police Court remain unavailable to the public. The Omaha Police Department and the city of Omaha's refusal to provide current access to these records bears further investigation in future projects on discrimination toward Omaha's largest minority population. Research at Omaha's Roman L. Hruska United States Courthouse revealed no documentation of federal discrimination suits filed by either Mildred D. Brown or Marvin Kellogg Sr.[8]

Because of possible public backlash against the university, Creighton administrators insisted that the De Porres Club convene elsewhere. The club "moved its meetings off campus due to [the] controversy." As the organization's sponsor, Markoe was aware of several college professors and citizens finding fault with the program. Outsiders viewed the organization as a bunch of radical crackpots disturbing the peace. The interracial association was even accused of fostering mixed dating, designed to culminate in biracial marriages. Several Creighton priests ostracized Markoe. It began in the Jesuit university's dining hall. Markoe somehow always ended up eating alone. He heard the not-so-quiet mumblings; his colleagues labeled him "the nigger lover" and "nigger Markoe." Undaunted by the lack of support from his fellow professors and the university, Markoe temporarily moved the club to a storefront office on Twenty-Fourth Street, but the rent money proved difficult to raise. The *Star*'s owner invited the De Porres Club into the newspaper office building, which was also her home. She informed Markoe that he did not need money to operate out of her business. The De Porres Club planned to meet at the *Star* on Friday nights. Brown announced the organization's new arrangement on the front page of her weekly. "Through the courtesy of Miss Mildred Brown," the De Porres Club would be meeting at the newspaper office for the foreseeable future.[9]

Father Markoe and Mildred Brown became the parents of the De Porres Club. Reverend Kenneth Vavrina of Saint Benedict the Moor Church saw Markoe as the father of Omaha's civil rights movement. The priest led demonstrations down Twenty-Fourth Street, long before residents understood what was happening on the northern side of the city. Vavrina, the leader of northern Omaha's largest black Catholic congregation, understood Markoe's dual role in the black community and the De Porres Club. Serving as a priest, Markoe had neither a wife nor a child, but he mentored white club president Denny Holland. Because the activist liberal arts student recently lost his father, he regularly asked Markoe for paternal advice, especially when Holland received hate mail threatening to kill him because of his involvement in the association. Mildred was the mother figure in the De Porres family. The *Star*'s owner became the organization's staunchest ally. Interacting with the De Porres organization became a shining part of the publisher's life. When club members invited activist organizations, such as the

Friendship Houses of America, to Omaha, Brown provided rooms for their meetings at her Carnation Ballroom. She hired Holland as a *Star* reporter, photographer, advertising salesperson, and driver. Employing the club's president as her chauffeur allowed Brown the time to teach him salesmanship while acting as a surrogate mother. When Holland married Jean Waite, a De Porres Club reporter, the *Omaha Star* not only ran a long article on the nuptials but also accompanied it with a large wedding photograph of the happy couple.[10] New opportunities for the twosome and the rest of the activist organization quickly emerged with the discovery of a state law.

The De Porres Club jumpstarted northern Omaha's equality campaign when it discovered an old but valuable legal precedent. The 1893 Nebraska Civil Rights Statute supplied necessary legal leverage against discrimination:

> All persons within this state shall be entitled to a full and equal enjoyment of the accommodations, advantages, facilities and privileges of inns, restaurants, public amusements, conveyances, barber shops, theaters and other places of amusements; subject only to the conditions and limitations established by law and applicable alike to every person. Any person who shall violate the foregoing section by denying to any person, except for reason by law applicable to all persons, the full enjoyment of any of the accommodations, advantages, facilities, or privileges enumerated in the foregoing section, or by aiding or inciting such denials, shall for each offense be deemed guilty of a misdemeanor and be fined in any sum not less than twenty-five dollars nor more than one hundred dollars and to pay the costs of the prosecution.[11]

To convince the city of Omaha to prosecute violators, club members distributed hundreds of handbills documenting the civil rights statute. The *Star*'s publisher supported the organization's activism by paying for the printing of the flyers and publicly stated, "I believe in economic measures, like boycotts, to achieve goals. A business man who won't hire you, but wants to rip you off, shouldn't be patronized." Brown encouraged De Porres members to file discrimination suits against local venues, such as Harry's Tea Club, Pignotti's Donut Shop, the Paxton Hotel, Eppley Airfield, and the Greyhound bus station; sometimes the De Porres organization had between eight and ten simultaneous different suits. African American Bertha Calloway recalled visiting Pignotti's Donut Shop with a white friend named Peggy. The server refused to acknowledge them. The two girls asked the owner, Pignotti, to come to their table. The following conversation ensued: Peggy said, "Don't you know me Mr. Pignotti, [we] go to the same church." Pignotti replied, "Yes, I know you but I'm not serving them, you're gonna have to leave." Peggy said, "In the name of Christ, how can you do this?" He answered, "Hey, if I serve them I'll lose business, I'm not gonna start serving colored people in here." Calloway let him know she had the right to file charges. Pignotti replied, "I don't give a damn whether you file charges against me or not, I'm not serving you." Calloway filed charges at Omaha's Police Court. During Pignotti's lunch break the following day, an officer served him with a warrant. At the court proceedings Pignotti pointed to Calloway and said, "That's the one that had me arrested like I was a common criminal. All I did, [was say] I'm not serving colored in my place." Judge Palmer replied, "Well, I don't blame you but you're gonna have to pay [the] $25 fine." The judge turned to Calloway and said, "Now that De Porres Club, what are you guys up to? Are you all Communist or something?"[12]

During the tenure of the club, members assured the city of Omaha that it was a patriotic American organization and refused to react to the practice of red-baiting. Their strategy was common for those harassed during the Cold War years. The fear of interracial organizations dabbling in communism was not so farfetched. During the 1930s the prevalence of blacks joining the Communist Party earned it the southern epithet "the nigger party," especially in Brown's home state of Alabama. The De Porres Club weighed the benefits of becoming members of the American Communist Party but Father Markoe dissuaded members by stating that he would "rather do business with the devil himself to stop racism" and that communism would not change

Omaha's discriminatory practices. Besides, he disclosed, the club was already under FBI investigation.¹³

The FBI maintained daily surveillance of the De Porres Club. Holland recalled how the mail to the De Porres Club arrived resealed and the telephone lines were tapped. Federal agents kept logbooks and eventually directly questioned Holland. He informed the FBI that there were several members whom he viewed as "confused individuals," such as club vice president and *Star* reporter Harold Tibbs. They did not know if they were communist or not, but just because the interracial organization supported civil rights did not mean its members were more apt to join the American Communist Party. The De Porres Club, however, took special precautions to keep communists and communist-front organizations from infiltrating the local organization. Nationally, some Americans, such as Georgia's governor, Herman Talmadge, claimed communism as a rationale for supporting segregation of the races: "If Communists supported racial integration, could there be any clearer sign of its immorality?" The fear of being labeled un-American kept many civil rights groups from protesting too loudly about racial inequality.¹⁴

In March 1950 the De Porres Club explained its moral stance by staging a nonfictional play, *Trial by Fire*. Written by Father George Dunn, a friend of Father Markoe's, the production focused on the true story of the Short family moving into an all-white neighborhood in Los Angeles, California. In December 1945 the family died when a mob firebombed their home. Although witnesses testified to instances of racial hate and the murders of the four family members, the jury ruled that no crime was committed because the Shorts were told to "get out while the getting was good." The dramatic presentation accurately portrayed what Stephen Grant Meyer's *As Long as They Don't Move Next Door* claimed was "the worst incident of racial violence against a black moving into a white district of Los Angeles." The Omaha play proved timely because a similar incident, albeit less severe, had recently occurred on the Near North Side. Woodrow Morgan, a World War II black fighter pilot and prisoner of war, bought a home in one of the city's covenanted white neighborhoods. Before the Morgan family moved into its new home, neighbors hurled several bricks through the windows of their house and threatened them with harm. Markoe and the club arrived the morning of Morgan's intended relocation and seated themselves on the front porch. Looking imposing in his clerical collar, the priest told inquiring neighbors, "We're here to welcome the new family." The Morgan family moved into their home without any more trouble.[15]

In an attempt to involve the black neighborhood, the *Star* and the De Porres Club targeted businesses practicing discriminatory employment. The group focused on sensitive entry positions, such as counter clerks and drivers, which were highly visible to the public. The *Star* staff, its publisher, and the club quickly earned the label of troublemakers. They started with the Near North Side's Edholm-Sherman Laundry, located at Twenty-Fourth and Erskine Streets, one block away from the *Omaha Star* building at Twenty-Fourth and Grant Streets. The business owner refused to hire black employees. Brown published an account of Mrs. Edholm's conversation with a club member. The laundry owner disclosed that even though 70 percent of her clientele were black, her policy was not to hire black men and women: "The white people might object to a Negro waiting on them." Although the club members were flabbergasted with the proprietor's logic, Brown validated the laundry owner's right to hire whomever she chose but noted that if Edholm did not change her beliefs soon it would be a great loss to the community. After another week of Edholm continuing her unfair hiring policy, the *Star* supported the club's Do Not Patronize campaign, because the newspaper had no alternative other than asking the black community to boycott the business. By October the club's campaign resulted in a surprising result: the owners of the Edholm-Sherman Laundry put it up for sale.[16]

Excited by their success, Brown and the De Porres Club attempted collective activism against Omaha's Central High School in December 1950. The secondary institute was the alma mater of Mildred's foster daughter, Ruth Harris Kellogg. As an organization member, Brown paid for the printing of four thousand handbills that described why the activist organization needed to protest the high school's production:

> This is discrimination. Negroes at Central are not allowed full and equal participation in some activities at this school. How is it that the opera tonight, put on by the student body, has no Negro students in the cast? The last road show here humiliated the Negro students by presenting a degrading black face in the show. Isn't it about time for public school officials to catch up with public opinion on this matter? With democracy on trial all over the world is it not time to eliminate on the local scene that which is against the spirit of democracy and thus weakens her at home and abroad?

Members managed to hand out three hundred of the missives to opera attendees before police officers warned the club protestors that they were not allowed to distribute the flyers on school property. Denny Holland keenly remembered what happened next. A man strode up to him and accused him of being a communist. Holland replied, "May God have mercy on your soul." The club's president had never seen anyone so full of hate. It was the closest he ever came to violence. But it was worth it; the next Central High School production featured students of color. The De Porres Club sent the school a letter of congratulations.[17]

Buoyed by their success, the club and the *Star* next pursued the Coca-Cola bottling company. Brown met with the general manager, Mac L. Gothard, on May 7, 1951. The *Star*'s owner informed Gothard that the club was launching a Don't Buy Coca-Cola campaign and that she completely agreed with its activities. In fact, she told Gothard, "Every thinking person in Omaha should support the De Porres Club."[18]

Not everyone who lived in northern Omaha agreed with Brown's assessment of the De Porres Club. Peter C. Doss, advertising manager of the *Omaha Guide* newspaper, the *Omaha Star*'s competition, met with Gothard and informed the bottling company's manager that most black residents did not support the boycott. Shortly after this conversation, Charles Chapman Galloway, the *Guide*'s publisher and Brown's former boss, met with De Porres Club members. Galloway stressed the importance of the black press and mentioned how local newspapers with agendas had the power to mold opinions. Brown ignored Galloway's thinly veiled judgment of her newspaper. However, after Doss's Coca-Cola ad featuring the soft drink company's two token temporary black hires ran in Galloway's *Guide*, she publicly accused Doss of being an Uncle Tom. The newspaper publisher's instincts proved correct. According to FBI records, Doss visited its Omaha office. FBI agent Edward Abbott knew Doss quite well since the latter designed the 1941 Omaha Negro Directory. It provided a much more comprehensive publication of Omaha's black population than the Omaha City Directory. The FBI used the black directory to create a list of subversive black men and women for city of Omaha administrators. Rapid Printing and Mailing Company, the same company that printed the *Omaha Star* from 1938 to the late 1970s, published Doss's directory. Therefore, when Doss supplied incriminating evidence against the De Porres Club, the FBI listened. Doss informed FBI agent John Barnes that the club caused "discontent and disunity among the Negroes ... and hate between the white [sic] and Negroes."[19]

Brown and her staff stayed up most of the night printing a rebuttal in an extra edition of the *Star*. The June 8, 1951, special issue displayed an image of a smiling Gothard shaking hands with his two new *permanent* black assembly line employees. Although it was not documented, Brown and the De Porres Club used their influence with the Coca-Cola manager to ensure the job security of the new hires. The *Star* quoted the regional corporate manager insisting that "the De Porres Club didn't have anything to do with our hiring Negroes." Fourteen years later, in 1965, Gothard publicly amended his previous comment during a *Star* interview: "If there is anything I can say about the De Porres Club, it is that they were ahead of their time. The methods and pressures they used were not thought of in those days. I was shocked by their tactics. I was ignorant of the whole thing."[20] The club had cleverly undermined their seemingly unstoppable opponent.

Energized by their employment victory, De Porres members and the *Star* confronted the Omaha and Council Bluffs Street Railway Company (O&CB). Since Nebraska's and Iowa's pioneer days, the O&CB bus system was a prominent fixture. Its electric streetcars crisscrossed through Omaha, northern Omaha, and Council Bluffs, Iowa. In the early 1940s the Omaha Urban League challenged the local corporation's steadfast refusal to hire black bus drivers. The league, also accused of ties with the American Communist Party, questioned Chester Colvin, the streetcar's personnel manager, about the company's unfair hiring practices, but to no avail. It was not until the De Porres Club and Brown challenged the O&CB's racist policies in 1952 that reform eventually occurred. The streetcar management attempted to defend its discriminatory rule by using stereotypical rhetoric: "No white woman would be safe on a street car if there was a black [man] driving." The club protested the O&CB's unfair practice by printing and distributing flyers. The *Star* even provided irate readers with the home addresses and telephone numbers of the company's officials. Needless to say, shortly thereafter, the O&CB purchased its last full-page ad in the *Star*.[21]

Brown responded to the O&CB company ending business with the *Star* by printing a blanket statement addressed to Omaha's city commissioners. She warned Omaha's administrators that her *Star* would run a tireless campaign for civic and economic improvements for the Near North Side. Brown encouraged *Star* readers to send editorials to the *Omaha World-Herald*'s Public Pulse column. Brown updated Near North Side readers of nationwide progress elsewhere by printing stories of successful bus campaigns, such as a protest in Missouri: "The St. Louis Company now is accepting applicants for bus and street-car operators regardless of race, creed or color. It is Omaha's turn now." To encourage racial solidarity for the De Porres Club, she made sure articles concerning the organization's bus protest ran in the *Kansas City Call* and the *St. Louis Argus* black weekly newspapers.[22]

The *Star* publisher and the club devised a progressive strategy, *four years* before the famous 1955 bus boycott in Montgomery, Alabama. As a De Porres Club Street Railway committee member, Brown instructed her readers, "Don't ride Omaha's buses or streetcars. If you must ride, protest by using 18 pennies." It was a similar strategy later used in Alabama by Dr. Martin Luther King Jr. and his wife, Coretta Scott King, who was a close friend of Brown's. De Porres Club leaflets repeated her words; the club's FBI file still contains a copy of the flyer. The club advised local merchants to stockpile pennies to aid the protestors. As the boycott campaign, or what ministerial activists in Philadelphia later dubbed as selective patronage, stretched into its second year, Brown asked her subscribers to donate money to the cause. "It is obvious that we are gauged for a long campaign. A campaign of which can be won only through much hard work, planning, and finance of which must come from the Near North Side Citizenry." In a grassroots tactic used later in Montgomery, De Porres Club participants organized car pools to ensure black Omahans stayed off the buses. Realizing the importance of communication during the boycott, Brown kept readers notified by printing the club's daily activities.[23] She printed summaries of the De Porres Club's weekly minutes and upcoming activist events, featured articles charting the club's successful actions against employment discrimination, published members' editorials critical of racism, and printed letters sent to business owners refusing service to black Omahans. In return, the association provided exclusive pictures and sensational news stories every time it picketed a discriminating business.

On March 3, 1952, the De Porres Club voted to affiliate with the Congress on Racial Equality, better known as CORE. James Farmer and Bayard Rustin had founded the Chicago-based multiracial civil rights organization in 1942. CORE encouraged boycotts and protests by sending representatives to train leaders of smaller associations, such as the De Porres Club. Because CORE specialists taught strategies and techniques to local civil rights protestors, local movements became linked to the larger national civil rights movement. Club members elected Brown as their CORE spokesperson. CORE made a difference by engaging participants, especially college students. CORE's Journey of Reconciliation campaign nonviolently challenged segregation, while

1. Mildred Brown in front of the *Omaha Star* building, circa 1985. Reprinted with permission from the *Omaha World-Herald*.

2. (*above*) Mayor Mike Boyle presenting the Key to the City plaque to Mildred Brown, June 1, 1984. Reprinted with permission from the *Omaha World-Herald*.

3. (*opposite top*) Somerville Courthouse, Somerville, Alabama, 2008. Photograph by the author.

4. (*opposite bottom*) Louisville and Nashville Railroad Company train station, Hartselle, Alabama. Courtesy of Morgan County Archives, Decatur, Alabama.

L. & N. R. R. Depot, Hartselle, Ala.

5. (*top*) Miles Memorial College, Fairfield, Alabama, 2008. Photograph by the author.

6. (*bottom*) Malone AME Church, Sioux City, Iowa, 2009. Photograph by the author.

7. Downtown Omaha, Nebraska, circa 1900. Reprinted with permission from the *Omaha World-Herald*.

8. (*above*) Lynching death of Will Brown (no relationship to Mildred Brown), September 28, 1919. Reprinted with permission from the *Omaha World-Herald*.

9. (*opposite top*) Intersection of Twenty-Fourth and Lake Streets, 1943. Reprinted with permission from the *Omaha World-Herald*.

10. (*opposite bottom*) *Omaha Star* newspaper carriers posing in front of the *Omaha Star* building, circa 1948. Reprinted with permission from the *Omaha World-Herald*.

11. (*top*) Mildred Brown's business card, circa 1970s. Courtesy of Omaha resident Edgar Hicks.

12. (*bottom*) Mildred Brown in her *Omaha Star* home (back of the office building), circa 1950s. Reprinted with permission from the *Omaha World-Herald*.

13. (*top*) Mildred Brown in her *Omaha Star* office, circa 1960s. Reprinted with permission from the *Omaha World-Herald*.

14. (*bottom*) Father Markoe and Mildred Brown, circa 1950s. Courtesy of Creighton University Archives.

15. (*opposite top*) Jewell Building (once housing the Dreamland Ballroom), northern Omaha. Photograph by Robert E. Samuels III.

16. (*opposite bottom*) President Lyndon Baines Johnson and Mildred Brown, 1965. Courtesy of Nebraska State Historical Society, RG5503-PH-O-3.

17. (*right*) The Near North Side neighborhood burning, June 26, 1969. Reprinted with permission from the *Omaha World-Herald*.

18. (*below*) Littleton Alston's bust of Mildred Brown in the Mildred Brown Strolling Park, 2009. Photograph by the author.

19. Mildred Brown standing between images of her mother and father in the living room of her *Omaha Star* home. Reprinted with permission from the *Omaha Star*.

its Freedom Rides garnered attention but ended in publicized violence. Brown's first assignment as a CORE representative consisted of presenting the club's arguments to the Omaha city council. Brown asked the council to encourage the O&CB to hire black bus drivers, especially since black men served as drivers during the current Korean war. But her referencing President Truman's 1948 desegregation of the military failed to impress Omaha's administrators.[24] The council recommended the *Star*'s publisher investigate the O&CB situation by speaking with the newly formed Mayor's Human Relations Committee. The chair of the city committee, who was none other than De Porres Club sponsor Father Markoe, commended Brown for her fearless presentation of facts concerning racial discrimination, but he was unable to increase pressure on the streetcar company to hire black drivers. By November 1952 De Porres Club picketers were marching in front of the railway company headquarters. Several of the picket placards echoed Brown's words from her earlier meeting with the city council: "Negro G.I.'s drive tanks, jeeps and trucks. Why not buses and street cars in Omaha?" The other boycott signs read, "Let's all defeat Communism by making democracy work in Omaha." The club cleverly deflected red-baiting against the O&CB's discriminating policy, while Brown reinforced her commitment to the black community:

> It is this paper's duty to take a stand on vital issues. We are convinced that two great evils facing us are racial discrimination and racial segregation. This paper will expose and oppose these evils. We accept this not only as a right but as a duty. The price of the duty which we accept comes high. It would be financially more profitable for us to remain silent. In the past few months we have opposed racial discrimination as practiced by several business places. Others have found it to their liking to remain silent or to completely sell out. We have and still are losing money for taking the stand of exposing and opposing these evils.[25]

The club and the *Star* led the protests and continued encouraging the boycott against the transportation company for another two years.

Finally, the city of Omaha ended the O&CB controversy. In an attempt to force the railway corporation to adopt a fair hiring policy, the city council threatened to attach an antidiscrimination amendment onto the streetcar's franchise agreement. Hoping to prevent the necessity for a disclaimer, one that would financially hamstring the streetcar company even more, the O&CB hired three African American men as drivers. Omaha administrators trusted the street railway company's new hiring policy. Mayor Johnny Rosenblatt believed the company. He earnestly stated, "They have had a change of mind. I think we have got the thing licked." Warren Swiggart, Omaha's public property commissioner, agreed to leave out the policy amendment, since the additional clause would discriminate against the streetcar firm.[26]

O&CB company president James P. Lee insisted that their final decision to hire the three black employees was merely a coincidence. Lee also denied that the O&CB company's past refusal to hire applicants was because of their race. Apparently, previous applicants were either unqualified or failed to pass the required tests. Enraged, Brown asked her readers, "How gullible and naïve do they think people are!! For lo, these many years they have with utter disregard refused to hire Negro applicants. Suddenly they hire three and want you to believe they have never refused bus and train operator employment to anyone solely because of the applicant's race or color." A *Star* reporter interviewed Lee. When asked if he would let them go after the risk of his losing his franchise passed, he patronizingly responded, "These drivers can stay with the company as long as they want it if they do their job right and behave themselves." The O&CB even attempted to hire De Porres Club member and International Sweethearts of Rhythm trombonist Helen Jones Woods as a driver, but not knowing how to drive, she turned down their job offer.[27]

The first of the O&CB public hearings convened on August 17, 1954. The *Star* publisher, along with two hundred other Omahans, attended the meeting. Brown happily noted that the northern Omaha community sent representatives from every organization, club, and church group to the meeting. At the second hearing, on August 24, 1954, the city council made a motion to add an antidiscrimination clause to the company's amended franchise. The company would not be able to discriminate against applicants according to their color, creed, or race. O&CB administrators realized the immediate ramifications of the proposed clause. On the front page of the *Star*'s October 22, 1954, edition, the newspaper displayed a large photograph of an additional four black men hired as drivers by the O&CB Street Railway Company. Brown and the De Porres Club's hard-fought campaign was a success.[28]

One of the last protests spearheaded by the club and the *Star* concerned the discriminatory employment practices of Reed's Ice Cream Company. Initially, Brown's former first husband, Dr. Shirley Edward Gilbert, noted the discriminatory employment practices of the ice cream shop in the late 1930s. Almost thirteen years later, Bell Griffin, a representative of the De Porres Club, spoke with Reed's personnel manager about their discrimination against blacks. Mr. Becker assured Bell that he would think about hiring black employees. After two years of noncompliance, Holland wrote a letter to Reed's management. The *Omaha Star* printed his missive:

> This unfair policy of denying equal job opportunities to Negroes, especially because of your large number of Negro customers, has for too long stood in complete violation of the American ideal of equal opportunity. It is becoming ever more urgent that we live up to this ideal as Americans in Korea, regardless of color, fight and die to preserve democracy. Beginning Monday, January 19, unless we hear from you before then, we will stop supporting your unfair policy by not buying Reed's ice cream. We shall ask all our friends who believe in equal opportunity, regardless of color, to do the same until you open employment at all levels to qualified Negroes. We remain anxious to discuss a change of policy with you.[29]

The club and the *Star* insisted that Near North Side residents boycott the ice cream shop at Twenty-Fourth and Wirt Streets. Congregants at the Zion Baptist Church collected five-dollar donations from community members to end Reed's whites-only hiring practice. Protestors distributed handbills in front of the store. After one potential white customer read the De Porres flyer, he said, "My boy's life was saved by a Negro in Korea. As a small token of thanks to him, I'll tell my friends not to buy Reed's Ice Cream." The store's manager responded through the *Star*, "We don't care if they buy our ice cream or not." Near North Side resident Richard Artison remembered watching the demonstration against Reed when he was a young child. He witnessed Brown marching with the picketers. The *Star* owner stopped to talk with him and explained why he should not purchase ice cream from Reed's. He did not buy his customary treat. Later on, the *Star*'s publisher witnessed a woman asking a child to buy her an ice cream cone. The child asked the woman what was wrong with her. "Don't you know they don't hire our people at Reed's? I wouldn't go in there for no money." Max Brownell kept track of noncompliant residents. He noted the names of four young black men who read the club's handbill but still purchased ice cream. The *Star* not only printed Brownell's list, titled "Uncle Toms Supporting White Supremacy," but also promised to print photographs of those seen buying ice cream. The paper threatened to include patrons' names, license plate numbers, and the amount of time they spent in the store.[30]

By September 1954 the *Star* reported that few blacks were visiting Reeds, and hundreds of white patrons were turning away as well when they learned of the store's un–African American employment policy. Occasionally, club protestors needed the protection of the law when white citizens threw objects at them, although city police officers refused to stop Reed's feeble volatile outbursts at the picketers. Omaha's police watched from a block away but did not interfere. By January 1954, after nine months of protests and picketing, Reed's capitulated by hiring Virginia Dixon. The black salesperson worked the five-to-midnight shift. The De Porres Club and the *Star* proclaimed a victory. Insisting they held no grudges, organization members joined Brown in an evening celebration. The *Star* publisher treated them to an ice cream cone at Reed's.[31]

Although Brown and the De Porres Club's fair-employment campaign raised residents' hopes of attaining more rights, the black community showed signs of class factionalism. The *Star* owner addressed this neighborhood infighting issue with an editorial scolding readers for not working together: "Today we are deeply concerned with the role of the colored man in the advancement of democracy. Specifically, we refer to those colored citizens of Omaha who by good fortune in some cases and hard work in others are looked upon as leaders. We know there are those among the leadership who for some petty and selfish reasons are leaders in name only. Traitors and do-nothings are dangerous not only to the cause of non-whites but also to the cause of the nation."[32]

Omaha's black class system was causing a schism in the leadership of the Near North Side. Resident Joan McCaw Lincoln explained northern Omaha's hierarchy. Status depended on an individuals' employment and their place of worship. Elite blacks distanced themselves socially from their less advantaged sisters and brothers. Privileged people had private parties, kept their offspring away from supposed toughs, and spoke disparagingly of those who were less cultured in the neighborhood. Their upper-class black children in Omaha went to museums and attended the opera. The Saint Philip Church showcased their wealthy members by sponsoring the Coronation Ball at the Dreamland Ballroom, while the Saint John AME Church held a comparative event, the King Solomon Wedding. The two black high-society events were the equivalent of Omaha's Aksarben Ball, a yearly lavish affair held since 1895, which had a whites-only policy for many years. Although Brown belonged to Saint John, she was not originally on black Omaha's social A-list. Even though she was crowned queen at the annual Solomon ball for 1952–53, several of the black elite derogatorily nicknamed her "Miss Carnation" because of her oversized carnation corsages. She was not initially in the higher echelon of northern Omaha society because she slighted black elitist C.C. Galloway when she and her first husband took five *Omaha Guide* staffers with them when they founded the *Omaha Star* in 1938. However, as Dorothy

Glenn, co-owner of the short-lived *American Record* black weekly, explained, because the people of the Near North Side accepted the *Star* as an alternative to the *Guide*, eventually they accepted Brown as well. But it took awhile. The *Star* owner was not considered one of the crème de la crème until her newspaper firmly established her on the Near North Side.[33]

Several weeks after Brown's editorial on divisionism in the black community appeared, Holland wrote a follow-up article titled "Those Who Don't Make Mistakes." Addressing his remarks to readers disgruntled with the club and the *Star*, he wrote, "Spending all our time criticizing those who are in a position of leadership is like rocking a rocking chair, it keeps you busy but doesn't get you anywhere." Holland challenged readers, some of whom he knew to be biased, to "throw aside all pettiness and unite to work for common cause. . . . It is only those who do nothing who make no mistakes." Brown had worked long hours to appease community members critical of the *Star* and its association with the De Porres Club; some thought it too radical, others not enough. It confirmed her philosophy that there was no consensus among Omaha's black leaders. Brown's close friend Paul Bryant recalled decades later that she and the De Porres Club were simply practicing what she regularly preached to him: "Do right because it is the right thing to do. Don't do right in search of reward or in fear of retribution." Brown was more of a doer than a complainer. She would ask, "What can be done for that not to happen again; what could you do to prevent that from happening," instead of allowing the *Star* to become a diatribe against white residents. She was mindful that the *Star* needed to represent the black community, but she could not afford it becoming an inflammatory rag. *Omaha Star* writer Walter Brooks can still hear Brown talking about her shining years of activism. She talked incessantly about the De Porres Club and how it acted as a pivotal change. Her newspaper was crucial for mobilizing that change, simply because it existed.[34]

In October 1954 a special meeting took place at the back of the *Omaha Star* office. Because of Father Markoe's advanced age and

Denny Holland's family commitments, the De Porres Club had dwindled to only a few members. After seven years of protesting the eight remaining participants of the organization voted to disband. Brown's days of sit-ins, protests, marches, and boycott activism were over, and Father Markoe, who had a history of using the press to make change happen, was tiring.

Although the club reconvened in May 1955 for another five years, without Holland as its president the activities were limited. Markoe remained the club's sponsor until it permanently ended in the 1960s. It was time for other younger black male religious leaders to take over northern Omaha's fight. The Citizens' Coordinating Committee for Civil Liberties, better known as the 4CL, replaced the De Porres Club. Markoe, by now an elderly man, and Brown, only a decade and a half younger, served as members in the new activist organization but were not leaders.

Brown was well aware that her social cause editorializing was not always an acceptable action to white business enterprises that might be chief advertisers. Challenging mainstream Omaha proved costly for her business, but Brown was a woman of strong convictions. She walked a narrow financial line, wooing white advertisers while keeping black readers informed. The newspaper owner occasionally paid the price in lost revenue and broken windows. Denny Holland's son Matt remembers that Brown had a constant worry about money and the *Star* going out of business. Jean Waite Holland vividly recalled Mildred rushing out of the *Star* to stop utility workers before they shut off her building's electricity. She persevered despite her financial difficulties. She no longer picketed businesses, and the De Porres Club members no longer convened at the *Star* on Friday nights, but their years of boycotting together laid the foundation for Omaha's civil rights movement. It would be the next chapter in Brown's commitment to the Near North Side's struggle for equality.[35]

6

Restricted Housing and 'Rithmetic

The back of the postcard bore an insidious message: "If you want to stop communism in the USA see that restrictive covenants are enforced!" The mailed memorandum informed Omaha's Kountze Place residents in 1950 that it was their duty to keep the neighborhood free from a black invasion. Home owners could not afford to stay neutral. "Protective covenants can be enforced, if YOU will cooperate and contribute." The postcard campaign in the northeast residential area adjacent to the black neighborhood was the work of an anonymous hatemonger who made sure every Kountze Place resident received an instructional missive. Mildred Brown told her readers she believed the postcard perpetrator was most likely a neurotic crackpot, but members of the black community needed to take the mailing seriously. Its damaging rhetoric could exacerbate neighborhood fears and stereotypes by associating communism with a white person's right to sell a home to a black buyer. Brown warned her readers that they better grow up and support organizations like the NAACP that fought against this type of racial discrimination. Unfortunately, a majority of home owners in Kountze Place believed the contents of the postcards.[1] They affixed restrictive covenants, like the one found in Omaha's Douglas County Register of Deeds Office, to their deeds of sale: "This property is conveyed upon the express covenant that it shall never be sold or leased or permitted [to] be occupied by a colored person; nor shall it be used for carrying on a liquor business or for any other immoral or illegal use, and the grantees for themselves and their successors take title subject to having agreed to this covenant."[2] The Kountze Place residents fought to protect their all-white neighborhood population, and whether they thought this out of ignorance, racism, or the perceived threat of unpatriotic behavior or minority ownership did not matter. Restrictive covenants, already a common real estate addendum in many urban neighborhoods nationwide starting in the 1920s and continuing until the late 1960s, artificially segregated communities and inexorably led to enforced segregated parks and government-mandated public schools.

Mildred Brown used the *Omaha Star* as an instrument of racial solidarity to fight against restrictive covenants in the 1950s, which in turn led to the black community's desegregation of Omaha's Peony Park in the 1960s and the Omaha public school system in the 1970s. Brown's unique status, being the most visible and outspoken minority female leader in Omaha's black community during these decades, provided her with the opportunity of rallying residents of color through the impetus of the *Omaha Star*.

Before 1900 the nation's housing was available to anyone who could pay the price of the home. However, by 1902, the same year Alabama's delegates copied other southern states' constitutional amendments, which included Jim Crow disenfranchisement, mainstream newspapers were advertising limited housing sales earmarked for "colored buyers" only. The Great Migration and its subsequent perceived economic threat to the white population gave rise to a systematic enforcement of restrictive housing covenants in the 1920s. By devising residential restrictions, mainstream America sought to stop black encroachment, curtail integration, and maintain white dominance. Nebraska's state constitution, which was amended shortly after Will Brown's lynching in 1919, forbid discrimination in respect to the ownership, acquisition, enjoyment, possession, or descent of property, but it did little to stop determined local neighborhood residents. Indeed, it barely registered with the national population when the U.S. Supreme Court condemned restrictive covenants in the 1926 *Corrigan v. Buckle* decision. In fact, the lukewarm ruling tacitly *agreed* with white home owners' right not to sell their property to black buyers. If America's black community planned on fighting against restrictive covenants, it would need to happen on a local grassroots level.[3]

In northern Omaha Mildred Brown, a biracial figure, respected by young and old, rich and poor, became the key transitional grassroots leader. She fought against Omaha's restrictive covenant system by using the *Star* to educate her readers. Brown printed information concerning the imperfection of the federal ruling. The *Corrigan v. Buckle* decision inadvertently upheld the constitutionality of restrictive covenants, but, thankfully, the ruling lasted only from 1926 to 1948. She informed her northern Omaha readers when the Supreme Court replaced *Corrigan v. Buckle* with *Shelley v. Kraemer* by ruling racial covenants were invalid and citing the nefarious practice as a negation of the rights guaranteed in the Fourteenth Amendment. Brown published numerous articles about this landmark decision in several editions of her weekly *Star*. Ever the teacher, she taught her readers the nuances of this national ruling, but, more important, she explained why the decision was ultimately unenforceable as a federal law on several different local levels.[4]

In Omaha some white home owners and their real estate agents allowed race-restrictive covenants in their property deeds because of peer pressure. Brown explained to the black community that these residents and businesspeople were actually in danger of antagonizing other residents and jeopardizing their jobs if they allowed black home owners into an all-white neighborhood. Efforts like the postcard campaign sought to exert peer pressure to pledge the disciplined exclusivity of the white community. Specific race covenants banning black boarders or the division of houses into multiple apartments eliminated the slight possibility of individual minorities living in a white neighborhood as well.

Lois Stalvey, an Omaha housewife, challenged her home owner's association and its restrictive covenants by attempting to purchase housing for a black family in her neighborhood. She met with the black middle-class family, who attended her church, to understand why they wanted to buy a home outside of northern Omaha. They explained to her that 75 percent of the overcrowded housing in the Near North Side needed at least five hundred to a thousand dollars worth of repairs to make the homes acceptable dwellings. Stalvey and her husband almost succeeded in buying the couple a home, but once the real estate agent understood who was involved in the sale, he stopped the closing. The agent knew the rule: any realtor violating these discriminatory guidelines faced a penalty or expulsion from the Omaha Real Estate Board and lost access to the board's cross-listing services. The real estate agent then took his duties one step further and reported the Stalvey family's actions to their home owner's association. Even though the couple explained the situation to their residential organization, the real estate agent, and the board, Stalvey and her family were ostracized by their community to the point that they moved away from Omaha.[5]

Brown sent her *Star* reporters to interview the Omaha Real Estate Board after it denied allegations of racism toward financially solvent black home buyers. The board president, Harold Peterson, insisted that he did not allow the observance of restrictive covenants because the owner of a house generally made the final decision on selling or renting. The mainstream *Omaha World-Herald* daily also interviewed Omaha tycoon N. P. Dodge III, president of the city's largest real estate firm, and he concurred with Peterson and openly acknowledged a similar attitude in most of Omaha's white home owners. Dodge claimed that "the white man will trade and work with the Negro. He will purchase from a Negro clerk, ride in the same bus, eat in the same restaurant, and occupy the same hotel without noticeably affecting the economic security of these business firms. This same average white family will not purchase a house next to a Negro's home and if a Negro family buys next to him, he will move." Dodge admitted that several of his firm's neighborhood housing construction projects refused black home buyers. He saw these home owner association's decisions as a simple fact of community living. He blamed the white residents for not accepting blacks as their neighbors. But, once they did, it would be the last barrier to black first-class citizenship. By accepting the public's racist attitude toward open housing, Dodge refused to confront his own complicity in housing discrimination.[6]

Brown refused to accept the discriminatory housing situation and insisted the black community continue seeking a legislative act allowing open housing. She assured her readers, "We support the principle of legislation in this field which seeks open occupancy as a goal, and we suggest the time for it is ripe. She added that "most Negroes are not seeking integration. We simply want equal rights and justice. Whether Negroes want to move out of the ghetto has nothing to do with the correctness of open house legislation. The right to freedom of mobility should be there for him to use even if he doesn't." Brown did not demand the desegregation of neighborhoods, but she insisted black leaders, especially the NAACP, join her in demanding the right for Omaha's black residents to live in any Omaha neighborhood.[7]

Through the *Star* Brown publicly questioned the NAACP's slow reaction to challenging restrictive covenants, while she privately chided Laurence McVoy, the Omaha chapter's president, on his lack of action. Her reasoning to fight against the local housing restrictions was twofold. "Other races come into the GHETTO [her emphasis] and exploit us, but have their homes in restricted areas where Negroes aren't welcome to frequent. Others will not respect us until we show more 'togetherness and concern' for ourselves."[8]

The NAACP, the Near North Side's oldest black organization, was well aware of the Omaha Real Estate Board's racist practices and the discriminatory housing situation, but its policy was to stay moderate during city disputes. Former television talk show host Ben Gray explained the decades-long predicament of the NAACP, especially its presidents. He saw the NAACP leaders as agitators without a platform, because there was rarely a given group consensus on how to accomplish a protest. In the 1940s Omaha's NAACP had sought advice from its National Legal Committee on ways to circumvent restricted property addendums, but the local chapter refused to challenge the racial covenants on the grounds that there were no official policies for boycotting or picketing.[9]

As the sole owner of the *Star*, Brown did not have to consider any official organizational policies or need a member consensus to publicly fight against restrictive covenants. In 1963 she rallied her readers and demanded they petition for a Nebraska Fair Housing law. Loren Miller, renowned for his attorney role in *McGhee v. Sipes*, a sister case to *Brown v. Board of Education*, supported Brown's campaign with a *Star* editorial. He likened the separation between northern Omaha and the rest of the city to "walls unseen but as real and commonly believed to be as invincible as the wall that separates East Berlin from West Berlin." Miller agreed with Brown when he boldly stated that concomitant residential segregation and discrimination were luxuries Omaha and other metropolitan areas could no longer afford. Through the *Star* and the subsequent political unification of the black community, mainstream residents in the city of Omaha gained an understanding of the gravity of the housing situation, but it was not enough to support the passing of a city ordinance.[10]

In mid-November 1963 Omaha's city council rejected the Open Housing Ordinance with a four-to-three vote. The black community's hope that Nebraska's most diversified city would become the first urban center west of the Mississippi River to comply with President Kennedy's order for equal opportunity in housing was dashed. Brown fought against the setback by letting her readers know that the two black members of the mayor's biracial housing committee resigned after the council's negative vote, which she called a dastardly deed. The informal restrictive covenants implemented in neighborhoods surrounding the black neighborhood would continue isolating the Near North Side. Michael Harrington's *The Other America: Poverty in the United States* astutely documents how this type of isolation deliberately condemned black neighborhoods to political invisibility and a lack of protection from city and state statutes. Historian Robert Self shrewdly further summarizes in *American Babylon* that prejudiced property clauses and the white residents enforcing them were what kept blacks trapped in black belts throughout the 1960s. But northern Omaha's black community possessed hope. The isolated enclave had Brown as a community organizer and the Citizens' Coordinating Committee for Civil Liberties, a new local interracial activist group better known as the 4CL, as the means to strike down restrictive covenants.[11]

The 4CL, a latter-day De Porres Club concerned with Omaha's employment discrimination policies, was led by reverends Rudolph E. McNair and Kelsey A. Jones. Denny Holland, the former president of the De Porres Club, described the 4CL as a broader-based organization associating with all of the city's black ministers, not just the white and black Catholic priests. He saw the 4CL pretty much as an activist, local association connecting to the national civil rights movement. In the early 1960s Brown and an elderly Father Markoe, the founder of the now defunct De Porres Club, became members but were not officers. They regularly attended 4CL meetings and participated in discussions of how to end discriminatory policies, hiring practices, and housing covenants, but Holland remembers tension with the priest's presence. "The fact that he was white made it difficult for some people to know exactly what to do with him. He didn't fit into stereotypes as far as these are the good guys and these are the bad guys." The *Star* publisher regularly printed the association's activities in a similar manner to how she promoted the De Porres Club in the 1940s and 1950s. The 4CL's demonstrations, such as their sit-in at downtown Omaha's S. S. Kresge's lunch counter, were reported in a fiery *Star* article titled "4CL Vows to Continue Drive until Hell Freezes Over." Brown, as far as research for this project revealed, did not physically participate in the organization's boycotts, but she fully supported the 4CL as much as she had the De Porres Club. Omaha Housing Authority director Robert Armstrong explained Brown's strategy: "As a queen bee making the drones work, she made the necessary contacts. She knew how to put leaders in contact with each other. When the 4CL picketed, she did not need to be there."[12]

In 1963, when Reverends McNair and Jones requested an audience with Omaha's city council, the *Star*'s owner was not present; it was an all-male black assembly that presented the community's case. The 4CL religious leaders, state senator Edward Danner, and a young Omaha lawyer named Ernie Chambers, who lived in the Spencer Homes housing project, voiced the black neighborhood's frustration with their limited choices of crowded, dilapidated federal and private housing. They explained how residential segregation was systematically undermining the nationwide economic and social well-being of black Americans. Omaha's isolated black belt, which ran from Cumming Street to Bedford Avenue and Sixteenth Street to Thirtieth Street, was one of the most critical areas needing city improvements. Chambers described the Near North Side's housing conditions to the city council: "We live in places where there are large rats as you walk down the street, the snow is not cleared from the streets in the winter until it has begun to melt, the streets are not washed until it is raining, there are not stop lights at dangerous intersections . . . there is police harassing and brutality. These are the kind of things you do not want in your neighborhood." While the council appeared to listen to Chambers's words, they paternalistically responded that the residents living in the district were to blame for the squalid conditions. Chambers angrily appealed to the council's morals when he stated,

> It seems tragic to me that a group of people would have to have their rights submitted to the vote of those who are intent on depriving them of those rights. . . . We don't want them either, we are human beings first. You gentlemen all attend church, you are all professing Christians yet you can reconcile discrimination, segregation, bigotry and prejudice with your Christian faith, you can sing a song on Sunday in church, you are pillars in your community. You sit here making laws to rule men like me, well think about it because the day may come when I may be in a position to make laws to rule men like you.[13]

Mayor James Dworak refused to believe Chambers, and he did not recognize the leaders of the 4CL organization as representatives of the black community. Brown rallied her *Star* readers to the situation when she quoted Dworak, stating, "The 4CL apparently are a group of self-appointed citizens. . . . I am going to take the leadership in this matter. We'll see this thing [racial discrimination] evaporates very quickly." Brown publicized the 4CL's answer to the mayor and council's assessment of the black community: a pray-in at city hall the following week.

Resident Warren Taylor remembered watching the 4CL's nonviolent demonstration a few days later in downtown Omaha. He wished to join the assembled group, but as one of the first black secondary teachers hired in 1963 he knew participation could be grounds for losing his job at Omaha Public Schools. He had good reason to be worried.[14]

At the peaceful pray-in, Reverend Jones informed a *Star* reporter that the 4CL would continue holding protests until the mayor and council took proper notice: "We will "sit-in; kneel-in; pray-in; lay-in; wade-in; any of the other 'ins' because we want 'in' the full citizenship." Forty-nine participants were arrested on charges of disturbing the peace and holding an assembly. The charges against youths under eighteen were dismissed, and the adults were fined court costs and one dollar each. An agitated Reverend Jones stated that "Nebraska was now the Mississippi of the North." Speaking for the black community, he added, "In housing we want open occupancy, with no reservations and no unwritten covenants. We want guarantees for displaced minorities before any urban renewal is accepted." Brown, who did not attend the demonstration, met with members of the 4CL at Omaha's Mount Moriah Baptist Church to plan their next strategy. The organization decided to picket the offices of the *Omaha World-Herald*. As much as Brown's *Star* was unifying the black community against restrictive covenants, the mainstream newspaper's articles were solidifying Omaha's white community to keep the racist clauses.[15]

The 4CL held their *Omaha World-Herald* demonstration in front of the daily's offices. Picket signs pointed out the daily newspaper's responsibility to the entire Omaha community and demanded published appraisals of minority viewpoints. Although Brown stayed far away from the marching lines, she printed every word of Father Markoe's opposition to the white newspaper's rebuttal editorial, which cautioned against an open occupancy ordinance in the city of Omaha. Markoe, never one to speak subtly, told a small gathered crowd that the reason integrated housing appeared dangerous to the local population was because it might allow something scarier, namely, interracial marriage. Several people passing by heard Markoe explain that African

American state senator Danner was in the process of compiling Legislative Bill 179. If passed it would declare interracial marriage legal in Nebraska. The aging priest finished his monologue by informing listeners that in reality, lighter-skinned children, in this white dominated society of ours, fared better and had more places to go than darker-skinned children. There was nothing wrong with miscegenation. What was wrong was the fake social attitude toward it.

Brown, personally aware of the importance of the issue, published every word of Markoe's impromptu lecture. The *Star* displayed an oversized headline when the state legislature repealed the ban on interracial marriage at the end of 1963. It not only eliminated the previous legal provision prescribing racially mixed marriages as void but also reinstated the legitimacy of children born from such marriages. Without explaining her great-grandfather's life-altering will written before the turn of the twentieth century, Brown emphasized the importance of this key legality to her Near North Side readers. The Nebraska legislature had indeed settled the issue of interracial marriage, but the issue of interracial swimming continued creating an uproar at Omaha's largest amusement park.[16]

In the mid 1960s Brown and her *Star* led the fight to desegregate Peony Park's 4.5-acre beach with a pool and waterslide. For the previous several decades black high school students attending proms and after-prom parties at Peony Park had been allowed to dance, but they had not been permitted to swim in the park's oversized water pool. Near North Side resident Archie Godfrey remembers the discriminatory situation quite well: "You could go to the park but no one brought swimming trunks." Omaha's NAACP chapter had attempted to solve the situation in 1955 by having the municipal court convict Joseph Malec Jr., the park's owner, of racist behavior, but he paid his fifty-dollar fine and continued discriminating. NAACP members considered their options on how to desegregate the park but, as in the housing situation, were unable to gain a group consensus. Too many members feared losing their full-time jobs in the city of Omaha. Brown told her fellow recalcitrant NAACP members that she did not expect integration to be easy but that Nebraska's state nondiscriminatory statute and the federal law had already settled the integration question one hundred years earlier with the passage of the Civil Rights Act of 1875.[17]

Although NAACP adults failed to challenge the discriminatory situation, Bertha Calloway, the NAACP's youth group organizer and Brown's secretary, became the leader of Peony Park's successful integration. With the help of community volunteers, she led two carloads of black adults and teenagers, including Archie Godfrey, to the front entrance of the amusement park. The first car in their small caravan stopped at the narrow gate. A white teenager, about Godfrey's age, refused to let the car enter. He nervously read a statement printed on a card: "Due to anticipated crowds, I can't let you into the Park." The younger black adults later learned that William J. Hotz Jr., the park owner's lawyer, wrote the inscription. The car's passengers pressured the white youth to admit he was discriminating against them. He refused and repeated his written sentence. Meanwhile, a second car with black passengers pulled up to the narrow exit gate, and another white youth with a matching card repeated the same sentiment. Since the park had only one entrance and one exit, a line of impatient drivers behind the protestor's cars pressed on their car horns. The black teenage driver at the entrance gate took the keys out of the ignition and put them in his pocket. He refused to move his vehicle. Park officials called the Omaha police, who brought police dogs. Under the supervision of the officers and their accompanying canines, the parked vehicles were towed away from the entrance and exit of Peony Park. The NAACP youth group's first integration attempt had failed, but Brown encouraged them to try again.[18]

The newspaper publisher spoke with the NAACP youth group about the power of racial solidarity and encouraged the disappointed teenagers to write an article for her *Star*. She suggested to the youths, several of whom were ministers' children, that they include the names of blacks and whites involved in the incident. The teenagers created a simple statement of what transpired at the park and how they would continue protesting its restrictive racial policy. Brown published it in the *Star*. Peony Park's owner responded to the *Star*'s article with an editorial. The publisher updated her readers by letting them read how Malec Jr. intended to convert the amusement park into a country club with private memberships and a whites-only policy. At an emergency NAACP meeting adult members considered the state of affairs but wavered on their options. Mildred informed her constituents that she would write to the NAACP's headquarters if a decision was not quickly forthcoming. She met with NAACP president McVoy and convinced him to engage a lawyer and sue Peony Park's owner. Malec Jr. defended his racist stance by claiming twenty-five telephone callers warned him "they would stop swimming at Peony if he started admitting blacks.... His whites-only policy was based on simple economics, not on any prejudice."[19] Brown made sure his response and the *Star*'s subsequent publicized boycotts reached northern Omaha residents and city of Omaha administrator's offices. Within weeks of fewer visitors to the park and thus lower profits, Malec Jr. opened the entire park to any customer. Looking back on the situation, Godfrey stated, "If Mildred Brown's paper had not been there, we wouldn't have had any traction in the community." She used the *Star* as public leverage during the desegregation of the park, and she continued using it after the city of Omaha printed its minority report.[20]

A Report on Discrimination in Housing for Minorities in Omaha, Nebraska, 1965 mirrored the city reports issued in 1946 and 1954. The study noted that blacks in northern Omaha "have made increasingly greater gains in the occupancy of new neighborhoods" but that it did not "by any means mean that Omaha is becoming more highly integrated." Report committee members concluded for the third time that nonwhite neighborhoods were more dilapidated, deteriorated, and lower in property value than most of the white neighborhoods. The homes of nonwhite owners were worth $6,455, which was nearly half the value of the homes owned by whites ($11,700), and there were twice as many (6.2 percent) dilapidated homes in the Near North Side as compared to the 3 percent in the city of Omaha. The report showed that 80 percent of black Omaha residents still lived in the nine-tract area known as the Near North Side and that the ghettoization of northern Omaha continued mainly because the black population in Omaha was increasing with nowhere to go. White residents were fearful their city was being overtaken by poor black southern migrants. The committee's solution was to enforce an open occupancy ordinance that would prohibit conspiracies between Omaha's real estate companies. However, they cautioned that "breaking custom based on prejudice never has come easy and the real problem revolves around the means of bringing the policy into being. The professionals in the real estate market are concerned over the centuries old right of a property owner to dispose of his property as he wishes within the bounds of the truly critical interests of society in general." The committee admonished community leaders like Mildred Brown to patiently remind her readers that it was "incumbent upon all educated people in Omaha to foster the established findings of Anthropology, namely that color does not change the personal characteristics or intelligence of a man."[21] Brown and the black community already knew this to be true; they were still waiting for the rest of Omaha to accept it as a fact.

Omaha did accept open housing and ban housing discrimination, but not until the federal government created Title VIII of the national Civil Rights Act of 1968, better known as the Fair Housing Act of 1968. The law created national open housing and banned racial discrimination and segregation in federally funded housing projects. In 1969 Nebraska followed the federal example and offered the option of open housing to its registered voters. Brown's *Star* proudly informed her readers that the Eightieth Session of Nebraska's Unicameral Legislature created the state's open-housing ordinance by approving Open Housing Legislative Bill 718 with a vote of thirty-eight to six. In a front-page banner, she announced that Senator Edward Danner had the satisfaction of being one of the cowriters of the successful law. His approved bill prohibited "discrimination based on race, creed, color, national origin, or ancestry in the acquisition of housing" throughout the state of Nebraska. It was unlawful for any bank or loan association to redline or deny financial assistance based on said discriminatory criteria. The Omaha Housing Authority complied with the federal law by offering applicants a free-choice policy to pick their housing project and neighborhood. Residents appreciated the liberty to live wherever they chose, especially since Omaha's four housing project complexes were unsafe and undesirable locations by the mid-1960s. After this success Brown and community activists turned to another intractable institution: the Omaha public school system.[22]

At the turn of the twentieth century, Omaha Public Schools (OPS) hired two black women teachers, Lucinda Gamble and Eulalia Overall. In 1901 Gamble married John Albert Williams, an Episcopalian priest and publisher of the *Omaha Monitor* newspaper, and promptly quit teaching. Overall, the other young black instructor relinquished her societal rights as an educator when she married in 1910. Between 1910 and 1939 OPS did not hire any black instructors and the city of Omaha's policy for employing black educators outside of northern Omaha's segregated schools was nonexistent prior to 1963. But with the assistance of Mildred Brown and the insistence of the 4CL, the OPS teaching staff was integrated in 1963 and the entire public Omaha student body was desegregated in 1976.[23]

In 1953 Mildred Brown began her confrontation with the OPS system. She could not fathom why Omaha's public school system was "short 200 teachers and yet would not hire black teachers for grade and high school employment." Even with the 1954 *Brown v. Board of Education* decision, OPS superintendent Harry Burke refused to hire black educators at the public schools. At a public meeting in northern Omaha, Burke claimed that the school board had previously offered several black educators teaching positions in West Omaha but these potential hires refused their offers due to a lack of bus transportation from their isolated neighborhood in northern Omaha. Brown confronted Burke that day by tartly replying, "Negroes who can't get bank loans for houses can get them readily for automobiles." Warren Taylor, who later became Lothrop Elementary School's black principal, questioned Burke's explanation in private. Burke informed Taylor that he was "moving too fast" concerning black employment. In fact, the superintendent admitted he discouraged the Omaha School Board from hiring minority teachers. The white administrator insisted that "black people preferred to have black teachers all in the black community to be examples for black children."[24]

Superintendent Burke's stereotypical reasons for not hiring black teachers were unacceptable rationales for Brown. She pointedly asked her readers, "How long are we going to permit segregation of school teachers in Omaha? The superintendent in Columbus, Ohio is considering the use of Negro teachers. . . . What about the superintendent in Omaha, Nebraska?" Five years later, in 1959, Brown's *Star* printed a large photograph of protesters Dorothy Eure, Mercia Smith, and Marguerita Washington, the *Star* publisher's niece and recent permanent houseguest, picketing OPS's predominantly black Omaha Technical High School with signs reading "Guilty, Who? the Omaha Public School system, Of What? Discrimination." Photographs also showed the young women handing out flyers stating, "Little Rock—No, Omaha," which referred to the Little Rock Nine's desegregation of what was once known as "America's Most Beautiful School," Central High School in Little Rock, Arkansas. Brown knew that she needed to be careful in her fight against OPS. As a practical businessperson she knew the *Star* financially existed through its advertisements, and many of her advertisers were white local businesspeople. The Little Rock Nine's integration fight led by Daisy Bates was successful, but it resulted in corporate managers retracting advertisements and causing the demise of Bates's newspaper, the *Arkansas State Press*. Despite Brown's activist handiwork, the northern Omaha protest campaign did not change Burke's racist hiring policy. There would be no black teachers as long as he was in charge, although the OPS administrator once taunted Warren Taylor by stating, "If you could get Marion Anderson to apply, I might consider it."[25]

It was not until after Burke's sudden death in early 1963 that conversations about hiring black educators prompted meetings between northern Omaha community members, including Brown, and the Omaha Public School Board. Paul Miller, the new superintendent, mollified the community's frustration with the shortage of minority educators by promising Brown that in the following school year of 1963–64, black teachers would teach at the senior high level. In 1963 OPS did indeed hire a number of black educators, but the school district's student body remained predominantly segregated until 1976.[26]

Some educational institutions, such as Little Rock's Central High School, integrated, albeit with massive protests, within a few years after the 1954 *Brown v. Board of Education* outlawed segregation, but schools in the city of Omaha, similar to many other urban districts, ignored the federal mandate. The mandated integration of OPS started when Eugene Skinner, OPS's first black assistant superintendent in 1969, criticized the city's failure to hire African American teachers to teach in predominately white schools. Mildred Brown did not participate in the OPS federal court case, but *Omaha Star* editor Charles Washington and former De Porres Club president Denny Holland served as plaintiff witnesses. Judge Albert Schatz, U.S. District Court for Nebraska, found OPS guilty of intentional segregation.[27]

Superintendent Miller received a federal court order to formulate a plan to peacefully desegregate the public schools between April 17, 1972, and September 1, 1976. Implementation of said plan would commence on September 7, 1976. OPS assigned Board of Education Task Force president Norbert Schuerman to desegregate Omaha's public school system. Schuerman felt that his job was easier than in other urban systems because in "our case, the school district was to receive permission from the court to implement a plan initiated on a local level; every other city had outside consultants that the court had appointed." Schuerman worked with court case plaintiffs and community members to implement desegregation plans within Omaha's schools. *Star* staffer Bob Rodgers and the school principal, Katherine Fletcher, assisted him in desegregating OPS, the eighty-first largest school system of the nation's 130 largest districts. Brown helped Schuerman by running front-page articles updating her readers on the desegregation progress, printing notices of school visitations sponsored by the Omaha Council of Parents and Teachers, and announcing city-wide open houses. While the majority of Omaha children affected by bussing were black public-housing residents, OPS's white student enrollment dropped from 53,527 students in 1976 to only 41,911. OPS teacher Mary Jo Monahon explained these statistics: "Blacks were coming too close, which caused white flight. Neighbors worried about blacks, fear and property values." Despite the white migration into Omaha's suburbs and private schools, the Concerned Citizens for Omaha, an interracial group consisting of city of Omaha and northern Omaha residents, distributed hundreds of bumper stickers saying, "Let's Make It Work!" to accepting residents of Omaha.[28]

Mildred Brown and the *Omaha Star* assisted the 4CL and northern Omaha residents in "making it work" by successfully challenging restrictive covenants and desegregating Peony Park and the Omaha public school system in the 1950s, 1960s, and 1970s, respectively. She was on the sidelines as a member of the 4CL; however, her role as the leading community organizer through her use of *Star* articles, 4CL updates, and editorials provided the integral conduit of community communication. Her newspaper created a unified generational voice that sustained the racial solidarity necessary to change several of the city of Omaha's worst racist practices. Unfortunately, the crowded, financially stressed Near North Side citizenry's overall frustration with daily inequality was on the verge of exploding. The late 1960s national and local black power movement ushered in the most tumultuous decade in North Omaha's history.

Part 3 **Transferring Ownership to the Community**

7
Changing Strategies for Changing Times

Music blared from the doorway of the dilapidated empty unit in the Logan Fontenelle Housing Project. It was the summer of 1969, the year following the Fair Housing Act, which finally gave northern Omaha residents open housing, the right to choose where they wanted to live in the city. However, like many other impoverished black residents, the parents of Vivian Strong did not have the financial means to leave their low-income government housing. Mildred Brown, like most residents of the Near North Side, originally thought the Fontenelle apartment buildings "were a good idea, but [they became] a den of criminals." It was like "assigning people to a dead end." The violence in this project was sporadic and created uneasiness; residents called it "Vietnam." Project dwellers lived in an atmosphere of terror, afraid to report crimes or testify in court. On the fateful warm evening of June 24, 1969, white officer James L. Loder was driving his police cruiser through the black neighborhood toward the project. He was responding to a public disturbance call of loud music. As the police officer approached the partially vacant dwellings, several black children ran out of a doorway. One of them was fourteen-year-old Vivian Strong. Loder did not shout at her to stop. According to him, "she was running away from the scene, [and] we were supposed to shoot." He aimed his gun at the back of her head and pulled the trigger. Strong's sister Carol, who was nearby, will forever remember seeing her older sibling crumpled on the ground. Vivian died instantly. The death of this "skinny little girl" started a riot, the third of its kind in three years, and the worst racial disturbance in Omaha's history. Approximately fifty predominantly white-owned businesses and numerous parked automobiles sustained extensive fire damage. The looting, destruction, and burning of the Near North Side's Twenty-Fourth and Lake Streets central business district resulted in one fatality, twenty-seven injuries, sixty-six arrests of black residents, and $925,000 worth of damage.[1]

Keeping Omaha's black community uplifted and informed between the mid-1960s and late 1970s proved a challenging task for Mildred Brown. As a woman in her later sixties, Brown did not identify with the new generation of assertive black male leaders in the black power movement. Their nationwide separatist, militant, and occasionally violent campaigns for political, economic, and cultural control of the black community were already driving a deeper wedge into the black generational gap. "We Shall Overcome" was fast becoming "We Shall Overrun." To a certain degree Brown supported northern Omaha's Black Panther Party for Self-Defense, but she steadfastly maintained that Dr. Martin Luther King Jr.'s nonviolent approach to change was the best for the black community. Nevertheless, she persevered by revising her strategies to fit the changing times. She used the *Star* to encourage and unify black residents during Omaha's three race riots and campaigned against a freeway project that would physically divide the already isolated black community. Keeping the black and white communities informed on a weekly basis was her greatest black power contribution to the people of Omaha. The *Star* was "command central," and Brown strategically operated it during the city's most emotionally tense decade. She assigned herself to the helm of the newspaper instead of participating in rallies. After all, she stated, "you do not put your generals on the front line." She used her access to the powerful white and black men managing the city of Omaha and northern Omaha to promote nonviolent solutions to the problem of black inequality.[2]

Omaha's third racial disturbance was just one of the 239 riots that rocked the United States in the turbulent 1960s. Before the decade a race riot had meant whites lynching blacks and destroying black properties, but in this era a race riot came to mean black residents attacking white owners and destroying their businesses in the ghetto.

Hugh Davis Graham's study, "On Riots and Riot Commissions: Civil Disorders in the 1960s," concluded that isolated black ghettos were the foundation of unrest. However, he contended, not only did white institutions maintain the ghettos but also white society as a whole condoned the ghettos. It was a classic case of organized white supremacy fusing with individual "not in my backyard" attitudes; black Americans occupied mainstream-sanctioned enclaves while a portion of the white populace pretended it was unaware of the minority community's geographic and therefore financial oppression. Black rioters throughout the country were conveying a message to white America: ghetto politics as usual were no longer working.[3]

City of Omaha ghetto politics were no longer working in northern Omaha either, especially after the Cudahy, Armour, and Swift meatpacking plants closed their doors in 1967, 1968, and 1969, respectively. The Near North Side was a crowded black community that suffered great social and economic inequality. In the 1960s approximately thirty-five thousand people of color, a third of whom were unemployed, lived in one square mile of Omaha's total forty-five square miles of city. Ill will flowed from the frustrated residents, especially toward northern Omaha's former Jewish residents. The central business district, the Twenty-Fourth and Lake Streets corridor, contained more than two hundred shops and service venues, and most of these businesses were predominantly owned by white Jewish shopkeepers who no longer resided in the neighborhood. It was only a matter of time before the isolated minority community exploded.[4]

Brown recognized the potential for violence in northern Omaha. In the spring of 1965 she attempted to forestall possible rioting by asking Mayor Axel Vergman Sorensen to discuss his intentions toward the black community. After all, Sorensen, who had recently been sworn in for a four-year term at Omaha's downtown civic center, had publicly promised to "faithfully and impartially perform the duties of the office of Mayor of the City of Omaha according to law and to the best of my ability." Sorensen assured Brown he would keep his word. She in turn informed her readers that she believed in the mayor's commitment to the community, telling them she was "interested in the economics of the situation and the welfare of my people." She made this point more apparent in a peaceful public march in northern Omaha over a year later.[5]

Brown remained committed to nonviolence, although others in the national black community, particularly young black men, were growing disillusioned with the philosophy and strategy of nonviolence. In mid-June 1966 the Southern Christian Leadership Conference's Dr. Martin Luther King Jr., the Congress of Racial Equality's Floyd McKissick, and the Student Nonviolent Coordinating Committee's Stokely Carmichael led a massive crowd of men and women as they completed James Meredith's aborted March against Fear. The thirty-one-year-old Meredith, best known for desegregating the University of Mississippi in 1962, was seriously injured with birdshot from a racist sniper when he had attempted a solo protest march from Memphis, Tennessee, to Jackson, Mississippi, two weeks earlier. It was during the second publicized concluding march that local police in Greenwood, Mississippi, arrested Stokely Carmichael. After his release an enraged Carmichael, spouting the philosophies of black nationalism and Omaha-born Malcolm X's teachings, strode through the small town's park and shouted, "This is the twenty-seventh time that I've been arrested. I ain't going to jail no more. The only way we gonna stop them white men from whuppin' us is to take over. What we gonna start sayin' now is Black Power!" In a nationwide show of solidarity, many black communities throughout the United States supported Carmichael's more aggressive stance. Within days of Carmichael's statement, northern Omaha black male leaders organized a late-afternoon march down the center of Twenty-Fourth and Lake Streets; their silhouettes were joined by the stately female figure of Mildred Brown. Rudy Smith, now the *Omaha World-Herald*'s first black photographer, depicted the march in several panoramic photographs. Smith's images documented Brown's commitment to the Near North Side, even though the national black power movement caused her, and many other women leaders, to lose authority in their black communities. The prominent roles of civil rights activists such as Brown's close contemporaries Dorothy Height, Septima Clark, Ella Baker, and Daisy Bates declined with the rise of male chauvinism.[6]

Mildred was a mature, seasoned fighter, but her gender was barely allowed to play a part in the black power movement's masculine deployment of power, punishment, and violence. Although the mid-1960s movement was an extension of earlier civil rights activism in the 1940s and 1950s, its dominant black male leadership tended to exclude black women activists and organizers such as Brown. Black power became a symbol of self-determination, self-defense, and black manhood. David Rice, the deputy minister of information for Omaha's *United Front against Fascism*, a splinter Black Panther Party organization, explained the overall goal of the militant movement in the extremist underground newspaper, the *Buffalo Chip*. Starting in December 1967 Rice and his fellow writers created the radical monthly as a free expression of poetry, quizzes, artwork, and noncensored articles as an alternative to what they termed the so-called fantasy stories appearing in the *Omaha World-Herald* daily. Its only similarity to the *Omaha Star* was its ten-cent price. Rice informed readers from the headquarters of the short-lived newspaper in downtown Omaha, "Black Power does not want to take over the United States or kill off all the white people. We [men] just feel that it is impractical to live under a democracy without being able to fully partake of all its fruits. Negroes want the whole pie—every liberty described in the Constitution and every responsibility." But black power leaders did not want women like Angela Davis and Kathleen Cleaver as equals. Indeed, the movement's nationalism popularized submissive black women as the inspiration for strong black male leadership.[7]

It did not surprise Rice that Brown's news coverage of Omaha's role in the black power movement "was pretty much slim to none." She did not associate with the movement's macho ideology. Black Panther Frank Peak reasoned that "we have always had friends at the *Star* [who] will slip things into the paper for us but as far as stepping out and giving us any kind of overt support, no there hasn't been any. I suppose a lot of that was due to the issue of advertising. Miss Brown played it cool, it was a conservative town." Peak misunderstood Brown's actions. As a friend and fervent follower of Dr. Martin Luther King Jr., she repeatedly promoted nonviolent assertiveness and legislature as the solutions to racism. Her stance concurred with many others in the black community who saw the black supremacy mentality in the movement as divisive. Brown chose to ignore the more aggressive tactics of the predominantly young black male–led movement by generally not reporting them in her *Star*. President Lyndon Baines Johnson complimented Brown on her publishing choices at a National Newspaper Publishers Association conference in 1965. Johnson appreciated her decision to forego sensationalizing Omaha's racial tension. It cost her newspaper sales, but it demonstrated her commitment to uplifting Omaha's northern community. She thanked Johnson for his praise but in her four subsequent meetings with him at the White House in 1966, 1967, and 1968, she advised him that he, as the top male office holder in the land, needed to take immediate and forceful action in the area of civil rights, or there would be more violence. Her words proved prophetic for the Near North Side.[8]

The first riot between the black community and the Omaha police began in the early hours of July 4, 1966. The downtown Omaha police station received an anonymous phone call. It concerned a disturbance in the Safeway parking lot. The recently constructed grocery store not only provided northern Omaha with the necessary elements of employment and infrastructure but also offered teenagers a central meeting space. According to Harl Dalstrom's *A. V. Sorensen and the New Omaha*, "The parking lot was the place to go for most of the youths. Most of these guys were too young to hang out in the bars and they had no other place to go. There was not a single recreational facility in that whole area of the city." When the police arrived, several young adults were lighting fireworks. Details of what happened next remain sketchy. Although the *Star* and the *World-Herald* barely reported the uprising, northern Omaha residents saw three days of chaotic fighting between residents and the city of Omaha police; [9]

people sustained injuries and the police arrested 122 black rioters. Property damage incurred was minimal. There were no fires and the only gunfire occurred when several times police officers fired warning shots into the air.[9]

Brown deliberately decided not to publicize the first Omaha uprising. She informed her readers, "I don't like crime. I don't condone crime. If I have to report it, I put it in the smallest article possible," which was precisely the size of the brief paragraph titled "Public Mass Meeting Sunday." It briefly explained the cause of the first riot as the result of unemployment. The youth who engaged in the July Fourth weekend outbreak wanted job training, recreation facilities, and an end to verbal and physical police abuse. Brown informed her readers that there would be a public mass meeting to discuss the disturbance. Sponsors of the meeting included the National Association for the Advancement of Colored People (NAACP), the Urban League, the Citizens' Coordinating Committee for Civil Liberties (4CL), and the Zion Baptist Church. Wilbur Phillips, former De Porres Club attorney and current NAACP lawyer, authored the small paragraph in the *Star* concerning the first riot. Brown deliberately did not post an editorial nor did she comment on the first riot. Instead, as a conciliatory diplomatic gesture, she shrewdly printed a public statement from Mayor Sorensen. He wished to salute those who brought the July Fourth incident to an end and express his pride in the majority of black citizens who exercised good judgment during the rioting. The *Star* duly reported the city administrator promising to make amends through increased minority employment and newly constructed recreational facilities. Brown's refusal to reiterate stereotyped characteristics of the black population by printing the negative side of issues or sensationalizing northern Omaha's local news confused some residents. They were unable to see that there was no reason for her to reinforce the given discourse of her day; it incorrectly blamed crime on race, not on racism and poverty.[10]

Barbara Hewins-Maroney, a University of Nebraska at Omaha professor, questioned Brown's seemingly tepid inclusion of national and local civil rights demonstrations. Hewins-Maroney reasoned that the publisher was "out for money for herself" and that Brown had failed to publish articles concerning negative issues because she did not want to harm her relationship with local white advertisers. Bertha Calloway, Brown's secretary, validated a portion of Hewins-Maroney's conjecture by explaining the age-old dilemma of the black press: "Black newspapers did not play the role that they could have played in supporting the struggles of black people" due to the issue of advertising and local politics. Brown knew she could not afford to lose revenue or her newspaper. The mainstream *Omaha World-Herald* did indeed shut down the *South Omaha Sun* newspaper for being too vocal against the city of Omaha administrators. But the allegations against Brown caring only about money were inaccurate and ignorant. In earlier eras she had not shied away from calling out white businesses that discriminated against blacks for fearing of losing ad revenue. Reading through fifty years of microfilmed *Omaha Star* newspapers clearly shows that from the time Brown cofounded the *Star* in 1938 until her passing in 1989, she maintained her philosophy of printing only positive news; it was a commitment many of the younger black activists, including Hewins-Maroney, were unaware of in the 1960s. Brown's *Star* reflected the respected identity most of its readers wished to attain, even though another racial uprising in 1968 widened the split between the populations of white and black Omaha.[11]

On March 4, 1968, almost two years after the first riot, a second riot occurred in Omaha's downtown civic center. The catalyst was a visit from presidential-hopeful George Wallace. Because of the Alabama governor's racist reputation, Holy Ghost Church reverend Jack McCaslin chaperoned Near North Side youth to the auditorium packed with 5,400 attendees. According to McCaslin, Wallace's inflammatory oration that day incensed the group of approximately forty teenagers, especially when the Dixiecrat gestured at them and stated, "Those responsible for a breakdown of law and order are not the majority of American people, but a group of activists, militants, and Communists." After listening to their responding booing and catcalls,

Wallace asked the local police to escort the minority students out of the auditorium. Several officers grasped the backs of metal chairs and swung them at the small group. Youths stumbled through the barrage of police, flying chairs, and angry epitaphs and escaped through the exit doors. A few hours later the police paid a visit to McCaslin; they arrested him and charged him with inciting a riot. The white priest's arrest and the particulars of the riot received mention in the *Omaha Star*. Brown acknowledged the police brutality, but she focused on praising the mobilization of church and community leaders, as well as government and agency officials who proactively eliminated the triggers for another long, hot summer by designing a community model for law and order.[12]

Reverend McCaslin maintained his parish's good relations with the *Star*'s owner. He appreciated Brown, whom he labeled as "a classy dame who supplied the public with the complicated angles of the North Side." As one public servant to another, he thought he understood the publisher's quandary. "She made her living from the *Star* but needed the white businesses' advertising." He knew Brown was a middle-aged divorced woman earning a comfortable living as a newspaper owner, but as an ardent subscriber to black power's masculine ideology, he considered the paper's lack of local news disturbing. McCaslin also perceived that the mainstream *Omaha World-Herald* newspaper was "not giving us what the *Star* should have. It should have been more militant."[13]

Instead of printing editorials challenging the black community to fight against inequality, Brown published proestablishment nonbiased articles, such as a piece mentioning Mayor Sorensen's opinion of the second uprising. She did not soften Sorensen's rationale for the uprising but merely reported exactly what he stated: "Wallace came to town to make a speech and a group of priests and nuns organized these young people to break it up. . . . The important issue was freedom of speech. The police had every right to remove them from the auditorium." However, she did question Sorensen's statement that the police handled it superbly, especially the arrest of six black youngsters the evening after the debacle. Racial tension among city administrators, the police, and the black community continued escalating.[14]

Omaha officials initially expected another riot after Dr. Martin Luther King Jr.'s assassination on April 4, 1968. The demise of one of the Big Six caused riots in Washington DC and 129 other metropolitan cities, but northern Omaha remained peaceful. Indeed, an editorial in the *Daily Nebraskan*, the University of Nebraska at Lincoln's newspaper, warned Omaha of an imminent rebellion. "Omaha is seething and an abyss has opened between city hall and 24th Street. It is certain Near North Side residents will no longer sit placidly and fan themselves during the long summer days. The Wallace riot spewed out only a small amount of the steam rapidly collecting in the ghetto pressure cooker." The Near North Side's lack of rioting was one of the reasons presidential-hopeful Robert Kennedy visited the black community three weeks later during his campaign. Mystified, the *Omaha World-Herald* newspaper asked reporters to explore the Near North Side's lack of reaction by interviewing several black residents. Archie Godfrey, a twenty-year-old student at the University of Nebraska at Omaha at the time, explained why a riot did not come to fruition: "Individuals decided that one way to show their respect to Dr. King's family and his philosophy of nonviolence was not to participate in any rioting." Brown, whose family had known the civil rights leader personally, praised the black community for properly memorializing the slain leader. "We ought therefore to do more than grieve for him, we ought to think about his life and death . . . his integrity, his calm, and his self respect." She encouraged readers to properly honor Martin King, which was how she privately referred to him, by not resorting to aggression. Local and national leadership were essential for understanding the level of violence present throughout the United States.[15]

President Lyndon Johnson appointed an eleven-member National Advisory Commission on Civil Disorder, led by Illinois governor Otto Kerner, to study the nationwide occurrence of rioting. The March 1968 Kerner Report concluded "that the United States was moving toward two societies, one black, one white—separate and unequal. Prominent among the causes that the commission identified for this growing racial inequality was residential segregation." The report defined the type of rioter involved in the black power movement. "A young black male. Unskilled and underemployed, he was also a typical local resident (possessing a typical arrest record) rather than a southern emigrant or an outside agitator. His targets were police and symbolic white property." Bob Armstrong, Omaha Housing Authority director, later recalled that "the people in the projects were afraid of the police and the police were afraid of people who lived in projects. The two sides never communicated." Lack of communication proved to be a major issue during Omaha's third and worst race riot.[16]

This last riot started on June 24, 1969. Initially, the *Omaha World-Herald* reported Vivian Strong's death as a female suspect running away from a burglary and downplayed the horror of Loder, a white police officer, shooting Strong, an innocent, unarmed black teenager. Instead, the mainstream paper focused on Strong's divorced mother, who was supposedly difficult to reach after the shooting; she was at North Sioux City's dog track in South Dakota. Saint Benedict's white reverend Ken Vavrina was shocked when he attended police officer Loder's preliminary hearing. The judge charged the thirty-year-old officer, who viewed "the whole incident as a shame," with manslaughter and "just slapped Loder's wrist" by posting bail at five hundred dollars. The low bail figure, which was the same amount the court set for each of the seventeen people arrested for looting, caused outrage to descend on the courthouse audience. Angered, Father Vavrina and several of the black men at the trial "walked away talking about how to make a Molotov cocktail."[17]

Burning and destruction followed the court's bail decision. Ronald Blumkin, grandson of Nebraska Furniture Mart's Russian Jewish founder Rose Blumkin, witnessed the third riot from a unique perspective on the top of Omaha's downtown Peter Kiewit Plaza building, where he was celebrating his twenty-first birthday. Blumkin vividly remembers looking down at northern Omaha's skyline and seeing flames. "It was a glow. It was like sitting in a skybox at Lincoln's

Memorial Football Stadium; almost like watching a movie but it was real." One of the first stores torched was Herman's Grocery, a Jewish establishment that allowed buying goods on credit with interest. Although charging was generally an accepted transaction, some black customers regarded it as the black "little man buying goods and services provided and financed by *the man*." The rioters targeted Jewish storeowners, which affected many of the shops on the Near North Side.[18]

Brown believed destroying the heart of the black community was not the way for the frustrated residents to demand equality. She and Max Brownell attempted to reason with the rioters during the three long days of burning and looting. The destruction stretched for ten city blocks on Twenty-Fourth Street between Ohio and Seward Streets. Brown told rioters, "No good will come of this burning. It is destroying the black neighborhood." The rioters destroyed a total of fifty white-owned shops and stores. Similar to the three days of looting and burning during northern Philadelphia's riot in August 1964, a disproportionate number of the demolished shops were owned by Jewish businesspeople. In *Up South*, Matthew Countryman explained that these types of riots, the kind that caused millions of dollars worth of damage, focused on a common enemy. In Omaha's and Philadelphia's case, the enemy was not the Jewish shopkeepers. The rioters' enemy was the white establishment, "most visible, best symbolized and most vulnerable behind the plate glass [store] windows in the black ghetto." As Champer Jack, an old-time northern Omaha resident, sadly reminisced, "The Jewish people, they were good to blacks, but the blacks were misinformed." For the moment, the black community was also past listening to Mildred Brown and the city of Omaha officials.[19]

Brown's centrally located *Star* was never in danger of destruction. Omaha's Black Panther Party members, such as Edward Poindexter, protected black-owned establishments. Poindexter recollected standing guard over the newspaper office and the Greater Omaha Community Action headquarters, adjacent to the *Star*. The *Omaha World-Herald* printed a photograph of Poindexter and two other rifle-armed Black Panther members. Ironically, Benny Johnson, a *Star* staffer, took the image; it never appeared in the *Star*, because Brown would not approve of its possibly violent message. Inside the *Star* building, longtime employee Shirley Harrison remained unconcerned for her safety. She knew many of the rioters. They were former *Star* newspaper carriers and they respected Brown, the *Star* building; even Brown's Cadillac, parked in front of the office, went untouched.[20]

The destruction of the predominantly white Jewish–owned properties was a strong indication of the Near North Side's frustration with unequal rights. Black Panther David Rice described Omaha's third uprising as an act of financial despair and an "act of rebellion. There was a grievance, not only [Vivian Strong's] murder that started it but other murders, acts of brutality by the police and support of those acts by the prosecutor's office and the courts. Many African American people felt as though they had no recourse but to take it to the streets."[21] A dean of the University of Nebraska at Omaha, Mary Mudd, believed the third riot "happened due to the insensitivity of the people in power. The local government misunderstood the people of the black community. The people did not have any hope. People did not have much to lose," and they showed it through the obliteration of white Jewish businesses that catered to the black community.[22]

Because of police barricades most black and white Omaha residents viewed the destruction of the north Twenty-Fourth Street community through photographs printed in the *Omaha World-Herald* newspaper. The mainstream daily sent black photographer Rudy Smith to document the burned destruction on the first night of the riot. Knowing it was unsafe to walk in the street, since someone could mistake his camera for a gun, Smith remembers walking through the alleys of his neighborhood. Two national guardsmen approached him, and one of the men told Smith to "come here, nigger." When he complied, the soldier held a gun to Smith's head and walked him around a building to where the new Omaha mayor, Gene Leahy, was assessing the situation. After Smith explained that he worked for the *Omaha World-Herald* newspaper, the guardsmen allowed him to leave the devastated area. Smith returned after the riot ended two days later and photographed what was left of the smoldering business infrastructure. The city of Omaha began the process of evaluating the fire damage caused by what Mayor Leahy termed "the recent spasms in the ghetto area."[23]

Brown did not condone the third demonstration against racial inequality but instead focused her *Star* on the death of Vivian Strong. Brown, as was her modus operandi during the 1950s, did not pen an open letter to the community but reprinted a statement from the president of the Urban League denouncing the senseless fatal shooting of Strong. According to the *Omaha World-Herald*, Strong was a distant girl who had a heart condition, which would have eventually necessitated major surgery. Besides her medical condition, according to the mainstream newspaper, Strong "had a discipline problem. She seemed to resent anyone trying to make her behave herself. But she certainly wasn't incorrigible." Through Brown's strategy of reporting the injustice of Strong's death, she sought to counter the denigration of Vivian Strong's character.[24]

But Brown was far from indifferent concerning the third riot. During an interview with a *Dundee and West Omaha Sun* newspaper reporter, she frankly told him, "We're behind other cities—even many of the southern cities." Within weeks, when the black community demanded the city of Omaha create reform measures to avoid another riot, Brown published activist Ernie Chambers's list of ten necessary changes. His petition included relieving Officer Loder of his duty, paying a hundred-thousand-dollar compensation to Strong's mother, and keeping "all white cops out of the black community altogether." Chambers and thirty other black outraged and angry citizens had already submitted the list to Mayor Leahy, but the *Star*'s publisher wanted to make sure everyone in Omaha knew the contents of the petition. Although Brown was two generations older than Chambers and did not always agree with his politics, she respected him enough to give his proactive words the entire front page of the *Star*. Mayor Leahy did not publicly comment on the list, but he complimented Brown for "keeping the public informed on all subjects in this rapidly changing world," even though the city did little to clean up the riot's destruction.²⁵

As Omaha's black community broke down in crisis, Brown suffered her own personal calamity. First, she discovered that Brownell, her husband, had betrayed her, and, second, the *Star* almost declared bankruptcy. Between 1947 and 1969 Brownell and Brown presented an image of a happy couple. But Brown was twenty-three years older than Brownell, and she worried about her appearance. She did leg-lift and sit-up exercises while still in bed and drank milk of magnesia to purge herself after each meal. Imagine her dismay when Brownell became interested in her niece Marguerita Washington. The tall, slender Kansas City native was seven years younger than Brown's husband. Their love affair existed for only a short while before Brown discovered it. Brownell and Washington left Omaha for a few years in the early 1970s, but eventually they returned. He continued his job as the *Star*'s office manager while living with Washington. It was a painful situation for Brown, but it ensured the longevity of the newspaper. Brownell, who realized his adulterous error too late, spoke highly of Brown; he never stopped loving her. The second crisis in Brown's life was less emotional, but far more financially critical.²⁶

Due to a corrupt accountant, Brown's personal finances during the last riot became entangled with her business capital. She owed the Internal Revenue Service fifteen thousand dollars of back taxes. Normally, Brown would have had the assets to pay the taxes, but a previous purchase of an expensive property in Omaha left her with few liquid resources.²⁷ She attempted to borrow money from a local bank but was unable to secure a loan. The situation became tense when Brown announced that not only did one of the bank's board members own an Omaha newspaper but also someone from the board had approached her and asked the price of her *Star*. The unnamed person told Brown she would have to sell it eventually to pay her taxes. The *Star*'s owner responded, "Don't you bet on that; you're talking to Millie Brown."²⁸ Eventually, her financial situation resolved itself when an anonymous white advertiser paid the *Star*'s back taxes.

Brown hoped the city of Omaha would help to reconstruct the destroyed Near North Side. She informed readers that although Twenty-Fourth Street looked like a rag doll, it could be quickly renovated if black and white residents pulled together. Brown, together with several leaders of the Omaha Ministerial Alliance and the Mid-City Business and Professional Association, met with the city council on September 19, 1969, to say, "We are concerned because ten percent of the citizens of our city have been the victims of over one-third of all the reported crimes of our city.... We do not want nor are we asking for police brutality. We are not asking for the unwarranted harassment of Black citizens. We want more and better qualified police who will do their job well." Besides their desire for equal and good law enforcement on the Near North Side, the delegation wanted answers concerning the rehabilitation of Twenty-Fourth Street. The storeowners who had lost their shops were choosing not to reopen, rebuild, or sue the city of Omaha, even when it became apparent that no insurance monies would be forthcoming. Too many insurance vendors cancelled their policies shortly after the riot.[29] The northern Omaha group wanted to know why nothing was being done to rebuild the black community's infrastructure: "Why with the disturbances we have experienced did not the State of Nebraska apply for the Federal Government Re-Insurance funds that 35 other states applied for, rather than force many of our home owners and businesses to do without or pay exhorbitant [sic] insurance premiums."[30] The city council minutes indicated no response from the city administrators to the Near North Side leaders, other than council president Fred Jacobberger commending the small group for taking an interest in northern Omaha's problems and for bringing the issue to the council's attention. It seemed northern Omaha was on its own financially.

After waiting for more than eight years for the city to rebuild northern Omaha, Brown proclaimed 1977 as the year when Omaha officials should replace their rhetoric with concrete action and assist the Near North Side. "The City has allocated money to upgrade the business districts of other sections of Omaha. It is time that they find funds to aid in the revitalization of a once thriving business area." Brown used the *Star* to educate the community about the $7.5 million dollars offered by President Jimmy Carter for distressed cities. She maintained, "Omaha can't be viable and safe until something is done to 'undistress' the black community.... It is time that the City Government stop playing games concerning the needs of the black community and start actualizing the lip service it has historically given to problems of the area." Citing the Federal Community Development Block Grant funds, she noted that five hundred thousand dollars went to South Omaha renewal and ninety thousand dollars went to a northwest shopping plaza, while only forty thousand dollars found its way to the Twenty-Fourth Street and Lake District business area. Brown chastised her readers and blamed them for the unequal distribution of monies. "If Blacks had been properly registered in great numbers, the city council would not have dared to give us a measely [sic] $40,000 of the revitalization of No. 24th St., instead they would have come and asked you what do you want." The city council eventually decided that Omaha's Public Works Department needed to redesign, update, and beautify the black community's North 30th Street to improve commercial and business opportunities. According to Omaha City Relations director Buddy Hogan, efforts were made to rehabilitate northern Omaha's property, but Omaha's administration provided only limited time, expenditure, and assistance. At the same time a new threat arose within the black neighborhood.[31]

Starting in the early 1960s Omaha officials decided it was necessary to connect Omaha and its subdivisions with a freeway, even though one of the three proposed routes would bisect the black community. Residents of Omaha had the choice of a freeway running north, west, or south. Omaha's sizable Catholic community quickly capsized the western freeway plan because it would wreak havoc on Saint Cecilia's cathedral, which was directly in its path. Therefore, city ballots in the 1970s had only the northern or southern routes as choices. Omaha voters picked the northern freeway. The selected corridor would run through north Omaha's Twenty-Fourth and Lake Streets and thus

Changing Strategies for Changing Times 159

divide the black community. Moreover, northern Omaha residents denounced the northern freeway proposal because it would displace four hundred structures, the majority of which were black households. Black home owners and businesspeople living in the area would soon be unable to sell their property and therefore unable to relocate elsewhere.[32]

City of Omaha officials ignored the angst of the black neighborhood. The northern freeway was a matter of economics: black northern Omaha's community property was less expensive than mainstream Omaha's neighborhoods. It had the lowest home values and, like so many other cities, the highest concentration of segregation, which meant those affected by the freeways were mostly black residents. The table indicates the amount of segregation in several of the largest cities in the United States between 1940 and 1970. Omaha's segregation percentage had not varied much during the three decades of restrictive covenants and two years of open housing after 1968.

Table 1. Nonwhite-white segregation indices by year (%)

	1940	1950	1960	1970
Chicago	95.0	92.1	92.6	88.8
Kansas City	88.0	91.3	90.8	88.0
Los Angeles	84.2	84.6	81.8	78.4
Omaha	89.5	92.4	92.0	90.7
Birmingham	86.4	88.7	92.8	91.5
Memphis	79.9	86.4	92.0	91.8
New Orleans	81.0	84.9	86.3	83.1
Miami	97.9	97.8	97.9	89.4

Source: Taeuber and Taeuber, *Residential Segregation*, 40.

Fighting against the city of Omaha's plan to build the northern freeway through the black community was a David-versus-Goliath contest that Mildred Brown knew was futile. Therefore, she used her *Star* to update the community on the upcoming roadway and promised readers to "help every man in the firm belief that all are hurt as long as anyone is held back." She did not call for a mass protest. She was a realist.

Brown knew she was the voice of the black press in Omaha, and she knew when to pick her battles. James Suttle, transportation engineer for the northern freeway's construction, explained that Brown had to go along with the city's plans to stay in business and continue championing the black community. Brown's biggest concern was making sure the black residents were not pawns in a chess game of community development and housing relocation.[33]

Her *Star* published the times and dates of the Nebraska Department of Roads and the Nebraska Highway Commission's public hearings for black and white Omaha residents wishing to attend the northern freeway meetings. Engineer James Suttle and the freeway architectural firm who employed him, Henningson, Durham, and Richardson, led the well-attended discussions. At the last of these meetings, northern Omaha resident Carl Tyler organized a walkout to prevent the firm from claiming community acceptance. Tyler refused to be counted as accepting the city plat buyouts that allowed land speculators to buy the northern freeway's displaced property for a hundred dollars an acre. Suttle lamented Tyler's action to *Omaha World-Herald* reporters: "Carl timed his comments at about the time some of the people were ready to leave." The engineer refused to accept that Tyler and other residents were fighting against the northern freeway. Brown's *Star* remained steadfastly silent but continued to supply construction and home displacement news concerning the upcoming freeway.[34]

As a resident of northern Omaha, Brown circulated and promoted recently elected state senator Ernie Chambers's petition against the northern freeway, but as the *Star*'s publisher, she did not print the contents of it. Her power in the black community, diluted by the black power movement's focus on male leadership, was better employed by combining it with Chambers's influence. His Committee against the North Omaha Freeway petition denounced the northern freeway for seventeen reasons, including, "The freeway is part of a 25 year-old plan to drive Black people from this land by dividing, disrupting and destroying the Black community structure. By drawing traffic away from 30th and 24th Streets, it will harm existing businesses" and provide scant political support, because "the black vote will be seriously diluted or weakened as more people are being driven from the area." Election commissioner Lee Terry Sr. was indeed talking about gerrymandering the two black school board districts.[35] Brown signed the petition on line forty-six out of fifty petitioners and volunteered the *Star* office as one of several community buildings circulating the petition. Despite Chambers's public efforts and Brown's private assistance, the northern freeway construction plans proceeded as scheduled. Omaha's city council upset northern Omaha residents even more when it tactlessly decided to name the almost-completed roadway the Dr. Martin Luther King Jr. Expressway.[36]

Angry Near North Side residents refused to acknowledge the newly named freeway and dubbed it instead the "North Omaha Berlin Wall" and the "White Folk's Northwest Passage." Resident Herman Pearson voiced what many in the community considered was obvious. The freeway split everything in the neighborhood, and it was done deliberately by the city. The *Omaha World-Herald* attempted to placate northern Omaha's opinion and validate the benefits of the northern freeway for the entire Omaha population by compiling the *1979 Consumer Preference Study*. Prior to the city publication, Brown wrote an editorial in the *Star* that read, "People in need of better housing conditions need—and deserve—more than another study. They need results with immediacy." It was too late. Along with the riots, the damage the completed northern freeway caused was already reversing the progress the black neighborhood had attained in the early 1960s.[37]

Encouraging racial uplift, unifying the black community, and using the *Star* to keep the city of Omaha and northern Omaha informed were difficult tasks during the predominantly male black power movement of the mid to late 1960s and the divisive urban renewal of the 1970s. But Mildred Brown managed to fulfill these priorities by changing her leadership strategies. She used the *Star* to print positive news articles in spite of Omaha's three race riots and to assist residents contending with the northern freeway splitting the black community. Instead of taking to the streets, an aging Brown supported black equality through the *Star*. She deliberately chose when to publicly support the newer generation of black male activists, such as the local Black Panther Party and 1970s-elected senator Ernie Chambers, and when to ignore their aggressive tactics. The *Star*'s presence during this tense decade was integral to the well-being of the community. Brown used the newspaper as a public primer; she taught her readers how to effectively respond to and fight against racism. By the end of the 1970s, Brown was tiring from her years of activism, organizing, and strategizing, but she refused to consider retirement.

8

The Death of an Icon

Driving past the corner of Twenty-Fourth and Lake Streets, one can almost imagine the thriving Near North Side community before it perished in the burning and destruction of the 1969 race rebellion. Today, the Near North Side remains only a shadow of its former potential. However, evidence of its upbeat past lingers on a one-block section of Twenty-Fourth and Grant Streets. The short strip of roadway bears the title "Mildred Brown Street." The *Star* publisher, as well as Father Markoe and the De Porres Club, are no longer, but the results of the successful collective battles they fought still exist. The numerous newspaper youths, whom Brown encouraged through advice, respect, and employment, have grown into middle-aged adults. Brown's voice, now barely a whisper in the *Omaha Star* newspaper, continues her goal of equality. The *Omaha Star* building earned its rightful place on the National Register of Historic Places for being a center of social history, ethnic heritage, and mass communication during the civil rights movement. Matt Holland, the son of deceased De Porres Club president Denny Holland, applauded the building's national status. "The building means a lot of history to Omaha, not just the black community. The *Star* is an icon. Like the bus seat that Rosa Parks sat on. It's that tangible." Mildred Brown was a courageous leader and a practical dreamer. The *Omaha Star* newspaper was her dream. She made it happen for herself and the city's black community.[1]

In the last week of January, in 1989, an older but energetic Mildred Brown sat down on her office couch for an interview with Jeff Reinhardt, the white editor of Omaha's mainstream *New Horizons* magazine. It was a chilly, snowy afternoon, and their twilight meeting at the *Omaha Star* building was the one time slot Brown had available in her busy schedule that day. Reinhardt admired Brown's numerous displayed awards, including the Key to the City plaque given to her the night black and white Omaha honored her in 1984. His gaze dropped to the photo albums on the coffee table, and before he could stop himself, he picked up one of the volumes and started thumbing through the first pages. Images of the newspaper owner with Jackie Robinson, Richard Nixon, and Hubert Humphrey stared back at him. Looking over Reinhardt's shoulder, Brown softly reminisced, "I guess I've met everybody who's anybody." Her successful networking extended to managing the *Star*'s twenty-three staffers, operating the weekly within her monthly budget of fifty thousand dollars, and maintaining its circulation of 30,865 subscribers in thirty-nine states. Her *Star*, she said, was the longest-operating black newspaper in Nebraska's history because "we don't write anything derogatory, and we portray our role models." During her fifty-year tenure, she had been up against several stiff obstacles, but she had no fear, because the *Star* had broken down discrimination in Omaha. At the end of the interview, Paul Bryant, a young man whom Brown fondly called her foster son, arrived at her office and home. Bryant was driving her to the evening's special entertainment. She was attending the Dr. Martin Luther King Jr. Day celebration at Omaha's downtown civic center. Reinhardt bid Brown good-bye and thanked her for the interview. As he departed through the newspaper office's front door, he asked Brown one last question: "When will you retire?" She did not hesitate. "I'll be at the *Omaha Star* until God takes me."[2]

In the meantime though, Brown needed to decide who she would pick as the successor of her newspaper. She had started worrying about who would take over the *Star* in the 1970s. It would take an excellent staff person to operate the *Star*, because Mildred Brown and the *Omaha Star* were one and the same entity. But no one in her nuclear family was still alive or well enough to take over the newspaper. Annie "Anna" Washington, her older sister, had died almost two decades earlier on October 20, 1970, in Kansas City, Missouri, and her youngest sibling, Willie "Bill" Brown, had died on June 13, 1975, at age sixty-two. Her second-best choice was her first husband, Dr. Shirley Edward Gilbert, but he had died on April 16, 1976, in Saint Louis, Missouri. His adult children from his second marriage, Shirl and Roslyn, had the right to take over the newspaper, but they were uninterested in operating it. Her only other family candidate was her brother Bennie, but he had Alzheimer's and was barely able to take care of himself. Therefore, Brown began considering people she trusted in northern Omaha's black community.[3]

Brown's choices for a *Star* successor among the Near North Side's black residents were limited. Charlie Washington, her longtime editor, was a logical choice, but he had passed away three years earlier in 1986. Her foster grandson, Marvin Kellogg Jr., considered running the *Star*, but he was too busy managing his family's Kellogg's Market. *Omaha World-Herald* photographer Rudy Smith and city relations director Buddy Hogan each hoped to purchase the *Star*. Brown listened to their offers and joked, "Anything is for sale for the right price," but she refused to seriously consider someone buying her *Star*. Probably her favorite candidate was thirty-one-year-old Paul Bryant. He expected to succeed Brown. She had groomed him from the moment she met him seven years earlier. He was so close to Brown even his own mother was jealous of their friendship, but he was not close enough. Mildred Brown was a product of her parents' strong family upbringing. She wanted a relative operating the *Star*.[4]

The one person who understood her better than anyone else in the black community was her former second husband, Noel Maximilian Brownell. He had worked at the *Star* and stayed by her side, albeit in different capacities, for forty-three years. Max knew the newspaper business and Bennie, Mildred's one surviving sibling, approved of him. However, Max had kept a quiet social, political, and economic profile in Omaha for a reason. A recent thorough check through Nebraska's naturalization records at the Nebraska State Historical Society revealed why Max refused to have his picture in the *Star* and did not own a driver's license. He was an undocumented immigrant, and it was even doubtful his legal name was Noel Maximilian Brownell. Indeed, according to Nicole Bryan, from the National Library of Jamaica, no family with the surname "Brownell" owned a sugarcane plantation in Montego Bay during the last decades of the twentieth century. Signing over the *Star* to Max would entail legal paperwork, and neither Mildred nor Max could explain this discrepancy.[5]

Brown, the ever resourceful businessperson, the organized leader who successfully created a black weekly newspaper with scant financing, cultivated thousands of subscribers, and raised many of northern Omaha's youth as newspaper carriers, ultimately chose, according to the evidence researched for this five-year project, not to appoint anyone to succeed her as the owner, publisher, and editor of the *Omaha Star* newspaper. By not naming a successor and not writing a will, she forced whoever took over the *Star* to fight for it in the courts. Similar to her grandfather Millard Breeding having to fight for his rightful inheritance in 1899, her successor would have to defend his or her right to live in Brown's home and manage the *Star*.[6] It would not be long before the competition began.

When Paul Bryant telephoned the newspaper office on Thursday, November 2, 1989, he learned his newspaper mentor, his beloved Aunt Millie, had died in the early hours of that morning. Her death was a surprise to him and the black community. Residents in the neighborhood, who thought Brown was seventy-six, not her actual eighty-three, did not perceive her as an elderly woman. Her robust health and constant energy belied either of her ages. Dr. Laurence Zacharia, Brown's physician, had seen her in his office a week before her passing, and he had pronounced her "healthy enough to be managing the *Omaha Star*." Indeed, Mildred had recently returned the previous Sunday from a Miles Memorial College alumni reunion in Fairfield, Alabama. Reba Shelton, her first cousin, had spoken with Brown the day before her death, and Brown said she was feeling well, even though she had a slight head cold.[7] It seemed a vague malady to cause her death.

Several family members and residents of the Near North Side mentioned possible foul play in Mildred Brown's sudden demise. According to the Omaha police report, Max Brownell found Brown's body in her bed at the newspaper office, but the *Star* reported only that the deceased Brown was discovered by a close family friend. It made sense that Max placed the telephone call to the police at 5:55 a.m., because even though he cohabited with Washington, he was still working at the *Star*. What was unexplainable was his early morning presence in Brown's home, especially since she rarely awoke before 11 a.m. The police report outlined Brown's death as follows: "Brown, in bed, had been dead for at least 2 hours. She was on her back in bed in the southwest bedroom dressed in bedclothes. We conversed with her employee [Brownell] who stated that Brown had been feeling poorly, having both a cold and the flu." The police officers checked the locks on the doors, did not note any type of struggle, and counted the number of pills in Brown's heart medication vials, making sure the correct amount from the date of the prescription existed. Because they did not detect anything out of the ordinary, the police deduced Brown died at approximately 2:30 a.m. Coroner Dr. Thomas Haynes, who did not view her body, listed Brown's cause of death as coronary atherosclerosis, better known as hardening of the arteries. While her body was being delivered to northern Omaha's Myers' Funeral Home, her remaining family members were planning her funeral. The Near North Side's fearless female gladiator who always wore a white corsage was gone.[8]

While news of Mildred Brown's death spread quickly to leaders in the black and white communities, her family contended with writing her obituary. The *Omaha World-Herald*, the *Omaha Star*, and newspapers as far as Saint Louis, Birmingham, and Decatur printed the story of Brown's life and death, and Omaha's city council declared her memory an inspiration to future civic leaders. The council passed a resolution recognizing Brown's invaluable contributions through the *Omaha Star* and to the black community's decades-long struggle to reduce racial discrimination and increase their socioeconomic conditions in Omaha. Family members made the proper arrangements for Brown's large funeral, but it was not a financial burden. The black matriarch of the Near North Side had left a sizable estate. The total value of Brown's property at the time of her death was $127,395. This amount did not include Brown's fur coats, jewelry, and closets full of hats, shoes, and dresses. As the sole owner the *Star*, the *Star* building, three other pieces of property in Omaha, a home in Chicago, and her grandfather's long ago inheritance in Decatur, Alabama, Brown died a financially comfortable woman.[9]

Because Mildred Brown was the Near North Side's closest persona to a black female icon, her funeral was the largest in northern Omaha's history. It began at 10:00 a.m. at the Saint John AME Church on November 6, 1989. Several members of the Alpha Phi Alpha black fraternity carried her casket past approximately four hundred mourners. The eight pallbearers walked slowly to the tune of Isaac Watt's 1707 black spiritual, "When I Can Read My Title Clear." Governor Kay Orr, Nebraska's first female governor, eulogized the *Star*'s owner. The assembled crowd listened to Orr reflect on how Brown provided her community with "enormously effective leadership in the cause of social justice." Orr placed Brown among leading Nebraskans, regardless of race, who had selflessly dedicated their life to their fellow human beings.[10]

Reverend Dorsey McCullough, Brown's pastor at Saint John, proudly officiated at the publisher's funeral. McCullough's sermon focused on Esther 4:11. He paralleled Sister Brown to the Hebrew Bible's Queen Esther. The Jewish royal leader had also used the power of the pen to create a voice for her people. McCullough pointed to the deceased Brown, laid out in a bright red dress and a large carnation corsage, and said she was standing before her people one last time. After the pastor's sermon, it was time for the black community to walk past Brown's coffin. Longtime *Omaha Star* employee siblings Shirley Harrison and Catherine Jones joined the reverse receiving line to pay their last respects. When they approached Brown, Catherine bent over the open casket and kissed her employer's cheek good-bye. The gray-haired sisters, who each worked at the *Star* for fifty years, sadly watched as the pallbearers loaded Brown's remains into the limousine hearse.[11]

Brown's burial and wake demonstrated her respected status in Omaha. Her funeral processional was lengthy, with at least sixty-five cars following the hearse. Kathy Brown Battiste, Brown's niece, vividly remembered her aunt's last ride to Omaha's Forest Lawn Cemetery. The cavalcade of vehicles was a testimony to Mildred's place in Omaha. It was the first time Battiste witnessed a funeral procession with a police escort. The caravan slowly wound its way through the streets of northern Omaha into the now-desegregated cemetery grounds and stopped at Section 1, Woodlawn. Brown's unpretentious gravesite was within walking distance of adopted daughter Ruth Harris Kellogg's gravesite. Richard E. Dragoun, president of Omaha's Fraternal Order of Police, spoke at the burial. He commended Brown's lifelong commitment to the community, concluding, "With her known professional qualities, humor, caring and concerned attitudes, she will be sorely missed, by the black community as well as the city of Omaha. We sincerely hope she receives the rest she deserves." After the burial, Dr. Rodney Wead, a former *Star* newspaper carrier, held a wake for Brown in the historical Jewell Building. It seemed a fitting end to honor Brown at the site that once housed the Dreamland Ballroom.[12]

Five days after her aunt's death, Marguerita Washington took over the *Omaha Star* by filing a personal representative quitclaim deed at the Douglas County Courthouse on November 7, 1989. Brown had not considered Washington as her successor. She had forgiven Max for his indiscretion, but Brown did not forget or forgive Washington's betrayal. Brown's anger toward her niece was insurmountable. But Brown was gone, and within the month readers noticed a new sentence in the *Star* staff section. Underneath the words "Mildred D. Brown, Founder" appeared the phrase "Dr. Marguerita L. Washington, Acting Publisher." Washington made several other changes to the newspaper. She altered its name from the *Omaha Star* to the *Omaha Star, Inc.* and filed paperwork listing William Brown Jr., Brown's nephew, as president and herself as secretary and treasurer of *Omaha Star, Inc.* While she owned the *Star*, she did not edit or publish it. Washington, by profession a teacher, continued teaching her special education students at OPS's Central High School until 1998. Max Brownell served as the *Star*'s editor, and musician and journalist Preston Love Sr. acted as the newspaper's publisher until their deaths in 2000 and 2004, respectively. Since the beginning of this project in 2005, thousands of *Star* photographs, known as slicks, which could have provided an illustrated historical timeline of the Near North Side's progress, were destroyed. It was time, Washington said, to "throw out the old and bring in the new," but, thankfully, she kept some images for sentimental value.[13]

Early in 1990 Omaha's Douglas County Probate Court approved Marguerita Washington as the self-assigned personal representative of Mildred Brown's estate. Brown's niece had little sentimental attachment to the Breeding property and wished to sell Mildred's two hundred acres. On July 17 Washington telephoned Truman Clare, Brown's lawyer, and discussed the property's sale for division under Alabama's law statutes, but it was impossible to initiate a sale while Bennie Brown, the main property owner of the Breeding homestead, refused to sell.[14]

But that issue resolved itself on March 14, 1991, when Bennie D. Brown Sr. died in Chicago, Illinois. Like his siblings, Brown purposefully lied about his age. He claimed he was eighty, although he was eighty-two when he passed; even his son was unaware of his age until this project. Regardless of his actual age, Brown made sure there were no questions about the Breeding land. He left a will specifically spelling out his wishes for the property. David Winton, Bennie's sixth cousin, was not surprised. Winton recalled listening to Bennie as the elderly man fondly reminisced about picking blackberries with his mother, Maggie, on the Breeding acres. No one else in the family, including Mildred, visited the rural property more than once or twice prior to Bennie's death. The Breeding land was still a valuable piece of land, but it was more important to Bennie because of its sentimental value.[15] Bennie's last will and testament stressed this fact. He left a special message for his surviving family:

> I suggest to my wife and children that it is my desire that they do not sell the real estate, but keep the same for themselves and

their children, for the reason that I believe that *ownership of land is the most powerful force in American life* [my italics]. However, though it is my desire that they do not sell or otherwise dispose of the land, this shall not be construed as qualifying, modifying or restricting their right, title and interest in the land in any way or their legal right to sell or otherwise deal with or dispose of the land in any way they deem fit.[16]

While Bennie's family pondered the possible sale of the Breeding homestead, in 1992, after three years of family one-upmanship, the Douglas County Probate Court decided on the new owner of Mildred Brown's estate. It was a formality since Washington's lawyer and the court eliminated two of the three claimants. Lila Brown, the widow of Bennie D. Brown Sr., supposedly "had failed, neglected and refused to sign and return the estate Closing Receipt form for said stock certificate." On this technicality, the court eliminated Lila's one hundred shares of *Omaha Star, Inc.* stock valued at approximately twenty-five thousand dollars and negated her possible claim to Brown's estate. Financially destitute and physically exhausted from her struggle with cancer, Lila agreed to sell the Breeding homestead land. Then, in a situation similar to what Millard Breeding, Brown's grandfather, faced long ago with his brother Gus Breeding, the court eliminated Frederick Washington, Marguerita's brother, as non compos mentis, or not of sound mind. Frederick's fifty shares of *Omaha Star, Inc.* transferred to Marguerita. Because she already possessed an equal amount to his shares, Washington now owned two hundred shares of stock. The remaining claimant, William Andrew Brown, was allowed to keep his one hundred shares of stock.[17]

After the settlement of the estate, Max Brownell, known as a "day trader with horses," spent a majority of his after hours betting at the racetrack. Playing the ponies was a sport Brownell and Mildred Brown frequently enjoyed during their long common-law marriage. Near North Side resident Herman Pearson can still picture Brown purposefully striding into the Aksarben racetrack: "You could find her at the fifty dollar window." She would "dip into her purse, which was a disorganized tangle of money, gum and notes from a meeting, and bet on any horse with over 40 to 1 odds. She rarely won."[18]

In 1978 Mildred Brown delivered an important message to her readers on the bottom left-hand corner of the *Star*'s front page: "A voteless people is a hopeless people. People recognize only two things in politics and business: The BALLOT and the BUCKS. The Ballot and the Bucks are Weapons for First-Class Citizenship, Use and Spend Both Wisely." After years of activism, she realized that legislation was the best possible source of change. Her words remained on the *Star*'s front page for almost two decades after her death in 1989. As the respected owner of the *Omaha Star* and a seemingly tireless activist, leader, and organizer in the black community, Mildred Brown implored her fellow black residents to safeguard themselves from future city, state, and federal injustices by using their right to vote. The matriarch of the Near North Side wished to leave her loyal readers with a final piece of advice: "[I] cannot emphasize and state often enough how important it is for blacks to make use of their number. It is the most viable thing we have going for us."[19] She believed a legislative revolution, the same nonviolent solution preached by Dr. King, remained the key to future black equality in Omaha.

The *Star* became the most successful black newspaper in Nebraska's history and the longest-running black newspaper founded by a black woman in the history of the United States. Mildred Brown partially owed her two lifetime achievements to her strong-willed ancestors, especially William and Sopharina Breeding, her great-grandparents; and Millard Breeding, her courageous grandfather. Their actions taught her that she *can* fight and triumph against racism. Using this knowledge, she involved herself in northern Omaha's black community, and the residents, in turn, benefited from her matriarchy and supported her *Omaha Star*. Brown deconstructed the Sapphire stereotype, while her usage of the politics of respectability created an image of an intelligent, well-dressed, businesswoman with an aggressive selling style. She earned the respect of white and black residents and business owners in Omaha through her newspaper's participation in the nationwide Double V campaign during World War II, the De Porres Club campaigns against discriminatory employment practices in the late 1940s and 1950s, and the 4CL's successful battles against restrictive housing covenants, Peony Park's racist policy, and the Omaha public school segregated system.

Perhaps her proudest achievement was uplifting the black community's children. Mildred Brown subscribed to what historian Elsa Barkley Brown called the ethic of socially responsible individualism, especially concerning the youth of northern Omaha. Whatever the separate status of individuals like herself achieved in the community, Brown's real social value derived from her connections and contributions to the larger group. Her role as a successful businessperson allowed her to hire numerous newspaper carriers, but it was her example and motherly teachings that nurtured several generations of adult achievers. Former salesperson Royce Keller was the first person in his family to attend college. Brown made that happen for him by telephoning Creighton University and talking to its president. Today, Keller is a retired air force colonel. Former *Omaha Star* newspaper carrier Cathy Hughes credits Brown with giving her a transistor radio and teaching her the importance of compassion. Mildred Brown was "a friend of anybodies." If a homeless person approached the *Star* door needing a meal, she would holler, "We're right here" while bringing out a meal and digging in her purse for money. Then she would turn to Cathy and say, "There for the grace of God go us." Today, Hughes is the multimillionaire owner of Radio One, a radio conglomerate with sixty-nine radio stations in twenty-two U.S. cities. Brown's youth achievements include a long list of reverends, doctors, businesspeople, elementary school teachers, secondary school instructors, and college professors who each cherish and remember her taking the time to talk with them when they were children and giving them valuable advice as she gently pushed them forward to their own advancement. *Star* staffer, and now retired Creighton University associate dean, Charles Rucker applauded

Brown for the confidence she gave him and for what she achieved in Omaha. She was "an icon and a successful black businesswoman for challenging the mainstream newspaper and maintaining a respected presence during a time when it was almost impossible to be a black professional, regardless of gender."[20]

In her later years Brown struggled with maintaining leadership and adjusting her strategies to fit the more modern times. The masculine ideology of the black power movement, Omaha's three race riots, and the northern freeway that divided the black community into two under the guise of urban renewal left her with unresolved issues. At the end of her life, Brown, ever the achiever, was not completely satisfied. According to Joyce Young, her last secretary, "Brown probably died feeling that she did not reach her goal. She wanted our people to achieve more, be better educated, to work for higher wages. She wanted good for her people, and I don't think she saw it come to life in the magnitude she wanted it in."[21] While Brown worked tirelessly to demand equality and speak for the black community through the *Star*, in the twenty-first century, inequality, discrimination, and racism remain a dividing line between some of the city of Omaha's white populace and northern Omaha's black residents.

Mildred Brown and the *Omaha Star* made a difference in northern Omaha by creating a cohesive voice and a positive identity for the black community. Her affirmative newspaper agenda validated the black neighborhood's worth, while challenging stereotypes and in particular the *Omaha World-Herald*'s negative public imagery of the Near North Side's population. The *Omaha Star* provided news of social events and commentary that otherwise would not have appeared in any other Omaha publication. Brown's *Star* filled the media gap created by the mainstream *Omaha World-Herald*'s inconsistent coverage. In 1953 the *Omaha World-Herald* published zero photographs of black individuals and printed twenty-seven black news articles, five of which were positive toward the black community. However, in 1988 the city of Omaha's daily newspaper had increased its reporting of the Near North Side's daily activities to twenty-four images and ninety-one news items, although only twenty-eight of the stories were positive. If one considers that between 1953 and 1988, Omaha's black population increased by 63 percent while the city's white population grew by 17 percent, the *Omaha World-Herald*, which improved its minority reporting, still failed to provide even a partially equal amount of news consistent with the city's ethnic population growth.[22]

Black press expert Dr. Henry G. La Brie III once questioned Mildred Brown about the future of the black press in the Midwest and nationwide. She seriously thought about the black press and her *Star* for a moment and then slowly responded, "Well, it won't disappear in my time and you are much younger than I and it won't disappear in your time either. Unfortunately, I doubt it will happen in your grandchildren's time. There is a great need for the black press, for a long time to come." The need for black newspapers still remains today. As a twentieth-century pioneer in the black press, Brown championed the black community by providing weekly representation of northern Omaha's residents in her newspaper. Her *Star* editorially alternated between applauding and scolding Omaha and northern Omaha. She finally concluded that Omaha was "backward, but I don't think anybody planned it that way. There's hope here because there are so many wonderful people in Omaha. [It] has great potential for solving its problems and becoming one of the greatest cities in the country." Ultimately, her *Star* made the Near North Side not only matter to its residents but also visible to Omaha every week for fifty-two weeks, every year for fifty-one years. Brown never gave up on Omaha, her second hometown.[23]

On May 25, 2009, I visited with Mildred's cousin David Winton in Alabama, her home state. It was time to see the formerly owned Breeding property in the small rural northern town of Decatur. I had already met most of Mildred Brown's family, but I wanted to meet the ancestral nonliving members. After three hours of searching through the wooded land, Winton was unable to find the Breeding slave cemetery, but he located the Breeding family graveyard. Brambles, green moss, and thin white aspens surrounded what remained of the small cemetery. Hidden beneath northern Alabama's extensive foliage were the final resting places of Samuel Breeding, John Mason Breeding, William Breeding, and Sopharina Breeding. The latter two graves were basically unmarked, which made it difficult to ascertain their exact plots, but the important point was that they were buried together and not separated in the slave and family cemeteries. Their desegregated graves made me think of another burial plot, more than 850 miles away, in which another family member's grave resided in Forest Lawn Cemetery. Mildred Brown's small, flat tombstone covering the head of her plot stated only her name and the date she died. There were no sentences explaining her commitment to the black population of the Near North Side, no clever poem about Brown and the *Star*'s decades of being the black community's voice or a list of the civil rights she and residents successfully won over the years. The accolades were unnecessary. The achievements of the charismatic, stylish black female matriarchal leader who voluntarily and successfully occupied the transitional space between the white city of Omaha administration and the ghettoized area of northern Omaha live on through the community, the residents she deeply cared about, and her legacy, the weekly published *Omaha Star* newspaper.

Notes

INTRODUCTION

1. B. Brown, interview, August 6, 2008.
2. Woodward, *Strange Career*, 21; Pascoe, *What Comes Naturally*, 3; Dailey, *Age of Jim Crow*, 360–66. In 1967 the Supreme Court ruled that antimiscegenation laws violated the Fourteenth Amendment in the court case *Richard Perry Loving, Mildred Jeter Loving v. Virginia*, 388 U.S. 1 (1967). Marriage was ruled as a basic civil right fundamental to humankind's survival and existence. In Alabama alone, between 1883 and 1938, a total of 343 women and men were arrested on miscegenation charges. Even the late president Abraham Lincoln, the supposed champion of black rights, was "not in favor of black people intermarrying with white people." Myrdal, *American Dilemma*, 533; Dailey, *Age of Jim Crow*, xxix–xxx.
3. Woodward, *Strange Career*, 7; Du Bois, *Souls of Black Folk*, 134; Dailey, *Age of Jim Crow*, 68.
4. U.S. Department of Commerce, *Negroes*, p. 4, table 1; Massey and Denton, *American Apartheid*, 26; Grossman, *Land of Hope*, 35; Sitkoff, *New Deal for Blacks*, 35; Wright, *12 Million Black Voices*, 87, 36.
5. Berkin et al., *Making America*, 692–93; Grossman, *Land of Hope*, 14; Packard, *American Nightmare*, 109; Grossman, *Land of Hope*, 15; K. Boyle, *Arc of Justice*, 8; Gregory, "Second Great Migration," in Kusmer and Trotter, *African American Urban History*, 19–38.
6. Meyer, *Don't Move Next Door*, 116. Chicago's black belt community experienced fifty-eight bombings between 1917 and 1921, an average of one bombing every twenty days. Packard, *American Nightmare*, 107; K. Boyle, *Arc of Justice*, 98; Kornweibel, *Seeing Red*, 165–66. Federal Bureau of Investigation agents first assumed the rioting during the Red Summer was caused by IWW propagandists but after investigation realized it had nothing to do with the communist organization. Hoover did not believe his agents' reports and had them investigate black Americans involved in the riots anyway.
7. L. Bennett, *Before the Mayflower*, 396; *Omaha Daily Bee*, September

28, 1919; Menard, *Political Bossism*, 248. Menard contends that Brown was the victim of the Omaha politic machine. Larsen and Cottrell, *Gate City*, 169; FBI agent Edward Abbott, memo, August 19, 1943, Federal Bureau of Investigation, courtesy of David M. Hardy. According to the FBI memo, South Omaha Police Department captain Peter McGuire stated that the lynching of Brown "could of have been averted if prompt and effective measures had been taken [by] the police... [but] there was not an effective police organization in Omaha" during 1919. Agent Edward Abbott, *Omaha Daily Bee*, September 29, 1919.

8. J. Hirsch, *Riot and Remembrance*, 37, 53; Hale, *Making Whiteness*, 203.
9. Larsen and Cottrell, *Gate City*, 172; Department of the Army, "Survey of Race Situation: Nebraska and South Dakota," unpublished confidential file, U.S. Army Intelligence and Security Command, Freedom Information and Privacy Office; Meyer, *Don't Move Next Door*. See also Jones-Correa, "Racial Restrictive Covenants"; Goings and Mohl, *New African American*; and Mead, "Ecological Study."
10. Bloomfield, *Impertinences*, 65; Phillips, *AlabamaNorth*. See also Trotter, *Black Milwaukee*; and Cohen, *Making a New Deal*, 65, 58.
11. Biondi, *To Stand and Fight*, 113; K. Boyle, *Arc of Justice*, 21; Meyer, *Don't Move Next Door*, 40; Woodward, *Strange Career*, 100; Biondi, *To Stand and Fight*, 114; Meyer, *Don't Move Next Door*, 7.
12. Biondi, *To Stand and Fight*, 39. Black nationalist Ira Kemp was a street corner orator who created these successful consumer boycotts in New York City. *Omaha Star*, April 2, 1948; Myrdal, *American Dilemma*, 815; Cohen, *Consumer's Republic*, 48. Each Colored Merchant's Association city had a chain of at least ten stores. A. Battiste, interview, September 25, 2008. Andrew Cato Brown owned a grocery store for forty years at the corner of Jefferson Davis and South Holt Streets in Montgomery, Alabama. When he passed away in 1948, he was so wealthy he left a home for each of his three remaining brothers. Benjamin Brown, Mildred Brown's father, had already died in 1927.
13. Washburn, *African American Newspaper*, 143–44; Roberts and Klibanoff, *Race Beat*, 22; Simmons, *African American Press*, 69–80; B. Brown, interview, September 19, 2008; James G. Thompson, "Should I Sacrifice to Live Half American," *Pittsburgh Courier*, January 31, 1942.
14. Borstelmann, *Cold War*, 56; Simmons, *African American Press*, 83–84. The War Production Board reduced or denied newsprint supplies in a possible illegal attempt to curtail the black newspapers from printing editions. Director John Edgar Hoover, "Informant Coverage of Racial Conditions Internal Security," FBI memo, February 26, 1944, Federal Bureau of Investigation, courtesy of David M. Hardy; D. Lewis, *Du Bois*, 555–57; Simmons, *African American Press*, 89.

15. Cohen, *Consumer's Republic*, 59; Washburn, *African American Newspaper*, 167; Kornweibel, *Seeing Red*, 52; Biondi, *To Stand and Fight*, 6–7.
16. McGreevy, *Parish Boundaries*, 11; Boys Town Hall of History Archives. No school records of Brown's youths exist in the Boys Town archives. Angus, *Black and Catholic*, 6. Saint Benedict's high school's first class graduated in 1937. McGreevy, *Parish Boundaries*, 83; Kelley, *Hammer and Hoe*, 228, 109.
17. D'Angelo, *American Civil Rights Movement*, 222; Branch, *Parting the Waters*, 196; A. Hirsch, *Making the Second Ghetto*, 176; Robnett, *How Long?*, 71.
18. Borstelmann, *Cold War*, 190.
19. Carson, *In Struggle*, 215; Robnett, *How Long?*, 183; Sugrue, *Sweet Land of Liberty*, 379; Joseph, *Midnight Hour*, 176–209; Mumford, "Harvesting the Crisis," in Kusmer and Trotter, *African American Urban History*, 212; Olson, *Equality Deferred*, 58; Robnett, *How Long?*, 229.
20. Branch, *Parting the Waters*, 875; Woodward, *Strange Career*, 190; Cohen, *Consumer's Republic*, 373.
21. Polikoff, *Waiting for Gautreaux*, 61.
22. Mumford, "Harvesting the Crisis," in Kusmer and Trotter, *African American Urban History*, 212; Lyndon Baines Johnson Library, courtesy of Eric R. Cuellar.
23. Polikoff, *Waiting for Gautreaux*, 63; Cohen, *Consumer's Republic*, 170; A. Hirsch, *Making the Second Ghetto*, 10. See also Stalvey, *Education of a WASP*, which supplies an eyewitness account of housing racism in Omaha. Meyer, *Don't Move Next Door*, 8; Daub, interview; Sugrue, *Urban Crisis*, 45.
24. Kusmer and Trotter, *African American Urban History*, 8; Borstelmann, *Cold War*, 103; Benjamin Fine, "Troops on Guard at School," *New York Times*, September 25, 1957, 1; Sitkoff, *Struggle for Black Equality*, 31; A. Lewis, *Portrait of a Decade*, 51; Pach and Richardson, *Presidency*, 152–53; Wilkins, *Standing Fast*, 253–54; Borstelmann, *Cold War*, 93; Sugrue, *Sweet Land of Liberty*, 487; Harrington, *Other America*, 79.
25. Kusmer and Trotter, *African American Urban History*, 8; A. Hirsch, *Making the Second Ghetto*, 271; Kusmer and Trotter, *African American Urban History*, 9; Dewart, *State of Black America*, 185.
26. See Howard, "Then the Burning Began"; Larsen and Cottrell, *Gate City*.
27. Mildred Brown's personal motto has endorsed her *Omaha Star*'s promise to Omaha's Near North Side from 1938 to the present.
28. Martindale, *White Press*, 54.

1. A FAMILY OF FIGHTERS

1. William Breeding, file 307, Morgan County Archives; *Millard William*

Breeding v. James Breeding, 128 Ala. (Probate 1899), file 308, Morgan Country Archives.
2. Pascoe, *What Comes Naturally*, 2.
3. Pascoe, *What Comes Naturally*, 12, 11.
4. Breeding family genealogy, CSA Civil War rolls, M374, roll 5, courtesy of Andre Battiste; Winton, interview, May 25, 2009; Samuel Breeding, estate, file 305, Loose Documents, Probate Court Records, Morgan County Archives, courtesy of John Allison.
5. Marriage record, November 26, 1865, col. A1, Morgan County, 1865–71, Morgan County Archives; Winton, interview, January 22, 2009. Each year the Breeding family continues a traditional interracial family reunion. Pascoe, *What Comes Naturally*, 21, 135; Sandweiss, *Passing Strange*, 155.
6. A. Davis, "Don't Let Nobody," in Harley and the Collective, *Sister Circle*, 113. *Partus sequitur ventrem* refers to the legal status of children according to the legal status of their mother during the three centuries of American slavery. *Heritage of Morgan County*, 148; Morgan County Archives, courtesy of John Allison; Winton, interview, May 25, 2009; J. Jones, *Labor of Love*, 35; Gaspar and Hine, *More Than Chattel*; Cody, "Cycles of Work," 61–78.
7. *Breeding*, 128 Ala.; Robinson, *Dangerous Liaisons*, 61; Webb, *Two-Party Politics*, 2; Winton, interview, May 28, 2009; Webb, *Two-Party Politics*, 19, 9; William Breeding Estate Trial, Morgan County Archives.
8. U.S. Census, 1880, roll T9-27, p. 49, Church of Jesus Christ. Sophy was incorrectly listed as "Gopha" on the 1880 census. The children's "race" described them as "Mulatto." Breeding family genealogy, CSA Civil War rolls, M374, roll 5, courtesy of Andre Battiste.
9. Wormser, *Rise and Fall*, 27; Dewart, *State of Black America*, 141. The Colored Methodist Episcopalian Church originated in 1870 and changed its name to the Christian Methodist Episcopalian Church in 1954. Breeding family genealogy, CSA Civil War rolls, M374, roll 5, courtesy of Andre Battiste.
10. William Breeding, last will and testament, Morgan County Archives; Pascoe, *What Comes Naturally*, 11; Breeding, last will and testament, Morgan County Archives; *Breeding*, 128 Ala. Additional information supplied in an unpublished written account by David Winton.
11. In 1837 slave brick masons created Somerville's courthouse. David Winton gave the author a brick from this building. Wilson P. Breeding, 1907, file 300, Morgan County Archives, courtesy of John Allison.
12. Sixth Ground of Contest Amendment, October 9, 1899, *Breeding*, 128 Ala.; Amended ground of contest statement, filed by attorneys Samuel Blackwell and L. P. Troup, October 10, 1899, Morgan Country Historical Society; *Breeding*, 128 Ala.

13. John M. Breeding, Special Letter of Administration petition, August 2, 1899, Morgan County Archives; *Breeding*, 128 Ala.
14. *Breeding*, 128 Ala. Breeding, an ex-soldier in the Confederacy, possessed Confederate monies with a face value of more than two thousand dollars but only a street value of fifty cents. It was worth little but sentimental value. Probably more typical of the times, he possessed almost the same amount of Mexican currency and U.S. money. Trading with Mexico via the Gulf of Mexico constituted a lucrative trade market.
15. *Breeding*, 128 Ala.; *Heritage of Morgan County*, 75.
16. *Breeding*, 128 Ala.
17. *Montgomery Advertiser*, October 17, 1900; Kyle, interview. Kyle, the great-grandson of Oceola Kyle, described his relative as "a solid Democrat, Mason and a bit of a swashbuckler." *Montgomery Advertiser*, October 17, 1900, clipping file, courtesy of David Winton; *New Decatur Advertiser*, November 14, 1902, clipping file, Morgan County Archives, courtesy of John Allison.
18. Attorney J. Timothy Kyle and Morgan County archivist John Allison know of no other cases with a similar outcome in Morgan County. Pascoe, *What Comes Naturally*, 44. See also Gaspar and Hine, *More Than Chattel*; Robinson, *Dangerous Liaisons*, 61; Woodward, *Strange Career*, 43. George Henry White, North Carolina congressman, served from 1896 to 1901. He was the last black southern congressman until 1973.
19. Phillips, *AlabamaNorth*, 20; Webb, *Two-Party Politics*, 33, 9, 169; Hine and Thompson, *Shining Thread of Hope*, 193; D. Carter, *Scottsboro*, 197; Alabama, Revised Statutes (1931), no. 47, sec. 14. Sitkoff's *New Deal for Blacks* explains that no one living in Morgan County during this time could recall a black man serving on a jury. Woodward, *Strange Career*, 85.
20. Petition for letters of guardianship, return of jury and decree, April 14, 1903, Thomas Abstract Company, courtesy of Rick Pettey; Millard W. Breeding and Mary E. Jackson, marriage license, December 25, 1899, book D, 85, Morgan County Archives; Annie O. Breeding Windham, certificate of death, State of Alabama, *Index of Vital Records*, courtesy of Bennie Brown Jr.; U.S. Census, 1900, 1910, Church of Jesus Christ. Tommie Jackson did not appear as a member of the Breeding household in the 1900 census, but she was counted as part of the Breeding household in the 1910 census. *Omaha Star*, August 25, 1977. Annie Breeding Owens Windham passed in August 1977. Brown's "A Tribute to My Aunt" was one of the few instances in which she gave herself a staff writer's byline. Shelton, interview, January 25, 2009.
21. William Taylor (W.T.) Breeding, interview, May 25, 2009; Millard W. Breeding, estate, Loose Documents, Probate Court Records, Morgan County Archives, courtesy of John Allison.

22. William Taylor (W.T.) Breeding, interview, May 25, 2009; Millard W. Breeding, estate, December 3, 1907, Loose Documents, Probate Court Records, Morgan County Archives; warranty deed, October 14, 1968, book 810, 40, Thomas Abstract Company, courtesy of Rick Pettey. Tommie Gibson, Millard Breeding's stepdaughter from his second marriage, sold her deceased mother's larger portion of property to her uncle, Bennie Brown Sr., for two thousand dollars. U.S. Census, 1900, Church of Jesus Christ; Breeding family genealogy, CSA Civil War rolls, M374, roll 5, courtesy of Andre Battiste.
23. Benjamin J. and Maggie Breeding Brown, marriage license, November 25, 1901, document 303, Morgan County Archives; Shelton, interview, January 25, 2009; State of Alabama, *Index of Vital Records*. Mary Elizabeth Breeding died on June 8, 1947. Breeding family genealogy, CSA Civil War rolls, M374, roll 5, courtesy of Andre Battiste.
24. U.S. Department of Commerce, *Thirteenth Census*; U.S. Department of Commerce, *Fourteenth Census*. Millie Dee Brown's birth year was 1905, but since the state of Alabama does not possess birth certificates for anyone born prior to 1908, it is impossible to attain legal documentation to validate her year of birth. Brown's few remaining elderly relatives were unsure of her birth. The *Omaha Star* and the *Omaha World-Herald*, and her personal physician, Dr. Laurence Zacharia, recorded her birth year as 1915 or 1916, respectively.
25. Barbara Shores-Martin, interview, September 27, 2008. Mildred Brown's grandfather and Benjamin Brown were traveling ministers. The CME Church still moves ministers every two to three years. Shelton, interview, January 25, 2009.
26. *Omaha Star*, April 2, 1948. When Andrew Cato Brown passed in 1948, thousands paid their respects. Shelton, interview, January 25, 2009; Crittendon, interview.
27. Shelton, interview, January 25, 2009. Shelton's parents were Tommie Jackson and William Ira Draper. Millie's sister, Annie, called her a "country cousin" because they were not blood related. Superintendent's record of teachers, Bessemer City Schools. Brown incorrectly listed her birth date as December 20, 1907.
28. Catalog, Miles Memorial College Archives, courtesy of Shirley Epps. Miles Memorial High School and College was created by combining two high schools and then adding teaching certification for college-bound students. Shaw, *Woman Ought to Be*, 136; Department of Education, Division of Teacher Training, extension certificate, 1927, Jefferson County Board, courtesy of Anita Parkin. Brown attended Miles Memorial High School and College from 1921 to 1924 and earned a Class A Pre-Normal Alabama State Teaching Certificate.

29. State of Alabama, *Index of Vital Records*; Newbill, interview. The reference librarian at Birmingham Public Library verified the Birmingham city directory listing Maggie Brown as an African American woman employed as a matron in 1927 at Carrie Tuggle Elementary School in Birmingham. Fowalkes, interview. Fowalkes was a secretary at Tuggle from 1947 to 2009. Activist Angela Davis attended Tuggle school in the 1950s.
30. Shelton, interview, July 8, 2011; *Tennessee State Marriages*, 1780–2002, doc. 217, Giles County Court, courtesy of Carol; E. Boyle, "Feminization of Teaching." Howard University Registrar's Office employees Loretta Ransome and LaJuan Estes verified Dr. Gilbert attending Howard from 1924 to 1928. His admission papers noted his hometown as Nashville, Tennessee.
31. State of Alabama, *Index of Vital Records*. Maggie Breeding Brown's death was noted only as May 1929. Winton, interview, May 25, 2009; Wilson M. Breeding, 1907, file 300, Morgan County Archives. Millard Breeding started selling the timber in the early 1900s. Annie Mae Breeding Rovoal Owens Windham affidavit, September 21, 1970, book 847, 865–67, Thomas Abstract Company, courtesy of Rick Pettey.
32. Shaw, *Woman Ought to Be*, 17; D. Lewis, *Du Bois*, 536; J. Jones, *Labor of Love*, 156; Millie D. Brown, teacher application, Bessemer Public Schools, April 18, 1928, Jefferson County Board, courtesy of Birma Wilson and Anita Parkin; Trotter, *Black Milwaukee*, 32. The Knights of Pythias was a black fraternal organization created in 1892. Polk, *Polk's Chicago Summer*, 282; *Omaha Star*, May 6, 1976. Chicago Normal School (currently Chicago State University) was unable to verify school records for Mildred D. Brown Gilbert.
33. Azalia Mitchell Papers, 1898–1986, Iowa Women's Archives; *Omaha Star*, July 17, 1942; Document 100-3018, March 6, 1943, Federal Bureau of Investigation, courtesy of David M. Hardy. Mitchell served as an FBI informant during the 1940s. Polk, *Polk's Des Moines*, 420, 383. According to Lynda Walker-Webster, Saint Paul AME Church historian, the Gilberts' home is now a vacant lot created during 1960s urban renewal. Drake University's Alumni archivist Margie Davidson was unable to supply confirmation of Gilbert's matriculation. *Iowa Bystander*, May 22, 1931, June 5, 1931.
34. *Polk's Sioux City, 1934*, 151. Dr. Gilbert's pharmacy operated at 722 West Seventh Street. U.S. Department of Commerce, *Fifteenth Census*, 782; Banks, interview, November 25, 2008; *Polk's Sioux City, 1936*, 162.
35. Walker-Webster, interview. Walker-Webster explained that while the Saint Paul AME and Malone AME Churches were in different parts of Iowa, congregants relocated from Des Moines to Sioux City and vice versa. Banks, interview, November 25, 2008.
36. Sanford Community Center pamphlet, Sioux City IA, courtesy of George

Boykin. The Booker T. Washington Club became a subsidiary of the United Way in 1951 and was renamed the Sanford Community Center. Today it continues as a neighborhood settlement house targeting lower-economic minority youth between the ages of five and seventeen.

37. Civic program pamphlet, June 1, 1984, Omaha, courtesy of Matt Holland; Rev. David H. Harris, funeral program, courtesy of Kenneth Kellogg; M. Kellogg Jr., interview, April 22, 2009. Pastor Harris sent the Gilberts a monthly check to cover Ruth's expenses.

38. *Omaha Star*, October 27, 1988; Mildred Brown, interview by Henry La Brie III, August 27, 1971, digitized CD, Columbia University Archives; *Omaha Star*, October 27, 1988; Banks, interview, November 25, 2008. According to the Iowa State Historical Society, no known copies of the *Silent Messenger* remain. J. Anderson, *Philip Randolph*, 97; Smithson, "Omaha Star," 14; Banks, interview, November 25, 2008.

39. *Polk's Sioux City, 1937*, 115; *Omaha World-Herald*, September 7, 1968, clipping file, Douglas County Historical Society; *Omaha Star*, October 27, 1988; Workers, *Negroes of Nebraska*, 15; Tennessee Valley Authority deed, September 21, 1936, Thomas Abstract Company, courtesy of Rick Pettey. By 1914 each of Millard Breeding's surviving children either willed or sold their land to Maggie Breeding Brown and Annie Breeding Owens. On December 28, 1922, Annie Breeding Owens sold half of her portion to Maggie Breeding Brown for $250. On September 21, 1936, the Tennessee Valley Authority bought 13.2 acres of the Breeding property for $290. Eleven relatives, including Dr. Shirley Edward and Mildred Brown Gilbert, split the purchase payment.

2. INVOLVING THE COMMUNITY

1. Polk, *Polk's Omaha, 1940*, 277; *Omaha Star*, July 9, 1938. The *Omaha Guide* acknowledged the founding of the *Star* in an article dated July 23, 1938. *Omaha Guide*, July 30, 1938.
2. *Omaha Star*, July 9, 1938.
3. Polk, *Polk's Omaha, 1938*, 282; Brooks, "Great Migration," 9; U.S. Department of Commerce, *Fifteenth Census*, 65. Omaha's first black residents in 1880 migrated mainly from Oklahoma, Texas, Alabama, Mississippi, and Arkansas. *C.I.T. Corporation v. Mildred Gilbert*, doc. 349, no. 313, District Court, Douglas County NE.
4. Mead, "Ecological Study," 77; Wilkerson, "Urban League," 18; Trotter, *Black Milwaukee*, 31.
5. Ruth Lee Harris, transcripts, Central High School. Permission from Marvin Kellogg Jr., Harris's grandson, enabled the author to attain her file. Her school admittance date was February 8, 1937.

6. Stephenson, interview. Stephenson was the only black student to graduate from Omaha University in 1943. She became one of the first black teachers hired at Central High School in the 1960s. Dennis, interview. Dennis referred to serving as Central's quarterback as a "Jackie Robinson"; it was a "first" similar to Jackie Robinson being the first player breaking baseball's color line.
7. Ruth Lee Harris, transcripts, Central High School, courtesy of Marvin Kellogg Jr.; M. Kellogg Sr., interview, November 11, 2008. Saint Benedict the Moor remains Omaha's only black Catholic church.
8. Unpublished pamphlet, May 18, 1893, Jewish Press Archives; Mildred Brown, interview by Henry La Brie III, August 27, 1971, digitized CD, Columbia University Archives; Peterson, *Patterns on the Landscape*, 3.
9. Paz, "Black Press," in Suggs, *Black Press*, 225; Suggs, *Black Press*; Menard, *Political Bossism*, 255. Tom Dennison wanted to replace Edward Smith, Omaha's 1918 elected mayor, with his favorite politician, Jim Dahlman. The racial incident in 1919 made it appear that Smith was incompetent as a city official. Shaw, *Woman Ought to Be*, 19; city council minutes, August 19, 1980, doc. 3067, file 11591, Omaha City Council Archives.
10. Rhodes, interview, March 31, 2009; H. Smith, "Good," 9, courtesy of Warren Taylor; Cohen, *Making a New Deal*, 155; Workers, *Negroes of Nebraska*, 43. Cecilia Wilson Jewell entertained European audiences as a Fisk Jubilee Singer. Artison, interview. The Dreamland closed down in the late 1960s. H. Smith, "Good," 13.
11. Loewen, *Sundown Towns*, 129; J. Smith, *From Corps to Core*, 101, courtesy of Great Plains Black History Museum Archives, Nebraska State Historical Society; Meyer, *Don't Move Next Door*, 54; Loewen, *Sundown Towns*, 43. Roosevelt used the act to create seven new cities that explicitly excluded African Americans: Greenbelt, Maryland; Greenhills, Ohio; Greendale, Wisconsin; Norris, Tennessee; Richland, Washington; Park Forest, Illinois; and Boulder Dam, Nevada. Biondi, *To Stand and Fight*, 113; Stephen E. Szmrecsanyi, "The OHA Story: The Omaha Housing Authority, 1933–1995," unpublished manuscript, 10, Urban League of Nebraska Archives, courtesy of Stanley Timm; Heacock, "Social Significance," 43.
12. *Omaha Star*, July 9, 1938; Sitkoff, *New Deal for Blacks*, 67; Szmrecsanyi, "OHA Story," 29, 11. The Logan Fontenelle project and the Logan Fontenelle extension created 556 housing units. The city of Omaha constructed the Hilltop and Spencer Homes in 1951 and the Pleasantview project in 1953.
13. "Omaha Housing Authority: Scattered Site Housing Program Evaluation," pamphlet, 1997, University of Nebraska Archives. The city of Omaha created the Omaha Housing Authority in 1935. See also Momeni, *Minority Housing*, 1–6; Artison, interview; Larsen and Cottrell, *Gate City*, 216; A. Hirsch, *Mak-*

ing the Second Ghetto, 15; Hartman, *Near North Side Study*, 2. The Wagner Housing Act of 1937 attempted to maintain conditions in segregated housing by specifying that for every destroyed dilapidated unit of public housing one new unit must be built. Biondi, *To Stand and Fight*, 113.

14. U.S. Department of Commerce, *Sixteenth Census*, 2:636; Lemke-Santangelo, *Abiding Courage*, 16; Kerns, "Industrial and Business Life," 22; Workers, *Negroes of Nebraska*, 10; Larsen and Cottrell, *Gate City*, 222; Clark-Lewis, *Living In, Living Out*, 104; Brooks, "Great Migration," 9; Workers, *Negroes of Nebraska*, 24; Kerns, "Industrial and Business Life," 24.

15. Galloway, interview, December 19, 2008. As C.C. Galloway's secretary, Julia Sanford later married Boyd Galloway, C.C. Galloway's nephew. Suggs, *Black Press*, 230–31. According to Polk, *Polk's Omaha, 1938*, Mildred's occupation in the directory was listed as advertising manager of the *Omaha Guide*, while Shirley Edward's profession was listed as pharmacist. *Omaha Guide*, February 6, 1938, March 6, 1937.

16. Galloway, interview, December 19, 2008; Smithson, "*Omaha Star*," 51; Larsen et al., *Upstream Metropolis*, 276.

17. *Omaha Star*, July 10, 1953. Brown wrote an editorial reminiscing about the newspaper's founding on its fifteenth anniversary. *Omaha Star*, July 9, 1938, August 13, 1938.

18. M. Parks, interview, July 31, 2008; Polk, *Polk's Omaha*, 277; Hughes, interview, December 3, 2008; M. Parks, interview, July 31, 2008; M. Parks, interview, February 6, 2009; M. Parks, interview, July 31, 2008; Rodgers, interview; M. Parks, interview, July 31, 2008.

19. The *Star* originally opened at 2022 North Twenty-Fourth Street, but within three months it moved to its present location at 2216 North Twenty-Fourth Street. *Omaha Star*, July 16, 1938.

20. National Register of Historic Places registration form, sec. 8, p. 2, National Park Service, U.S. Department of the Interior, Nebraska State Historical Society, courtesy of Jill Dolberg; Adams, interview; M. Parks, interview, July 31, 2008; Rucker, interview; Washburn, *African American Newspaper*, 51; Rigby, interview; *Omaha Star*, August 13, 1938.

21. Warranty deed, book 807, 560, Register of Deeds Office, Douglas County Courthouse. Before the Gilberts rented the building in 1938, its 1922 brick one-story structure was the site of Alice and Allen Jones's funeral home. Suggs, *Black Press*, 232; *Omaha World-Herald*, September 7, 1968; *Omaha Star*, July 30, 1938.

22. *Omaha Star*, July 16, 1938.

23. *Omaha Star*, July 30, 1938. See also Larsen et al., *Upstream Metropolis*, 284.

24. Taylor, interview, September 23, 2008; M. Parks, interview, July 31, 2008; Lincoln, interview, April 19, 2009.

25. *Omaha Star*, July 16, 1938.
26. *Omaha Star*, August 27, 1938, August 2, 1940; Kornbluh, "Black Buying Power," in Theoharis and Woodward, *Freedom North*, 201; Biondi, *To Stand and Fight*, 39; Greenberg, *Or Does It Explode?*, 122; Kirby, *Black Americans*, 103; Cohen, *Consumer's Republic*, 44; Biondi, *To Stand and Fight*, 39; *Omaha Star*, September 3, 1938; Cohen, *Consumer's Republic*, 46.
27. *Omaha Star*, July 9, 1938, August 6, 1938; Smithson, "*Omaha Star*," 1; Washburn, *African American Newspaper*, 132; *Omaha Star*, August 14, 1942.
28. Cohen, *Consumer's Republic*, 47.

3. POLITICS OF RESPECTABILITY

1. *Omaha Star*, January 3, 1947, September 15, 1947; Wolcott, *Remaking Respectability*, 4–10; Higginbotham, *Righteous Discontent*.
2. Higginbotham, *Righteous Discontent*, 221, 187.
3. Giddings, *When and Where*, 81; Lynn, *Progressive Women*, 12.
4. M. Kellogg Sr., interview, November 25, 2008; M. Kellogg Jr., interview, April 22, 2009. Ruth and Marvin Kellogg had three sons: Kenneth, Marvin Jr., and Dale.
5. *Omaha Star*, April 2, 1943; La Brie, *Perspectives*, 29; J. Jones, *Labor of Love*, 253. See also Hine's *Hine Sight*'s chapter on World War II black navy nurses, 183–200; *Omaha Star*, April 16, 1943, July 9, 1943.
6. *Millie D. Brown Gilbert v. Shirley Edward Gilbert*, Divorce Decree Docket 373, no. 104, Journal 422, 201, August 20, 1943, District Court, Douglas County NE; Giddings, *When and Where*, 150; *Gilbert v. Gilbert*; Gilbert, interview, October 19, 2008; R. Davis, interview. Shirley Edward Gilbert disliked his first name and had it legally changed to Shirl.
7. Warranty deed, books 807, 470, pp. 560, 470, Register of Deeds Office, Douglas County Courthouse; *Omaha Star*, October 1, 1943, July 27, 1945.
8. A. Battiste, interview, October 5, 2008; A. Battiste, unpublished Brown family history. Julius Rosenwald, the founder of Sears and Roebuck and the Rosenwald Fund, gave Bennie Brown scholarship money to attend Drake University. B. Brown, interview, October 30, 2008. Most likely Noel Maximilian Brownell's name was an alias. B. Brown, interview, September 8, 2008. Brown's family deduced she followed her three siblings' tradition of lying about their age to make her accomplishments seem much larger. Hughes, interview, December 3, 2008; Bertha Calloway diary entry, February 9, 1947, courtesy of Bertha Calloway and her daughter, Beverly Shaw.
9. White, *Ar'n't I a Woman?*; Wexler, *Tender Violence*, 82; hooks, *Ain't I a Woman*, 71, 46–61; Morton, *Disfigured Images*, 6; hooks, *Ain't I a Woman*, 71; Mullings, "Images," in Zinn and Dill, *Women of Color*, 275.

10. Collins, "Meaning of Motherhood," in Staples, *Black Family*, 162; Collins, *Black Feminist Thought*, 178.
11. Adams, interview; Parr, interview, March 27, 2009; Reynolds, interview; Wead, interview; R. Smith, interview, August 27, 2005.
12. Hughes, interview, December 3, 2008; Bunting, interview.
13. Adams, interview; R. Smith, interview, August 27, 2005; Partridge, interview; Evans, *Born for Liberty*, 208; White, *Too Heavy a Load*, 186, 165.
14. See also Staples, *Black Family*; Washington, interview, May 24, 2009; *Omaha Star*, September 12, 1947; Collins, *Black Feminist Thought*, 192.
15. *Omaha Star*, July 9, 1938; Wolcott, *Remaking Respectability*, 4, 25; *Black Press*; Wolcott, *Remaking Respectability*, 241; *Omaha Star*, July 9, 1938, July 19, 1940; McSwain, interview.
16. Wolcott, *Remaking Respectability*, 5; Higginbotham, *Righteous Discontent*, 195; National Baptist Convention's fifteenth annual report of the executive board and corresponding secretary of the Women's Convention, 1915, in Higginbotham, *Righteous Discontent*, 195; Wolcott, *Remaking Respectability*, 8, 15.
17. Wolcott, *Remaking Respectability*, 3, 4.
18. Stephenson, interview; Wright, interview; Daniels, interview.
19. Galloway, interview, December 19, 2008. Galloway stated that prior to the founding of the *Omaha Star*, Gilbert did not wear a corsage. R. Smith, interview, August 27, 2005; K. Battiste, interview, October 22, 2008.
20. Bethune, "Century of Progress," 581; Walker, "Black Is Profitable," in Scranton, *Beauty and Business*, 254; Walker, *Style and Status*, 28, 256. Claude Barnett, founder of the Associated Negro Press, and William Ziff Sr., cofounder of Ziff Davis publishing, encouraged Walker's company to buy national ads to overshadow white competitors' ads. Burkhalter, interview; Peiss, *Hope in a Jar*, 237; Annie Lee Washington to Mildred Brown, December 24, 1969, courtesy of Bennie Brown Jr.
21. Walker, "Black Is Profitable," in Scranton, *Beauty and Business*, 262; Rice, "World of Illinois Panthers," in Theoharis and Woodward, *Freedom North*, 53; Walker, *Style and Status*, 191; Burkhalter, interview.
22. Hunter, *Politics of Skin Tone*, 6–9; Myrdal, *American Dilemma*, 105, 126. Myrdal, whose life spanned between 1898 and 1987, believed that there were separate white and Negro genes.
23. Peiss, *Hope in a Jar*, 208; Burroughs, "Not Color But Character," 277.
24. B. Brown, interview, September 19, 2008; Higginbotham and Weber, "Moving Up," in Chow, Wilkinson, and Zinn, *Race, Class, and Gender*, 144; Robinson, *Dangerous Liaisons*, 114–28.
25. Frazier, *Negro Family*, 420–87; White, *Too Heavy a Load*, 79; Hale, *Making Whiteness*, 22; White, *Too Heavy a Load*, 293.

26. Phillips, interview, October 12, 2008. While the author was visiting with Brown's family in Decatur and Bessemer, Alabama, she learned that Estée Lauder perfumes were a favorite of southern women. Ottley, *Lonely Warrior*, 220; W. Brown, interview; K. Battiste, interview, October 22, 2008; Hannah, interview. Hannah was the only one of William Brown's four wives to have a child. Higginbotham, *Righteous Discontent*, 190; Guy-Sheftall, *Daughters of Sorrow*, 40–43; Koehn, "Estee Lauder," in Scranton, *Beauty and Business*, 217–51.
27. Griffin, "Black Feminists," 34; Tyson, *Radio Free Dixie*, 1; Lee, "Anger," in Collier-Thomas and Franklin, *Sisters in the Struggle*, 151, 152.
28. Morris, "Local Women," in Theoharis and Woodward, *Groundwork*, 210; Gilkes, "If It Wasn't," in Zinn and Dill, *Women of Color*, 242.
29. Height, *Freedom Gates*, 295; Shaw, *Woman Ought to Be*, 202–4; Frazier, *Negro Family*, 443.
30. Mildred Brown Gilbert, permanent record transcripts, Municipal University of Omaha, Office of Registration, University of Nebraska at Omaha, courtesy of Matt Tilford. Brown's previous transcripts were from Chicago's Crane Junior College and Des Moines's Drake University.
31. N. Carter, interview. Municipal University of Omaha became the University of Nebraska at Omaha in 1968. N. Carter, interview.
32. Moynihan, "Study of Black Families," in Staples, *Black Family*, 8; Mullings, "Images," in Zinn and Dill, *Women of Color*, 273; Matthew, "No One Ever Asks," in Collier-Thomas and Franklin, *Sisters in the Struggle*, 240; Chalmers, *Crooked Places*, 162; White, *Too Heavy a Load*, 198; Wallace, *Black Macho*, 31; Mullings, "Images," in Zinn and Dill, *Women of Color*, 273; Rainwater and Yancey, *Moynihan Report*, 76. See also Moynihan, *Negro Family*, 30; White, *Too Heavy a Load*, 200; Carson, *In Struggle*, 148; Annie Lee Washington to Mildred Brown, July 8, 1969, courtesy of Bennie Brown Jr.
33. Ferguson, "Women's Liberation," in Lerner, *Black Women*, 590; hooks, *Ain't I a Woman*, 70.
34. K. Kellogg, interview, August 19, 2009; *Omaha Star*, April 30, 1948. The Carnation Ballroom opened on May 1, 1948. *Omaha Star*, April 29, 1949.

4. WORKING WITHIN HER SPACE

1. *Omaha Star*, November 9, 1989, 1; Rodgers, interview; Chambers, Steiner, and Fleming, *Women and Journalism*, 23; Washburn, *African American Newspaper*, 28–29. William Lloyd Garrison founded the *Liberator* in 1831. Stewart, "Throw Off Your Fearfulness," in Lerner, *Black Women*, 526. Stewart's lecture at the African Masonic Hall in Boston on February 27, 1833, was part of *Meditations*, 58–59. Lerner, *Black Women*, 323; Streitmatter, *Raising Her Voice*, 5. Ida

Baker Wells briefly became the nation's second minority editor when she co-published the *Memphis Free Speech* weekly; her short-lived Baptist newspaper circulated from 1889 to 1892.
2. E. Hicks, interview, August 12, 2007. Hicks cherishes Brown's business card. He subscribes to the *Star* as his way of thanking Brown. Roberts and Klibanoff, *Race Beat*, 13.
3. La Brie, *Perspectives*, 198; Hine and Thompson, *Shining Thread of Hope*, 226–27; Kathleen Cairns, e-mail message to author, October 29, 2007, March 14, 2010; Cairns, *Front-Page Women Journalists*, 78; Streitmatter, *Raising Her Voice*, 150; Gill, "1952 Vice Presidential Campaign," in Harley and Terborg-Penn, *Afro-American Woman*, 110; Washburn, *African American Newspaper*, 188. Bass was not a member of the Communist Party, but her support of communist ideals led to her forced sale of the *California Eagle*. The newspaper ran for eighty-six years. It was the previous longest-running black newspaper in the United States.
4. Preston Love, interview; Baker, interview; Simmons, *African American Press*, 5.
5. Washburn, *African American Newspaper*, 49; Workers, *Negroes of Nebraska*, 44.
6. Larsen and Cottrell, *Gate City*, 101. Gilbert Hitchcock founded the *Omaha Evening World* newspaper and then merged it with George Miller's *Herald* in 1889. Hitchcock then renamed the combined paper the *Omaha World-Herald*. Bloomfield, *Impertinences*, 61. The Nebraska State Historical Society archivist Linda Hein and microfilm manager Mary Waldemath confirmed Ferdinand L. Barnett as the editor and proprietor of the *Progress*. However, at my request, historian Beverly Guy-Sheftall contacted Paula Giddings, the leading expert on Ida B. Wells. Giddings confirmed that Barnett was the editor of the Omaha newspaper. He was not the same Barnett married to Wells but most likely an identically named family member. Workers, *Negroes of Nebraska*, 28.
7. Paz, "Black Press," in Suggs, *Black Press*, 219; Suggs, *Black Press*.
8. Bloomfield, *Impertinences*, 61; Angus, *Black and Catholic*, 4; Paz, "Black Press," in Suggs, *Black Press*, 223; Workers, *Negroes of Nebraska*, 44; unpublished narrative labels, Mildred Brown exhibition, September 12, 1991, Durham Museum Archives, courtesy of Robert Bodnar. Lucille Skaggs Edwards printed the *Aurora Magazine*, Nebraska's first black ladies journal, from 1906 to 1908.
9. Stevens, "World War II," in La Brie, *Perspectives*, 27. Statistics for the *Omaha Star* were unavailable since Brown's ledgers no longer exist. Dubofsky and Theoharis, *Imperial Democracy*, 5; Kirby, *Black Americans*, 223; Dubofsky and Theoharis, *Imperial Democracy*, 6; Borstelmann, *Cold War*, 36.
10. June 23, 1944, Federal Bureau of Investigation; *Omaha Star*, March 19, 1943;

June 23, 1944, Federal Bureau of Investigation; Department of the Army, "Survey of Race Situation: Nebraska and South Dakota," unpublished confidential file, U.S. Army Intelligence and Security Command, Freedom Information and Privacy Office; *Omaha Star*, February 5, 1943. See also FBI agent Edward Abbott, memo, June 24, 1943, Federal Bureau of Investigation; *Omaha Star*, June 24, 1943.
11. Ruth M. Weeks to FBI agent Edward Abbott, August 14, 1942, Federal Bureau of Investigation; *Omaha Star*, March 4, 1944; FBI agent Edward Abbott, memo, August 20, 1943, Federal Bureau of Investigation.
12. Washburn, *African American Newspaper*, 160. The Associated Publishers dissolved in the 1970s.
13. Simmons, *African American Press*, 79–80; *Omaha Star*, July 27, 1945.
14. Washburn, *African American Newspaper*, 177; *Omaha Star*, July 27, 1945; Pride and Wilson, *History*, 187; NNPA Board of Directors, meeting minutes, September 9–10, 1977, Moorland-Spingarn Research Center, courtesy of Joellen ElBashir.
15. Leavell, interview; Reeve, interview, December 18, 2008; Vogel, interview, November 6, 2008; John Smith, interview; Leavell, interview; *Lincoln Journal Star*, clipping file, Douglas County Historical Society, courtesy of Gary Rosenberg.
16. Daub, interview; Ottley, *Lonely Warrior*, 8; Lincoln, interview, April 13, 2009; Rodgers, interview. Brown gave Rodgers his first job as a sportswriter; he later became a famous sports columnist in Las Vegas. *Omaha Star*, October 18, 1946; White, interview. White's brother, James Seay, worked as the typesetter and printer for Galloway's *Guide*. The twenty-six-year-old World War II veteran died in a fire at the newspaper office on December 21, 1946. Cain, interview, September 11, 2008; *Omaha Star*, March 7, 1947. Cheeks's editorial, Ethiopia Today, supplied news on Ethiopia's modernization.
17. Myrdal, *American Dilemma*, 305; *Omaha World-Herald*, May 27, 1984; Lincoln, interview, April 19, 2009. The last issue of the *Omaha Guide* printed on August 3, 1956.
18. T. Davis, interview; D. Eure, interview, February 12, 2009; La Brie, *Perspectives*, 107; Harold W. Andersen, videotaped interview, 1997, Greater Omaha Chamber of Commerce, W. Dale Clark Main Library; Gottschalk, interview, November 20, 2007.
19. Simmons, *African American Press*, 45. Robert Vann, the *Courier*'s owner, was unable to purchase a car for the winner so he compromised by giving the winner money from his own pocket and several shares of *Courier* stock. La Brie, *Perspectives*, 110; Keller, interview, November 8, 2008.
20. Keller, interview, November 11, 2008.

21. Keller, interview, November 11, 2008; Myrdal, *American Dilemma*, 105. Southern whites referred to rising lower-class blacks as "uppity," whereas blacks labeled themselves as "biggity." Keller, interview, November 16, 2008; McSwain, interview.
22. Godfrey, interview, November 20, 2008; J. Young, interview; Thomas, interview, December 4, 2008. See also Wiese, *Places of Their Own*, 63; Adams, interview; Brooks, interview; Dennis, interview.
23. Armstrong, interview, October 6, 2008; Bryant, interview, October 31, 2008. Brown told Bryant that wherever she went she acted like a lady, especially the NNPA conventions, where no one wanted to be a "convention whore." It was too unprofessional. Phillips, interview, October 12, 2008.
24. Smithson, "*Omaha Star*," 21; Bryant, interview, October 31, 2008; Rudy Smith, interview, August 27, 2005; B. Hogan, interview, March 8, 2009; Rodgers, interview.
25. Westbrook, interview. Brown employed a chauffeur because in the accumulated time it would take her to find a spot and park her car, she could sell another ad. Westbrook, interview.
26. Truman Clare, interview, February 21, 2009. Clare acted as Brown's attorney from 1951 to 1989. L. Blumkin and R. Blumkin, interview, September 20, 2008.
27. La Brie, *Perspectives*, 198; La Brie, "Profile," 286; La Brie, *Perspectives*, 198.
28. Bunting, interview; Mildred Brown, interview by Henry La Brie III, August 27, 1971, digitized CD, Columbia University Archives; Armstrong, interview, October 6, 2008.

5. COLLECTIVE ACTIVISM AND THE DE PORRES CLUB

1. *Omaha Star*, June 27, 1952. See also Spencer, *Historic Photos of Omaha*, 36. The Omaha and Council Bluffs Street Railway Company's electric streetcars started transporting Omaha's and Council Bluffs' residents on November 1, 1888.
2. Biga, "Killing Jim Crow," 8; *Omaha Star*, February 27, 1948.
3. Lynn, *Progressive Women*, 51. Although a YWCA member's "race" was inconsequential, the YWCA chapters in Omaha remained segregated until the 1960s. Robertson, *Christian Sisterhood*, 128–52; *Omaha Star*, June 27, 1947, March 7, 1947, February 27, 1948.
4. J. Smith, "Omaha De Porres Club," master's thesis, 194. The exact number of club participants remains unknown, but there were several hundred members. De Porres Club press release, courtesy of Agnes Stark; P. Jones, *Selma of the North*; McGreevy, *Parish Boundaries*, 39–41; Mihelich, *History of Creighton University*, 259; Rhodes, interview, March 31, 2009; Lincoln, interview, April 13, 2009; Mihelich, *History of Creighton University*, 259. The Catholic Church

canonized Martin De Porres in 1962. McGreevy, *Parish Boundaries*, 64; *Omaha Star*, November 19, 1948; D. Holland, interview, September 14, 1982, in A. Smith, *Black Nebraskans*.

5. P. Jones, "Not a Color," 261; McGreevy, *Parish Boundaries*, 39–41.

6. *Omaha Star*, July 13, 1951; Cain, interview, May 3, 2009; White, interview; Szmrecsanyi, *Catholic Church*, 289, 286; Larsen et al., *Upstream Metropolis*, 297.

7. Calloway, interview, April 27, 1982, in A. Smith, *Black Nebraskans*; Dorothy Eure to Mildred Brown, June 1, 1984, clippings file, Nebraska State Historical Society; *Des Moines Tribune*, August 16, 1943; August 19, 1943, Federal Bureau of Investigation. The *Tribune* editor added a disclaimer: "We are not afraid, but we are ashamed to have to publish it. Incidentally, Jefferson was ashamed of slavery as were most of the Founding Fathers." *Omaha Star*, April 30, 1948. See also Spencer, *Historic Photos of Omaha*, 158.

8. Brown's foster daughter, Ruth Harris, married Marvin Kellogg Sr. Walter E. Harkert opened Harkert's Holsum Hamburgers at Dodge and Sixteenth Streets in 1925. M. Kellogg Sr., interview, November 25, 2008. Kellogg Sr. stated that Mildred Brown, African American Margaret Wright (Brown's dressmaker), and white Jean Waite (Denny Holland's future wife), along with two other white women from the De Porres Club, accompanied him to test the racial policy of the Harkert Café. *Omaha Star*, April 9, 1948. Police liaison Shelley Lesac informed the author that discrimination cases before 1980 exist in unfiled boxes in the basement of the Omaha Police Department, but she denied me access to these files. I then requested under the Nebraska Public Records Act the right to view these files, but Lesac failed to recall our earlier conversation and suggested contacting records manager Jane Alexander. Police chief Alex Hayes spoke with Alexander, and she also denied knowledge of any basement record files pertaining to discrimination cases in the 1940s, 1950s, and 1960s. United States District Court, District of Nebraska. A notarized certificate stated there were no criminal or civil records concerning the Central Violations Bureau. Courtesy of Denise M. Lucks, April 30, 2009.

9. Szmrecsanyi, *Catholic Church*, 293; Markoe, "Omaha De Porres Club"; FBI clipping file 100 OM 2225, vols. 1, 2, Federal Bureau of Investigation; B. Hogan, interview, March 8, 2009. Markoe initially earned these pejorative labels when he fraternized too much with the black soldiers under his command during the Spanish-American War. J. Smith, *From Corps to Core*, 19, courtesy of Great Plains Black History Museum Archives, Nebraska State Historical Society; Mildred Brown, interview by Henry La Brie III, August 27, 1971, digitized CD, Columbia University Archives; Harrison, interview; *Omaha Star*, October 27, 1950.

10. Vavrina, interview; M. Holland, interview. Denny Holland's father passed

away on March 3, 1952. D. Holland, interview, September 14, 1982, in A. Smith, *Black Nebraskans*; Brooks, interview; *Omaha Star*, January 19 1951. Brown owned the Carnation Ballroom during the 1950s. M. Holland, "Priest and the Troublemaker," 3; D. Holland, interview, September 14, 1982, in A. Smith, *Black Nebraskans*; *Omaha Star*, August 28, 1953. The courtship of Holland and Waite was surprising since Waite left Omaha the previous year to enter a nunnery. M. Holland, interview; Biga, "Killing Jim Crow."

11. *Compiled Statutes of Nebraska*, 283.

12. *Omaha World-Herald*, September 19, 1992; Calloway, interview, March 22, 1982, in A. Smith, *Black Nebraskans*.

13. Kelley, *Hammer and Hoe*, 92; M. Holland, interview. De Porres Club FBI files were gained through the Freedom of Information Act. FBI officials originally stated that the De Porres Club files were destroyed on January 1, 1990, March 1, 1990, and December 1, 1994, but a few documents remained for the author's perusal. Correspondence with author, July 31, 2009.

14. Reilly, "Few Who Have Acted," 5; Strategic Air Command to FBI agent Walter E. Taylor Jr., U.S. Government Office memo, December 20, 1950, file 100 OM 2225, vols. 1, 2, Federal Bureau of Investigation, courtesy of David Hardy; Isserman, *Hammer*, 4–9; Denny Holland, unpublished Omaha De Porres Club flyer, Great Plains Black History Museum Archives, courtesy of James Calloway and Tekla Johnson; Borstelmann, *Cold War*, 108.

15. *Omaha Star*, March 10, 1950; Markoe, "Omaha De Porres Club"; D. Holland, interview, September 14, 1982, in A. Smith, *Black Nebraskans*; *Omaha Star*, March 24, 1950; Meyer, *Don't Move Next Door*, 77; D. Holland, interview, September 14, 1982, in A. Smith, *Black Nebraskans*; J. Smith, *From Corps to Core*, 102, courtesy of Great Plains Black History Museum Archives, Nebraska State Historical Society; Angus, *Black and Catholic*, 57.

16. Countryman, *Up South*, 103; National Register of Historic Places registration form, National Park Service, U.S. Department of the Interior, Nebraska State Historical Society, courtesy of Jill Dolberg; *Omaha Star*, June 30, 1950; D. Holland, interview, September 14, 1982, in A. Smith, *Black Nebraskans*; *Omaha Star*, July 7, 1950, August 4, 1950.

17. *Omaha Star*, December 8, 1950; *Omaha World-Herald*, December 9, 1950; FBI clipping file 100 OM 2225, vols. 1, 2, Federal Bureau of Investigation; D. Holland, interview, September 14, 1982, in A. Smith, *Black Nebraskans*; *Omaha Star*, March 9, 1951, March 30, 1951.

18. Minutes of the De Porres Club, May 7, 1951, courtesy of Matt Holland. Holland's private collection includes De Porres materials and memos and all of Father Markoe's archival papers. *Omaha Star*, May 11, 1951.

19. Special agent John V. Barnes to Strategic Air Command, U.S. Government

Office memo, May 19, 1951, file 100 OM 2225, vols. 1, 2, Federal Bureau of Investigation, courtesy of David Hardy.

20. *Omaha Star*, March 25, 1949, May 11, 1951, April 3, 1944; Barnes to Strategic Air Command, memo, Federal Bureau of Investigation. The memo information came from a government missive titled "Foreign Inspired Agitation among the American Negroes in the Omaha Division." FBI informants observed Galloway frequently shopping the New World Book Shop, a known venue of Communist literature. Unpublished notes, Omaha De Porres Club Special Meeting, June 5, 1951, courtesy of Matt Holland; M. Holland, interview; *Omaha Star*, June 7, 1951; K. Davis, "Fighting Jim Crow," 246. See also J. Smith, "Omaha De Porres Club," *Negro History Bulletin*, 198.

21. Larsen and Cottrell, *Gate City*, 107; Workers, *Negroes of Nebraska*, 30. Omaha's Urban League was founded in 1928, and its first executive secretary was J. Harvey Kerns. FBI agent Edward Abbott report, June 6, 1945, April 25, 1945, file 100 OM 2225, vols. 1, 2, Federal Bureau of Investigation. According to FBI records, thirty-five of the approximately sixty-nine people attending American Communist Party meetings were black northern Omaha residents. One of the attendees was Galloway, publisher of the *Omaha Guide*. There were no manifestations of Japanese subversive activities among those attending. D. Holland, interview, September 14, 1982, in A. Smith, *Black Nebraskans*; *Omaha Star*, March 23, 1951.

22. *Omaha Star*, May 31, 1951, September 28, 1951, April 24, 1953, November 9, 1951.

23. *Omaha Star*, April 18, 1952; De Porres Club FBI clipping file 100 OM 2225, vols. 1, 2, Federal Bureau of Investigation, courtesy of David Hardy; B. Brown, interview, July 5, 2012; Countryman, *Up South*, 107; *Omaha Star*, May 16, 1952.

24. *Omaha Star*, June 27, 1952, March 7, 1952; Robnett, *How Long?*, 50–51; Height, *Freedom Gates*, 61; Eskew, *But for Birmingham*, 15. Reverend Fred Shuttlesworth, a Freedom Ride leader, was a star pupil of Annie Breeding Windham. *Omaha Star*, June 27, 1952; Eskew, *But for Birmingham*, 155–65.

25. City council minutes, June 17, 1952, December 12, 1952, November 2, 1952, November 28, 1952, doc. nos. 2665, 41363, Omaha City Council Archives.

26. City council minutes, August 10, 1954, doc. 4249, Omaha City Council Archives.

27. *Omaha Star*, July 30, 1954; Hughes, interview, August 3, 2007. Hughes's mother was Helen Jones Woods.

28. *Omaha Star*, August 27, 1954, October 22, 1954.

29. *Omaha Star*, April 6, 1951, January 16, 1953.

30. Denny Holland, unpublished press release, October 7, 1953, Great Plains Black

History Museum Archives; *Omaha Star*, January 16, 1953, January 30, 1953; Artison, interview, *Omaha Star*, May 8, 1953, May 22, 1953, April 30, 1953.
31. *Omaha Star*, September 4, 1953; D. Holland, interview, September 14, 1982, in A. Smith, *Black Nebraskans*; *Omaha Star*, July 10, 1953, January 29, 1954.
32. *Omaha Star*, February 5, 1954.
33. *Omaha Star*, January 9, 1953; Shaw, *Woman Ought to Be*, 54; Workers, *Negroes of Nebraska*, 29; Spencer, *Historic Photos of Omaha*, 132; *Omaha Star*, October 17, 1952; Lincoln, interview, April 19, 2009; Glenn, interview. William and Dorothy Glenn published *American Record* in Plattsmouth, Nebraska, from 1945 to 1948. Lincoln, interview, April 19, 2009.
34. *Omaha Star*, January 23, 1953; unpublished narrative labels, Mildred Brown exhibition, September 12, 1991, Durham Museum Archives, courtesy of Robert Bodnar; Bryant, interview, November 7, 2008; Brooks, interview.
35. M. Holland, interview; Biga, "Killing Jim Crow"; M. Holland, interview; Wolseley, *Black Press*, 5; Reilly, "Few Who Have Acted," 5; M. Holland, interview. Jean Waite Holland reminisced with her son Matt Holland. She has Alzheimer's and was unable to interview with the author. *Omaha Star*, October 29, 1954; unpublished draft for press release, courtesy of Agnes Wichita Stark; *Omaha Star*, May 27, 1955. After Denny Holland married Jean Waite (and subsequently fathered seven children), he was unable to afford serving as the unpaid president of the De Porres Club.

6. RESTRICTED HOUSING AND 'RITHMETIC

1. *Omaha Star*, March 24, 1950; Taylor, interview, December 5, 2008. During the late 1960s the Black Panthers referred to the Kountze Place's park as Malcolm X Park. The Kountze Place neighborhood was previously the site of the Trans-Mississippi Exposition of 1898.
2. Deed Record no. 586, January 17, 1930, Register of Deeds Office, Douglas County Courthouse. Although the Deeds Office contained numerous volumes of home sales with covenants, it was impossible to pinpoint the last seller who sold a restricted home in Omaha because properties were categorized by neighborhood, not by chronological order.
3. Loewen, *Sundown Towns*, 80; Pattillo, *Black on the Block*, 33; Nebraska Constitution, art. 1, sec., 25, 1875, amended 1920, Nebraska Constitutional Convention, 1919–20, no. 2, Douglas County Law Library, Douglas County Courthouse; Pattillo, *Black on the Block*, 34.
4. Wiese, *Places of Their Own*, 128. The NAACP's Thurgood Marshall and California attorney Loren Miller successfully ensured that the Supreme Court arrived at the same conclusion in *McGhee v. Sipes* as well. Supporters of open housing created the National Committee against Discrimination in Housing. McKen-

zie, *Privatopia*, 33–55; Massey and Denton, *American Apartheid*, 188; Jackson, *Crabgrass Frontier*, 208.
5. Sugrue, *Urban Crisis*, 45; Stalvey, *Education of a WASP*; *Omaha Star*, July 29, 1955; Sugrue, *Urban Crisis*, 46.
6. *Omaha Star*, February 28, 1963; *Omaha World-Herald*, July 10, 1963, clipping file, Douglas Country Historical Society.
7. *Omaha Star*, May 26, 1966. See also Smithson, "*Omaha Star*," 54; *Omaha Star*, June 2, 1967.
8. *Omaha Star*, March 29, 1963.
9. *Omaha Star*, March 29, 1963; Workers, *Negroes of Nebraska*, 29; Gray, interview, August 6, 2009. Gray serves the black community as a city of Omaha council member; NAACP documents revealed leadership struggles within the Omaha chapter between its founding in 1912 and the 1980s. NAACP Archives, courtesy of Tommie Wilson; *Omaha Star*, June 13, 1946.
10. *Omaha Star*, April 9, 1963.
11. City council minutes, November 12, 1963, doc. nos. 4058, 17290, Omaha City Council Archives; *Omaha Star*, March 29, 1963, November 15, 1963; Jones-Correa, "Racial Restrictive Covenants," 559; Harrington, *Other America*, 6; Self, *American Babylon*, 256.
12. Fletcher, interview; D. Holland, interview, September 14, 1982, in A. Smith, *Black Nebraskans*; *Omaha Star*, August 16, 1963, 1. S. S. Kresge exists today as K-Mart. Armstrong, interview, October 6, 2008.
13. Szmrecsanyi, "OHA Story," 168; Massey and Denton, *American Apartheid*, 2; *Omaha Star*, July 31, 1957. See also "The Improvement and Development Program Recommended for the City of Omaha by the Mayor's City-Wide Planning Committee," March 15, 1946, 160, University of Nebraska Archives; city council minutes, April 7, 1964, doc. nos. 1296, 807, Omaha City Council Archives. Seven years later the people of Omaha elected Ernest Chambers as a Nebraska state senator from 1971 to 2008. He remains the longest-serving state senator in Nebraska history.
14. *Omaha Star*, July 12, 1963; Taylor, interview.
15. Taylor, interview, September 23, 2008; *Omaha Star*, July 17, 1963, June 28, 1963, August 30, 1963, January 3, 1964.
16. *Omaha Star*, July 19, 1963, November 8, 1963, February 28, 1963, November 8, 1963, May 3, 1963. According to Nebraska's 1855 territory statute, it was "illegal for any Nebraskan of one-eighth or more of Negro, Japanese or Chinese blood" to marry a fellow white resident until 1963.
17. City council minutes, February 27, 1962, doc. 10931, Omaha City Council Archives. Peony Park president Joseph Malec Jr. beseeched the city of Omaha to buy his amusement park after the city council decided to build city-operated

swimming pools. Godfrey, interview, November 20, 2008; *Omaha Star*, October 14, 1955; C. Parks, interview; *Omaha Star*, May 24, 1963.
18. Godfrey, interview, November 20, 2008; Eure, interview, April 6, 1982, in A. Smith, *Black Nebraskans*.
19. Bristow, "Just Wanted to Swim."
20. Godfrey, interview, November 24, 2008. Malec Jr. did not want to lose another discrimination lawsuit, such as his earlier 1955 discrimination court case, *State of Nebraska v. Peony Park*. The fifty-dollar fine he paid was the largest possible fine assessed for a civil rights violation conviction.
21. *Report on Discrimination*, 1, 35, 19, 2.
22. *Omaha Star*, July 24, 1969. Brown listed each of the six "naysayers" with their names and Nebraska counties of representation. Open Housing Legislative Bill 718, Legislature of the State of Nebraska, eightieth sess., 1969, Douglas County Law Library, Douglas County Courthouse; *Omaha World-Herald*, September 5, 1967. See also Szmrecsanyi, "OHA Story," 73; Johns, interview. Johns's mother worked for "Mom Brown." Armstrong, interview, October 6, 2008.
23. Workers, *Negroes of Nebraska*, 34; "Omaha Public Schools Did You Know?" unpublished fact sheet, Omaha Public Schools Archives, courtesy of Collette March.
24. *Omaha Star*, May 22, 1953, January 4, 1953; Joslyn Castle brochure, Joslyn Castle Trust, Omaha. The public meeting was held at the former home of wealthy philanthropists George and Sarah Joslyn. Their opulent home served as OPS's headquarters from 1944 to 1989. Taylor, interview, September 23, 2008; *South Omaha Sun*, June 18, 1959, clipping file, Omaha Public Schools Archives; D. Holland, interview, November 19, 1982, in A. Smith, *Black Nebraskans*.
25. *Omaha Star*, June 4, 1954; *Dundee and West Omaha Sun*, September 17, 1959, clipping file, Omaha Public Schools Archives; *Omaha World-Herald*, July 7, 1959, clipping file, Omaha Public Schools Archives; LaNier, *Mighty Long Way*, xiv; Robnett, *How Long?*, 81. Every white advertiser, including Southwestern Bell Telephone and Arkansas-Louisiana Gas, pulled their ads from Bates's newspaper, which led to its demise in 1959. Fletcher, interview. Burke served as OPS superintendent from 1946 to 1963.
26. Omaha Public Schools' executive secretary of Human Resources, Cheryl Mayo, was unable to provide statistics demonstrating how many teachers of color the school system hired after 1965. She stated that OPS did not keep records of the ethnicity of its teachers.
27. Hale, *Making Whiteness*, 289. OPS also ignored the 1955 *Brown II* addendum decision outlining the implementation of nationwide desegregation. Omaha Public Schools intercommunication memo, May 2, 1997, Teacher Administra-

tive Center, Omaha Public Schools Archives; G. Bennett, "Court-Ordered Desegregation," 48, part of *United States v. School District of Omaha*.
28. City council minutes, August 24, 1976, doc. nos. 2432, 3949, Omaha City Council Archives. See also G. Bennett, "Court-Ordered Desegregation," 52. The study was part of the court case *United States v. School District of Omaha*, 565 F.2d 127 (1977); Schuerman, interview, June 19, 2009; "Historical Developments in the Desegregation of the Omaha Public Schools," unpublished pamphlet, November 12, 1975, 1, Urban League of Nebraska Archives; *Omaha World-Herald*, November 24, 1987, clipping file, Omaha Public Schools Archives. Even with the federal mandate and the black community's assistance, the 1987–88 school year statistics showed that OPS still employed 88 percent white teachers and only 12 percent black educators. *State of Black Omaha, 1989*, 71; *Digest of Educational Statistics*; *Omaha Star*, June 19, 1975, August 26, 1976. Schuerman was appreciative of Brown publicly supporting his efforts. Fletcher, interview; *State of Black Omaha, 1989*, xx; Monahon, interview; *Omaha World-Herald*, September 1, 1976.

7. CHANGING STRATEGIES FOR CHANGING TIMES

1. Daub, interview; Wirth, interview; *Omaha World-Herald*, February 9, 1969; Omaha Housing Authority file, Douglas County Historical Society; Fletcher, interview; *Omaha World-Herald*, June 25, 1969, June 29, 1969. Previous to Vivian Strong's death, two members of the black community filed charges of police brutality against Officer Loder; both charges were dismissed. Loder, interview. Loder confirmed he was the stepson of movie star Hedy Lamarr, although he mentioned they were not close. Fletcher, interview; *Omaha World-Herald*, June 28, 1969, June 30, 1969.
2. Honey, *Jericho Road*, 87; Bryant, interview, November 7, 2008.
3. Strain, *Pure Fire*, 129; Graham, "Riot and Riot Commissions," 16; Kusmer, "African Americans," in Goings and Mohl, *New African American*, 330.
4. Larsen and Cottrell, *Gate City*, 250; *Omaha Star*, July 21, 1950; Smithson, "Omaha Star," 61; Greenberg, *Or Does It Explode?*, 127.
5. City council minutes, May 24, 1965, doc. nos. 1881, 1551, Omaha City Council Archives; *Omaha Star*, May 28, 1965.
6. Joseph, *Midnight Hour*, 133; Robnett, *How Long?*, 179. Meredith's March against Fear originally took place on June 5, 1966. He ended the march after an assailant shot him in the legs, back, and neck. Joseph, *Midnight Hour*, 142; *Omaha Star*, June 23 1966. This newspaper edition marks the *Star* shifting its printing day from Friday to its current Thursday publication.
7. Joseph, *Midnight Hour*, 151; David L. Rice, "The Masque of the Black Death," *Buffalo Chip*, December 1, 1967, courtesy of the Wisconsin State Historical

Society. The newspaper lasted from 1967 to 1969. Fleming, "Black Women," in Collier-Thomas and Franklin, *Sisters in the Struggle*, 208.

8. Peak, interview, April 27, 1982, in A. Smith, *Black Nebraskans*; Strain, *Pure Fire*, 119; Nelson, "Mildred Brown," 31. Brown received similar appreciation from Hubert Humphrey, Richard Nixon, and Ronald Reagan. She offered them the same unsolicited advice she told Johnson in the 1960s. A photo album at the *Omaha Star* office contains photographs of Brown with Humphrey, Johnson, Nixon, and Reagan. E-mail message to author, July 19, 2012, Lyndon Baines Johnson Library, courtesy of Eric R. Cuellar. The White House recorded four instances of Mildred Brown meeting with President Johnson. Diary cards note meetings on May 27, 1966, with the president, Brown, and other representatives of the National Newspaper Publishers Association (NNPA); on March 17, 1967, the president, Brown, and other NNPA representatives met again; on March 23, 1967, the president met with Brown and the senior class of Holton Arms School, which included the daughter of nationally known feminist Liz Carpenter; and on March 15, 1968, the president met with Brown and thirty other NNPA members. The four meetings varied from five minutes to one hour and fourteen minutes. *Omaha Star*, March 19, 1965.

9. Sugrue, *Sweet Land of Liberty*, 327. Nearly every racial rebellion in the United States during the 1960s, except for those after the assassination of Dr. Martin Luther King Jr., were caused by a police incident. *Omaha World-Herald*, July 4, 1966; *Omaha Star*, January 10, 1963. In January 1963 the Safeway grocery store petitioned the Omaha Planning Board to rezone eight residential tracts into a commercial region. Store managers wished to build a half-million-dollar, twenty-thousand-foot store with parking spaces for 125 cars. Within three years the city designated the same Safeway store at Twenty-Fourth and Lake as needing rezoning to make way for a school, which did not materialize. Dalstrom, *Sorensen*, 204; *Omaha World-Herald*, July 7, 1966; Dalstrom, *Sorensen*, 205; Larsen and Cottrell, *Gate City*, 273.

10. Mildred Brown, interview by Henry La Brie III, August 27, 1971, digitized CD, Columbia University Archives; *Omaha Star*, July 29, 1966; city council minutes, February 27, 1962, doc. nos. 715, 10931, Omaha City Council Archives; *Omaha Star*, July 22, 1966, July 29, 1966.

11. Turner, interview, April 11, 2008; La Brie, "Profile," 123; Hewins-Maroney, interview; *Sun Newspapers, Inc. v. Omaha World-Herald Company*, 713 F.2d 428 (1983); Suburban Newspapers, Inc., and Rapid Printing and Mailing, Inc., United States Court of Appeals, Eighth Circuit, August 11, 1983. On June 14, 1983, the *Sun* sued the *Omaha World-Herald* for deliberate alleged anticompetitive conduct in violation of the Sherman Act; it won the case, but it was

too late to restart the South Omaha newspaper. The *Sun*, the Pulitzer Prize–winning weekly, had catered to a diverse population of mainly Latinos, blacks, and whites living in southern Omaha and had supported the *Omaha Star* by printing analytic articles concerning the residents of the Near North Side. Brown printed the court proceedings, especially since she used Rapid Printing and Mailing to publish her *Star*. The *Omaha World-Herald* owned this company, which printed the newspaper. M. Holland, with Jean Waite Holland, interview.

12. Larsen and Cottrell, *Gate City*, 274; McCaslin, interview.
13. McCaslin, interview.
14. Dalstrom, *Sorensen*, 237; *Omaha Star*, March 14, 1968.
15. Cole and Guy-Sheftall, *Gender Talk*, 85. Civil rights activist Anna Arnold Hedgman coined the phrase the "Big Six." She was referring to James Forman (SNCC), A. Philip Randolph and Roy Wilkins (NAACP), Martin Luther King Jr. (SCLC), James Farmer (CORE), and Whitney Young (National Urban League). *Omaha World-Herald*, clipping file, courtesy of Jeannie Houser. See also Wiese, *Places of Their Own*, 223; *Omaha Star*, April 11, 1968; *Daily Nebraskan*, April 11, 1968; Hubert Humphrey Papers, April 26, 1968, Hubert Horatio Humphrey Papers Collection, Minnesota Historical Society Archives. A memo typed during Vice President Humphrey's presidential campaign for the Democratic nomination mentioned his opponent Bobby Kennedy's whistle-stop campaign through the Midwest. Humphrey's aids noted, "*Omaha World-Herald* dislikes Bobby but because of its conservatism it is not too effective. Kennedy is spending a large sum of money in Omaha—is working the Negro sections very hard with registration drives and other activities. A private poll showed Kennedy edging Johnson with Humphrey next and McCarthy's votes weak. The Kennedy committee was preparing sample ballots and newspaper ads [targeting black newspapers, such as the *Omaha Star*] to identify their delegates." *Omaha World-Herald*, April, 10 1968; Daub, interview; *Omaha Star*, April 11, 1968; Godfrey, interview, November 20, 2008.
16. U.S. National Advisory Commission, *Kerner Report*, 1; Massey and Denton, *American Apartheid*, 4, 59; Graham, "Riot and Riot Commissions," 16; Szmrecsanyi, "OHA Story," 207.
17. *Omaha World-Herald*, June 27, 1969, June 25, 1969; Wisch, "Unnecessary Violence"; *Omaha World-Herald*, June 26, 1969, June 27, 1969; Vavrina, interview; Loder, interview. Loder was suspended from the Omaha Police Department until March 1970, when his trial in Douglas County's District Court found him innocent of any crime. Reinstated, Loder patrolled northern Omaha streets until the police forced him to resign in 1971. He then worked as a security guard at a gas station and a casino until he became a transportation secu-

rity officer at Omaha's Eppley Airfield for Homeland Security. Loder retired on September 11, 2010. City council minutes, January 26, 1971, doc. nos. 312, 243, Omaha City Council Archives.
18. L. Blumkin and R. Blumkin, interview, September 20, 2008. Memorial Stadium, home of the Nebraska Cornhusker football team, resides at the University of Nebraska in Lincoln. Fletcher, interview; Mason, interview.
19. *Omaha World-Herald*, June 26, 1969; Turner, interview, August 13, 2008; Countryman, *Up South*, 159; Nebraska Jewish Historical Society. NJHS records indicated at least a third of the damaged businesses were owned by Jewish businesspeople. Jack, interview.
20. Edward Poindexter to author, August 31, 2009; Harrison, interview.
21. David Rice to author, September 1, 2009. In 1970 the Douglas County District Court, with eleven white jurors and one black juror, sentenced Rice and Poindexter to life in prison for allegedly killing Officer Larry Minard. Brown, like many others in the black community, questioned the fairness of the trial and the validity of the conviction. She asked readers to withhold judgment on the verdict and instead support the newly created Black Legal Defense Fund, which could assist the two men better than a rally or another riot. Today, Rice and Poindexter remain incarcerated in the state penitentiary in Lincoln, Nebraska.
22. Mudd, interview.
23. Peak, interview, April 27, 1982, in A. Smith, *Black Nebraskans*; *Omaha Star*, July 3, 1969.
24. *Omaha Star*, June 26, 1969.
25. *Dundee and West Omaha Sun*, September 7, 1968; *Omaha Star*, June 28, 1969, July 31, 1969.
26. K. Battiste, interview, October 11, 2008; Hughes, interview, December 3, 2008; Spencer, interview, September 22, 2008.
27. Warranty deed, doc. nos. 1216, 423, Register of Deeds Office, Douglas County Courthouse. Brown's 1964 purchase of a property in Omaha had her financially strapped for liquid assets. For unknown reasons the property currently remains in Brown's name.
28. Smithson, "*Omaha Star*," 20.
29. *Omaha World-Herald*, August 7, 1971, courtesy of John Gottschalk; city council minutes, September 16, 1969, doc. nos. 3709, 2775, Omaha City Council Archives; Grice, interview, December 11, 2009.
30. City council minutes, September 16, 1969, doc. nos. 3709, 2775, Omaha City Council Archives.
31. *Omaha Star*, December 29, 1977, December 2, 1977, February 23, 1978. Brown's editorial posed Rabbi Hillel's famous first-century question: "If I am not for myself, who will be for me? And when I am for myself, what am 'I'?

And if not now, when?" City of Omaha resolution, October 13, 1981, Omaha City Council Archives; B. Hogan, interview, March 18, 2009.

32. *Omaha World-Herald*, April 30, 1970, October 15, 1966; North Freeway Right of Way file, Douglas County Historical Society; Sugrue, *Urban Crisis*, 47.
33. *Omaha Star*, March 14, 1974; James Suttle, interview; *Omaha Star*, April 5, 1978.
34. *Omaha Star*, September 6, 1973; *Omaha World-Herald*, May 7, 1974; North Freeway clipping file, Douglas County Historical Society.
35. Fact sheet against the North Omaha freeway, unpublished paper, NAACP Archives.
36. Resolution of city council member Bernie Simon's proposal to the city council, October 13, 1981, Omaha City Council Archives. The resolution passed while Mike Boyle was Omaha's mayor.
37. B. Hogan, interview, March 18, 2009; Pearson, interview; Thailing, *1979 Consumer Preference Study*; *Omaha Star*, March 9, 1978.

8. THE DEATH OF AN ICON

1. Rodgers, interview; Omaha Planning Department resolution, 387, March 30, 2004, City Council Office, courtesy of Sandy Kerwin; *Omaha World-Herald*, August 29, 2004, clipping file, Douglas County Historical Society. Council member Frank Brown, no relation to Mildred Brown, proposed the successful legislature to rename a section of Twenty-Fourth Street. *Omaha World-Herald*, January 13, 2008; M. Holland, interview; Dow, interview. Dow, a CBS broadcaster, was originally the emcee of Omaha's tribute to Mildred Brown on June 1, 1984. He cancelled that evening due to an asthma attack. Dow recently died of an asthma attack at the end of this project in August 2010.
2. Reinhardt, interview; National Register of Historic Places registration form, sec. 8, p. 3, National Park Service, U.S. Department of the Interior, Nebraska State Historical Society, courtesy of Jill Dolberg; *New Horizons*, February 1989, clipping file, Douglas County Historical Society; *Carolinian* (Raleigh NC), March 23, 1989, Great Plains Black History Museum Archives, courtesy of James Calloway and archivist Tekla Johnson; Reinhardt, interview; Daub, interview. Nebraska House of Representatives congressman Daub remembered Brown's role in the MLK federal holiday. Brown asked Daub to meet her at the store, which was how she referred to the *Omaha Star* building. She knew the MLK Day legislature bill was out of committee and going to the House floor for a vote. Daub's Democratic constituents, Nebraska senators John James Exon and Edward Zorinsky, were voting against it. Brown hoped Daub would vote for it. He did after giving it considerable thought. Brown responded to his decision with a simple, heartfelt thank you. *New Horizons*, February, 1989.

3. Mildred Brown, interview by Henry La Brie III, August 27, 1971, digitized CD, Columbia University Archives; Dow, interview; *Omaha Star*, October 22, 1970. Annie Washington was sixty-eight at the time of her death. *Omaha Star*, June 19, 1975, May 6, 1976, 1. Brown announced Gilbert's death by reprinting the *Saint Louis Argus* obituary in the *Star*. The funeral notice supplied no mention of his connection to Brown. The *Star* publisher, usually not one to skip mentioning family relatives, did not enlighten her readers either. She listed Gilbert's highest achievement as the founder of Omaha's Black Chamber of Commerce but did not mention his role as the cofounder of the *Omaha Star*. Gilbert, interview, October 9, 2008.

4. Charles Washington, a longtime *Star* employee, became the *Star*'s official editor in the 1970s. His off-and-on employment at the newspaper started in the 1940s, and while Brown appointed him as an editor in 1945, his administrational power fluctuated throughout several decades. Brown finally allowed Washington full rein as editor in the 1970s, but she retained the titles of publisher, founder, and owner for herself. M. Kellogg Jr., interview, April 22, 2009; R. Smith, interview, October 23, 2008; B. Hogan, interview, March 8, 2009; Bryant, interview, November 7, 2008.

5. B. Brown, interview, September 27, 2008; Omaha Immigration Records, 1900–60, RG 230, Naturalization Records, boxes 1, 2, Douglas County District Court, K Street Facility, Nebraska State Historical Society. Charlene Spencer, *Omaha Star* employee, noted that Brownell discussed his family's thriving business as late as 1999. K Street Facility, Nebraska State Historical Society; Noel Maximilian Brownell, death certificate, Office of Records, Douglas County Courthouse.

6. Washington, interview, June 15, 2005. Although Brown died intestate, without a will, Washington insisted to the author that Brown willed her the *Star*.

7. Bryant, interview, October 31, 2008; *Omaha World-Herald*, November 3, 1989, 44; Bryant, interview, November 7, 2008; Zacharia, interview; Borders, interview, May 27, 2009. Borders was a cousin of Mildred Brown. Shelton, interview, January 25, 2009.

8. *Omaha Star*, November 9, 1989, 1; K. Battiste, interview, October 22, 2008; anonymous, interview, March 26, 2009, Douglas County Coroner Office. The Coroner's Office explained that police officers needed to consider various factors before recommending an autopsy. Issues such as the person's age, health, and medical history needed consideration. It was not up to a family to decide on an autopsy, but the decision of the coroner. Omaha Police Division Report, November 2, 1989, courtesy of Pitmon Foxall. According to the police report, Brownell last saw Brown alive when she was watching television at 11:30 p.m. Lurlyn Johnson, Brown's elderly female boarder, who went to bed shortly

afterward, concurred with Brownell's statement. Dr. Tom Haynes was deputy county coroner at the time of Mildred Brown's demise. Mildred Brown, death certificate, Douglas County Health Department.

9. Request to Law Department, City of Omaha, November 6, 1989, p. 3, Omaha City Council Archives. Council member Fred Conley proposed the city resolution and the city of Omaha sent a certified copy of the resolution to Bennie Brown, her surviving sibling. Mildred D. Brown, probate estate, November 17, 1992, case 141-569, Probate Court, Douglas County Courthouse; Grice, interview, December 18, 2009; Brown, probate estate. On September 9, 1991, the County Court of Douglas County ordered $10,000 to Marguerita Washington from the estate of Mildred D. Brown, although the cost of Brown's funeral totaled $5,330. Register of Deeds Office, Department of Housing and Inspection Division, Douglas County Courthouse. At the time of this project, one piece of property still remained in Brown's name. A vacant lot, located at 5004 North Twenty-Fourth, lists Brown as the owner. The warranty deed showed that Brown purchased the plot of land on March 30, 1965. She paid $7,544.88 for it. A certificate of county court proceedings documented a petition to sell this real estate in April 5, 1990, but enforcement of an expensive city code improvement stopped the sale. Register of Deeds Office, bk. 919, p. 67.

10. Mildred D. Brown, funeral program, November 6, 1989, courtesy of Shirley Harrison; *Omaha World-Herald*, November 6, 1989, 13.

11. McCullough, interview, July 20, 2009.

12. K. Battiste, interview, October 11, 2008; Simpson, interview; Thomas, interview, February 25, 2009; *Omaha World-Herald*, November 12, 1989, clipping file, Douglas County Historical Society; city council minutes, August 19, 1980, doc. nos. 3067, 11591, Omaha City Council Archives. The Omaha City Planning Board approved the Jewell Building as a landmark of the city of Omaha.

13. Personal representative quitclaim deed, November 17, 1992, book 1862, 651, Register of Deeds Office, Douglas County Courthouse. The court awarded Marguerita Washington forty-five thousand dollars to serve as her annual salary to manage and operate the *Omaha Star* business. Washington continued teaching full-time for Omaha Public Schools until 1998. *Omaha Star*, December 7, 1989; domestic corporation occupation tax report, 2001–5, State of Nebraska, Secretary of State, State Capitol Building. The paperwork was filed on November 13, 1989. Portia Love, interview. Her father, Preston Love Sr., worked as a *Star* salesperson for twenty years. Brownell died of prostate cancer on September 20, 2000. Noel Maximilian Brownell, death certificate, Douglas County Health Department; *Omaha World-Herald*, February 21, 1991. Shirley

Chisholm, the first black congresswoman, spoke at the Durham exhibit's fundraising dinner for the *Mildred Brown and the Omaha Star* traveling exhibit. It opened on the second anniversary of Brown's death. Washington, interview, September 26, 2006.

14. Mildred D. Brown, probate estate, November 17, 1992, case 141-569, Probate Court, Douglas County Courthouse.

15. Bennie D. Brown Sr., funeral program, courtesy of Bennie D. Brown Jr.; B. Brown, interview, September 19, 2008. Brown met Julius Rosenwald, the founder of Sears, Roebuck, and Company, when he worked as a door attendant at the Grand Hotel on Mackinaw Island, Michigan. Bennie, similar to his siblings Millie and Willie, lied about his age. His falsehood allowed him to keep his prestigious four-year Sears college scholarship. Winton, interview, August 13, 2008.

16. Bennie D. Brown Sr., last will and testament, book 1756, 0929–31, Probate Records, Morgan County Courthouse.

17. Mildred D. Brown, probate estate, November 17, 1992, case 141-569, Probate Court, Douglas County Courthouse. The records contain an *Omaha Star, Inc.* stock receipt signed on March 16, 1992, by Lila Brown, but apparently she was negligent in signing the second stock receipt sent on October 2, 1992. Truman Clare, Mildred Brown's lawyer, guided the author through the correct procedure to locate these documents. Winton, interview, January 27, 2009. Marguerita Washington's lawyer, Dick McMillian, contacted Lila Brown about selling the Breeding land. It sold in two transactions to two different buyers. The timber rights sold first. This part of the sale was a continuing arrangement, which Millard Breeding had previously established in the early 1900s. Clearing the timber was a fairly easy procedure, especially after a tornado in the 1950s destroyed the Breeding house. The final timber sale was between Lila Brown, William Brown Jr., Marguerita Washington, and Champion International Corporation. The Breeding homestead sale is documented in the timber deed and real estate mortgage, security agreement and financing statement, books 1692 and 1757, 0412, 57–62, Probate Records, Morgan County Courthouse. After ninety-seven years of ownership, on November 11, 1998, the Breeding land, "Township 6 South, Range 2 West," ceased to exist. Lawyer Bennie Brown Jr. handled the sale. Marguerita Washington, Lila Brown, and William Andrew Brown Jr. sold the Breeding property to real estate magnates Christopher and Richard Pettey. The 407.67 acres of property sold for $231,000. A clause in the title deed forever allows descendants of the Breeding family access to the property's two small cemeteries. Mildred D. Brown, probate estate, November 17, 1992, case 141-569, Probate Court, Douglas County Courthouse. On November 19, 1992, Marguerita L. Washington became the

sole heir and devisee in intestacy from Frederick Washington. Domestic corporation occupation tax report, 2001, State of Nebraska, Secretary of State, State Capitol Building. According to this document, the president of the *Omaha Star, Inc.* is William Andrew Brown, and the secretary and treasurer is Marguerita Washington. William Brown stated that he has not received any monies or dividends from his one hundred shares of stock.

18. Rhodes, interview, March 21, 2009; Pearson, interview; Preston Love, interview.
19. *Omaha Star*, February 23, 1978; *Omaha Star*, March 16, 1978.
20. Shaw, *Woman Ought to Be*, 65. Brown treated Keller almost like a son. He said, "She treated a lot of people like that, and you would have to work pretty hard not to like her." Keller, interview, November 9, 2008; D. Smith, interview; Hughes, interview, December 3, 2008; Rucker, interview.
21. *Omaha Star*, October 27, 1988; Wirth, interview. For more than five decades, Brown shared her active social life and glittering evenings with her readers. J. Young, interview.
22. *Omaha Star*, February 25, 1988; National Register of Historic Places continuation sheet, National Park Service, U.S. Department of the Interior, Nebraska State Historical Society, courtesy of Jill Dolberg; Weston, "In Search of Parity," 50.
23. La Brie, "Future," 166; Beermann, interview; *Sun*, September 7, 1968, clipping file, courtesy of John Gottschalk.

Bibliography

ARCHIVAL SOURCES

Alabama State Historical Society, Montgomery AL.
Bessemer City Schools, Bessemer AL.
Bessemer Historical Society, Bessemer AL.
Birmingham Historical Society, Birmingham AL.
Birmingham Public Library Southern History Archives, Birmingham AL.
Boys Town Hall of History Archives, Boys Town NE.
Central High School, Omaha NE.
Church of Jesus Christ of Latter-Day Saints, Family History Center, Omaha NE.
Columbia University Archives, New York NY.
Creighton University Archives, Omaha NE.
Des Moines Historical Society, Des Moines IA.
Douglas County Courthouse, Omaha NE.
Douglas County Health Department, Omaha NE.
Douglas County Historical Society, Omaha NE.
Durham Western Heritage Museum Exhibit and Photographs Archives, Omaha NE.
Federal Bureau of Investigation, Records Management Division, Washington DC.
Freedom Information and Privacy Office, Fort George G. Meade MD.
Giles County Court, Pulaski TN.
Great Plains Black History Museum Archives, Lincoln and Omaha NE.
Iowa Women's Archives, Des Moines IA.
Jefferson County Board of Education Archives, Birmingham AL.
Jewish Press Archives, Omaha NE.
Love's Art and Jazz Center, Omaha NE.
Lyndon Baines Johnson Library, Austin TX.
Miles Memorial College Archives, Birmingham AL.
Minnesota Historical Society Archives, Minneapolis MN.
Moorland-Spingarn Research Center, Howard University Photograph Archives, Washington DC.

Morgan County Archives, Decatur AL.
Morgan County Courthouse, Decatur AL.
NAACP Archives, Jewell Building, Omaha NE.
Nebraska Government Records, Lincoln NE.
Nebraska Jewish Historical Society, Omaha NE.
Nebraska State Historical Society, Lincoln NE.
Omaha Chamber of Commerce, Omaha NE.
Omaha City Council Minutes Archives, Omaha NE.
Omaha Public Schools Archives, Omaha NE.
Omaha World-Herald Archives, Omaha NE.
Omaha World-Herald Photograph Archives, Omaha NE.
Register of Deeds Office, Omaha NE.
Sioux City Historical Society, Sioux City IA.
State Capitol Building, Lincoln NE.
Thomas Abstract Company, Decatur AL.
University of Nebraska at Omaha Archives, Omaha NE.
Urban League of Nebraska Archives, Omaha NE.
W. Dale Clark Main Library, Omaha NE.
Wisconsin State Historical Society, Madison WI.

PUBLISHED SOURCES

Anderson, Jervis. *A. Philip Randolph, a Biographical Portrait.* New York: Harcourt Brace Jovanovich, 1972.

Anderson, Reynaldo. "Practical Internationalists: The Story of the Des Moines, Iowa, Black Panther Party." In *Groundwork: Local Black Freedom Movements in America,* edited by Jeanne Theoharis and Komozi Woodard, 282–99. New York: New York University Press, 2005.

Angus, Jack. *Black and Catholic in Omaha: A Case of Double Jeopardy.* New York: iUniverse, 2004.

Barnett, Bernice McNair. "Invisible Southern Black Women Leaders in the Civil Rights Movement: The Triple Constraints of Gender, Race, and Class." In Chow, Wilkinson, and Zinn, *Race, Class, and Gender,* 265–87.

Beals, Melba. *Warriors Don't Cry: A Searing Memory of the Battle to Integrate Little Rock's Central High.* New York: Washington Square Press, 1995.

Bennett, Gary G. "A Study of Court-Ordered Desegregation in the School District of Omaha, Nebraska, 1972–1977." PhD diss., University of Nebraska at Lincoln, 1979.

Bennett, Lerone, Jr. *Before the Mayflower: A History of Black America.* Chicago: Johnson, 2007.

Berkin, Carol, Christopher Miller, Robert Cherny, and James Gormly. *Making America: A History of the United States*. New York: Houghton Mifflin, 2006.
Bethune, Mary McLeod. "A Century of Progress of Negro Women." In Lerner, *Black Women*, 113–27.
Biga, Leo Adam. "Killing Jim Crow." *Reader*, January 20, 2005.
Biondi, Martha. *To Stand and Fight: The Struggle for Civil Rights in Postwar New York*. Cambridge: Harvard University Press, 2003.
Bish, James. "The Black Experience in Selected Nebraska Counties, 1854–1920." Master's thesis, University of Nebraska at Omaha, 1989.
The Black Press: Soldiers without Swords. Directed by Stanley Nelson. Narrated by Joe Morton. San Francisco: California Newsreel, 1998. Videocassette (VHS).
Bloomfield, Susanne George, ed. *Impertinences: Selected Writings of Elia Peattie, a Journalist in the Gilded Age*. Lincoln: University of Nebraska Press, 2005.
Borstelmann, Thomas. *The Cold War and the Color Line*. Cambridge: Harvard University Press, 2001.
Boyle, Elizabeth. "The Feminization of Teaching in America." MIT Program in Women's and Gender Studies, 2004. http://web.mit.edu/wgs/prize/eb04.html.
Boyle, Kevin. *Arc of Justice: A Saga of Race, Civil Rights, and Murder in the Jazz Age*. New York: Holt, 2004.
Branch, Taylor. *Parting the Waters: America in the King Years, 1954–63*. New York: Simon and Schuster, 1988.
Bristow, David, "We Just Wanted to Swim, Sir." *Reader*, February 5, 2009.
Brooks, Walter V. "The Great Migration Brings Influx of Blacks to Omaha." *Dreamland: The Rich Legacy of African Americans in Omaha* 1, no. 3 (2006): 8–9.
Broussard, Jinx Coleman. *Giving a Voice to the Voiceless*. New York: Routledge, 2004.
Burroughs, Nannie. "Not Color but Character." *Voice of the Negro* 1 (July 1904): 277–79.
Cairns, Kathleen A. *Front-Page Women Journalists, 1920–1950*. Lincoln: University of Nebraska Press, 2003.
Carson, Clayborne. *In Struggle: SNCC and the Black Awakening of the 1960s*. Cambridge: Harvard University Press, 1981.
Carter, Dan T. *Scottsboro: A Tragedy of the American South*. Baton Rouge: Louisiana State University Press, 1969.
Chalmers, David. *And the Crooked Places Made Straight: The Struggle for Social Change in the 1960s*. Baltimore: Johns Hopkins University Press, 1996.
Chambers, Deborah, Linda Steiner, and Carole Fleming. *Women and Journalism*. New York: Routledge, 2004.

Chow, Esther Ngan-Ling, Doris Wilkinson, and Maxine Baca Zinn, eds. *Race, Class, and Gender: Common Bonds, Different Voices.* Thousand Oaks CA: Sage, 1996.
Clark-Lewis, Elizabeth. *Living In, Living Out: African American Domestics in Washington, D.C., 1910–1940.* Washington: Smithsonian Institution Press, 1994.
Cody, Cheryll Ann. *Cycles of Work and Childbearing Seasonality in Women's Lives on Low Country Plantations.* Bloomington: Indiana University Press, 1996.
Cohen, Lizabeth. *A Consumer's Republic: The Politics of Mass Consumption in Postwar America.* New York: Knopf, 2003.
———. *Making a New Deal: Industrial Workers in Chicago, 1919–1939.* Cambridge: Harvard University Press, 1990.
Cole, Johnnetta, and Beverly Guy-Sheftall. *Gender Talk, the Struggle for Women's Equality in African American Communities.* New York: Ballantine Books, 2003.
Collier-Thomas, Bettye, and Vincent Paul Franklin, eds. *Sisters in the Struggle: African America Women in the Civil Rights-Black Power Movement.* New York: New York University Press, 2001.
Collins, Patricia. *Black Feminist Thought: Knowledge, Consciousness and the Politics of Empowerment.* New York: Routledge, 2000.
———. "The Meaning of Motherhood in Black Culture." In Staples, *Black Family*, 157–66.
Compiled Statutes of Nebraska, Annotated 1893. Lincoln: Lincoln Paper House, 1893.
Countryman, Matthew. *Up South: Civil Rights and Black Power in Philadelphia.* Philadelphia: University of Pennsylvania Press, 2006.
Dailey, Jane. *The Age of Jim Crow.* New York: Norton, 2009.
Dalstrom, Harl. *A. V. Sorensen and the New Omaha.* Omaha NE: Lamplighter, 1989.
D'Angelo, Raymond. *The American Civil Rights Movement: Readings and Interpretations.* New York: McGraw-Hill / Dushkin, 2001.
Davis, Adrienne. "Don't Let Nobody Bother Yo' Principle: The Sexual Economy of American Slavery." In *Sister Circle: Black Women and Work*, edited by Sharon Harley and the Black Women and Work Collective, 103–27. New Brunswick NJ: Rutgers University Press, 2002.
Davis, Kathleen. "Fighting Jim Crow in Post–World War II Omaha, 1945–1956." Master's thesis, University of Nebraska at Omaha, 1992.
Department of Planning. *A Report on Discrimination in Housing for Minorities in Omaha, Nebraska, 1965.* Omaha NE: Henningson, Durham, and Richardson, 1965.
Dewart, Janet, ed. *The State of Black America, 1989.* New York: National Urban League, 1989.

Didonato, Gail. "Building the Meat Packing Industry in South Omaha, 1883–1898." Master's thesis, University of Nebraska at Omaha, 1989.
Digest of Educational Statistics. Washington DC: National Center on School Statistics, 1988.
Dittmer, John. *Local People: The Struggle for Civil Rights in Mississippi*. Urbana: University of Illinois Press, 1995.
Dubofsky, Melvyn, and Athan Theoharis. *Imperial Democracy: The United States since 1945*. Englewood Cliffs NJ: Prentice Hall, 1988.
Du Bois, W. E. B. *The Souls of Black Folk*. 1903. New York: Gramercy Books, 1994.
Edmondson, Ella L. J., and Stella M. Nkomo. *Our Separate Ways: Black and White Women and the Struggle for Professional Identity*. Boston: Harvard Business School Press, 2001.
Ehrenhalt, Alan. *The Lost City: Discovering the Forgotten Virtues of Community in the Chicago of the 1950s*. New York: Basic Books, 1995.
Eskew, Glenn. *But for Birmingham: The Local and National Movement in the Civil Rights Struggle*. Chapel Hill: University of North Carolina Press, 1997.
Evans, Sara. *Born for Liberty: A History of Women in America*. New York: Simon and Schuster, 1997.
Federal Writers' Project. *The Negroes of Nebraska*. Lincoln: Woodruff, 1940.
Ferguson, Renee. "Women's Liberation Has a Different Meaning for Blacks." In Lerner, *Black Women*, 587–92.
Fleming, Cynthia. "Black Women and Black Power: The Case of Rudy Doris Smith Robinson and the Student Nonviolent Coordinating Committee." In Collier-Thomas and Franklin, *Sisters in the Struggle*, 197–213.
Frazier, Franklin E. *The Negro Family in the United States*. Chicago: University of Chicago Press, 1939.
Gaspar, David Barry, and Darlene Clark Hine, eds. *More Than Chattel: Black Women and Slavery in the Americas*. Bloomington: Indiana University Press, 1996.
Gendler, Carol. "The Jews of Omaha: The First Sixty Years, 1855 to 1915." Master's thesis, University of Nebraska at Omaha, 1968.
Giddings, Paula. *When and Where I Enter: The Impact of Black Women on Race and Sex in America*. New York: Harper Collins, 1984.
Gilkes, Cheryl Townsend. *If It Wasn't for the Women*. Maryknoll NY: Orbis Books, 2001.
———. "'If It Wasn't for the Women . . .': African American Women, Community Work, and Social Change." In Zinn and Dill, *Women of Color*, 229–46.
Gill, Gerald. "The 1952 Vice Presidential Campaign." In *The Afro-American Woman: Struggles and Images*, edited by Sharon Harley and Rosalyn Terborg-Penn, 109–18. Port Washington NY: Kennikat, 1978.

Goings, Kenneth, and Raymond Mohl, eds. *The New African American Urban History*. Thousand Oaks CA: Sage, 1996.

Gordon, Linda. *Pitied but Not Entitled: Single Mothers and the History of Welfare, 1890–1935*. New York: Free Press, 1994.

Graham, Hugh Davis. "On Riots and Riot Commissions: Civil Disorders in the 1960s." *Public Historian* 2, no. 4 (1980): 7–27.

Greenberg, Cheryl Lynn. *Or Does It Explode? Black Harlem in the Great Depression*. New York: Oxford University Press, 1991.

Gregory, James N. "The Second Great Migration: A Historical Overview." In Kusmer and Trotter, *African American Urban History*, 19–38.

Griffin, Farah Jasmine. "Black Feminists and Du Bois: Respectability, Protection, and Beyond." *Annals of the American Academy of Political and Social Science* 568 (March 2000): 28–40.

Grossman, James. *Land of Hope: Chicago, Black Southerners, and the Great Migration*. Chicago: University of Chicago Press, 1989.

Guy-Sheftall, Beverly. *Daughters of Sorrow: Attitudes toward Black Women, 1880–1920*. Brooklyn: Carlson, 1990.

Hale, Grace Elizabeth. *Making Whiteness: The Culture of Segregation in the South, 1890–1940*. New York: Vintage Books 1998.

Harrington, Michael. *The Other America: Poverty in the United States*. New York: Simon and Schuster, 1997.

Hartman, Stella E. *Omaha Near North Side Study*. Omaha NE: United Community Services, Social Planning Unit, 1954.

Hayden, Dolores. *Building Suburbia: Green Fields and Urban Growth, 1820–2000*. New York: Vintage Books, 2003.

Heacock, Laura M. "The Social Significance of Public Housing with Special Emphasis on the North Side Project." Master's thesis, Municipal University of Omaha, 1938.

Height, Dorothy. *Open Wide the Freedom Gates*. New York: Perseus Books Group, 2003.

The Heritage of Morgan County, Alabama. Clanton AL: Heritage, 1998.

Hewitt, Richard. *The History of Omaha*. Omaha NE: Doss, 1954.

Higginbotham, Elizabeth, and Lynn Weber. "Moving Up with Kin and Community: Upward Social Mobility for Black and White Women." In Chow, Wilkinson, and Zinn, *Race, Class, and Gender*, 156–67.

Higginbotham, Evelyn Brooks. *Righteous Discontent: The Women's Movement in the Black Baptist Church, 1880–1920*. Cambridge: University of Harvard Press, 1993.

Hine, Darlene Clark. *Hine Sight: Black Women and the Reconstruction of American History*. Indianapolis: Indiana University Press, 1994.

Hine, Darlene Clark, and Kathleen Thompson. *A Shining Thread of Hope: The History of Black Women in America*. New York: Broadway Books, 1998.

Hirsch, Arnold. *Making the Second Ghetto: Race and Housing in Chicago, 1940–1960*. 1983. Cambridge: Cambridge University Press, 1998.

Hirsch, James. *Riot and Remembrance: The Tulsa Race War and Its Legacy*. Boston: Houghton Mifflin, 2002.

Holland, Matt. "The Priest and the Troublemaker." *Creighton*, Fall 2005, 2–4.

Honey, Michael. *Going Down Jericho Road: The Memphis Strike, Martin Luther King's Last Campaign*. New York: Norton, 2007.

hooks, bell. *Ain't I a Woman: Black Women and Feminism*. Boston: South End, 1981.

Hope, Lugenia Burns. "The Neighborhood Union, Atlanta Georgia." In Lerner, *Black Women*, 500–508.

Howard, Ashley M. "Then the Burning Began: Omaha, Riots, and the Growth of Black Radicalism, 1966–1969." Master's thesis, University of Nebraska at Omaha, 2006.

Hunter, Margaret. *Race, Gender, and the Politics of Skin Tone*. New York: Routledge, 2005.

Hutchinson, Earl Ofari. *Blacks and Reds: Race and Class in Conflict, 1919–1990*. East Lansing: Michigan State University Press, 1995.

Isserman, Maurice. *If I Had a Hammer: The Death of the Old Left and the Birth of the New Left*. Urbana: University of Illinois Press, 1993.

Jackson, Kenneth T. *Crabgrass Frontier: The Suburbanization of the United States*. New York: Oxford University Press, 1985.

Jargowsky, Paul. "Ghetto Poverty among Blacks in the 1980s." *Journal of Policy Analysis and Management* 13, no. 2 (1994): 288–310.

Jones, Jacqueline. *Labor of Love, Labor of Sorrow: Black Women, Work, and the Family from Slavery to Present*. New York: Basic Books, 1985.

Jones, Patrick. "Not a Color but an Attitude." In *Groundwork: Local Black Freedom Movements in America*, edited by Jeanne Theoharis and Komozi Woodward, 259–81. New York: New York University Press, 2005.

———. *The Selma of the North: Civil Rights Insurgency in Milwaukee*. Cambridge: Harvard University Press, 2009.

Jones-Correa, Michael. "The Origins and Diffusion of Racial Restrictive Covenants." *Political Science Quarterly* 115, no. 4 (2000–2001): 541–68.

Joseph, Peniel E. *Waiting 'Til the Midnight Hour: A Narrative History of Black Power in America*. New York: Holt, 2006.

Kerns, James Harvey. "Industrial and Business Life of Negroes in Omaha." Master's thesis, Municipal University of Omaha, 1932.

Kelley, Robin D. G. *Hammer and Hoe: Alabama Communists during the Great Depression*. Chapel Hill: University of North Carolina Press, 1990.

Kirby, John. *Black Americans in the Roosevelt Era: Liberalism and Race.* Knoxville: University of Tennessee Press, 1980.
Koehn, Nancy. "Estee Lauder: Self-Definition and the Modern Cosmetics Market." In Scranton, *Beauty and Business*, 217–53.
Kornbluh, Felicia. "Black Buying Power: Welfare Rights, Consumerism, and Northern Protest." In *Freedom North: Black Freedom Struggles outside the South, 1940–1980*, edited by Jeanne Theoharis and Komozi Woodward, 199–222. New York: Palgrave, 2003.
Kornweibel, Theodore Kornweibel, Jr. *Seeing Red: Federal Campaigns against Black Militancy, 1919–1925.* Bloomington: Indiana University Press, 1998.
Kusmer, Kenneth. "African Americans in the City since World War II." In Goings and Mohl, *New African American*, 320–68.
Kusmer, Kenneth, and Joe Trotter, eds. *African American Urban History since World War II.* Chicago: University of Chicago Press, 2009.
La Brie, Henry, III. "The Future of the Black Press: A Silent Crusade." *Negro History Bulletin* 36 (December 1973): 166–69.
———. *Perspectives of the Black Press: 1974.* Kennebunkport ME: Mercer House, 1974.
———. "A Profile of the Black Newspaper: Old Guard Black Journalists Reflect on the Past, Present and Future." PhD diss., University of Iowa, 1973.
LaNier, Carlotta Walls. *A Mighty Long Way: My Journey to Justice at Little Rock Central High School.* New York: Ballantine Books, 2009.
Larsen, Lawrence, and Barbara Cottrell. *The Gate City: A History of Omaha.* Omaha NE: Pruett, 1982.
Larsen, Lawrence, Barbara Cottrell, Harl Dalstrom, and Kay Dalstrom. *Upstream Metropolis: An Urban Biography of Omaha and Council Bluffs.* Lincoln: University of Nebraska Press, 2007.
Lee, Chana Kai. "Anger, Memory, and Personal Power: Fannie Lou Hamer and Civil Rights Leadership." In Collier-Thomas and Franklin, *Sisters in the Struggle*, 139–70.
Lemann, Nicholas. *The Promised Land: The Great Black Migration and How It Changed America.* New York: Vintage Books, 1991.
Lemke-Santangelo, Gretchen. *Abiding Courage: African American Migrant Women and the East Bay Community.* Chapel Hill: University of North Carolina Press, 1996.
Lerner, Gerda, ed. *Black Women in White America.* New York: Vintage Books, 1972.
Lewis, Anthony. *Portrait of a Decade: The Second American Revolution.* New York: Random House, 1964.
Lewis, David Levering. *W. E. B. Du Bois: Biography of a Race, 1868–1919.* New York: Holt, 1993.

Loewen, James. *Sundown Towns: A Hidden Dimension of American Racism.* New York: Simon and Schuster, 2005.
Lynn, Susan. *Progressive Women in Conservative Times: Racial Justice, Peace, and Feminism, 1945 to the 1960s.* New Brunswick NJ: Rutgers University Press, 1992.
Markoe, Father John. "Omaha De Porres Club." *Interracial Review*, February 1950.
Martindale, Carolyn. *The White Press and Black America.* New York: Greenwood, 1986.
Massey, Douglas, and Nancy Denton. *American Apartheid: Segregation and the Making of the Underclass.* Cambridge: Harvard University Press, 1993.
Matthew, Tracye. "No One Ever Asks What a Man's Role in the Revolution Is." In Collier-Thomas and Franklin, *Sisters in the Struggle*, 230–56.
McGreevy, John T. *Parish Boundaries: The Catholic Encounter with Race in the Twentieth-Century Urban North.* Chicago: University of Chicago Press, 1996.
McKenzie, Evan. *Privatopia: Homeowner Associations and the Rise of Residential Private Government.* New Haven: Yale University Press, 1994.
Mead, James. "An Ecological Study of the Second Ward of Omaha." Master's thesis, Municipal University of Omaha, 1953.
Meditations from the Pen of Mrs. Maria W. Stewart. Washington: n.p., 1879.
Menard, Orville. *Political Bossism in Mid-America: Tom Dennison's Omaha, 1900–1933.* Lanham: University Press of America, 1989.
Meyer, Stephen Grant. *As Long as They Don't Move Next Door: Segregation and Racial Conflict in American Neighborhoods.* New York: Rowman and Littlefield, 2000.
Mihelich, Dennis. *The History of Creighton University, 1878–2003.* Omaha NE: Creighton University Press, 2006.
Momeni, Jamshid. *Race, Ethnicity, and Minority Housing in the United States.* New York: Greenwood, 1986.
Morris, Tiyi. "Local Women and the Civil Rights Movement in Mississippi: Re-visioning Womanpower Unlimited." In *Groundwork: Local Black Freedom Movements in America*, edited by Jeanne Theoharis and Komozi Woodward, 193–214. New York: New York University Press, 2005.
Morton, Patricia. *Disfigured Images: The Historical Assault on Afro-American Women.* New York: Greenwood, 1991.
Moynihan, Daniel. *The Negro Family: The Case for National Action.* Washington DC: U.S. Department of Labor, 1965.
———. "The Study of Black Families." In Staples, *Black Family*, 18–24.
Mullings, Leith. "Images, Ideology, and Women of Color." In Zinn and Dill, *Women of Color*, 265–90.
Mumford, Kevin. "Harvesting the Crisis: The Newark Uprising, the Kerner Com-

mission, and Writings on Riots." In Kusmer and Trotter, *African American Urban History*, 203–18.

Murphy, Sara Alderman. *Breaking the Silence: Little Rock's Women's Emergency Committee to Open Our Schools, 1958–1963*. Fayetteville: University of Arkansas Press, 1997.

Myrdal, Gunnar. *An American Dilemma: The Negro Problem and Modern Democracy*. Vol. 1. 1944. New York: Pantheon Books, 1962.

Nelson, Deanne. "Mildred Brown." *Omaha Magazine*, November–December 1992.

Olson, James S. *Equality Deferred: Race, Ethnicity, and Immigration in America since 1945*. Belmont CA: Thompson, 2003.

O'Reilly, Kenneth. *Racial Matters: The FBI's Secret File on Black America, 1960–1972*. New York: Free Press, 1989.

Ottley, Roi. *The Lonely Warrior: The Life and Times of Robert S. Abbott*. Chicago: Regnery, 1955.

Pach, Chester, Jr., and Elmo Richardson, *Presidency of Eisenhower*. Lawrence: University Press of Kansas, 1991.

Packard, Jerrold. *American Nightmare: The History of Jim Crow*. New York: St. Martin's Press, 2003.

Pascoe, Peggy. *What Comes Naturally: Miscegenation Law and the Making of Race in America*. New York: Oxford University Press, 2009.

Pattillo, Mary. *Black on the Block: The Politics of Race and Class in the City*. Chicago: University of Chicago Press, 2007.

Paz, Denis G. "The Black Press and the Issues of Race, Politics, and Culture on the Great Plains of Nebraska, 1865–1985." In Suggs, *Black Press*, 213–42.

Peiss, Kathy. *Hope in a Jar: The Making of America's Beauty Culture*. New York: Holt, 1998.

Peterson, Garneth, ed. *Patterns on the Landscape: Heritage Conservation in North Omaha*. Omaha NE: Klopp, 1984.

Phillips, Kimberley L. *AlabamaNorth: African-American Migrants, Community, and Working-Class Activism in Cleveland, 1915–1945*. Chicago: University of Illinois Press, 1999.

Polikoff, Alexander. *Waiting for Gautreaux: A Story of Segregation, Housing, and the Black Ghetto*. Evanston IL: Northwestern University Press, 2006.

Polk, Ralph Lane. *Polk's Chicago Summer, 1929 City Directory*. Southfield MI: Polk, 1929.

———. *Polk's Des Moines and Polk County, Iowa, City Directory, 1931, 1932*. Des Moines: Polk, 1932.

———. *Polk's Omaha Douglas County, Nebraska, City Directory, 1938*. Omaha NE: Polk, 1939.

———. *Polk's Omaha (Douglas County, Nebraska) City Directory, 1940*. Omaha NE: Polk, 1941.
———. *Polk's Sioux City (Woodbury County, Iowa), City Directory, 1934*. Detroit: Polk, 1934.
———. *Polk's Sioux City (Woodbury County, Iowa) City, Directory, 1936*. Omaha NE: Polk, 1936.
———. *Polk's Sioux City (Woodbury County, Iowa), City Directory, 1937*. Omaha NE: Polk, 1937.
Pollak, Oliver. *Jewish Life in Omaha and Lincoln: A Photographic History*. Chicago: Arcadia, 2001.
Pride, Armistead, and Clint Wilson II. *A History of the Black Press*. Washington DC: Howard University Press, 1997.
Radford-Hill, Sheila. *Further to Fly: Black Women and the Politics of Empowerment*. Minneapolis: University of Minnesota Press, 2000.
Rainwater, Lee, and William Yancey. *The Moynihan Report and the Politics of Controversy*. Cambridge: MIT Press, 1967.
Reilly, Bob. "It Has Been the Few Who Have Acted, Who Have Saved Us from Unspeakable Scandal." *Creighton University Window*, Winter 1995–96.
Rice, Jon. "The World of Illinois Panthers." In *Freedom North: Black Freedom Struggles Outside the South, 1940–1980*, edited by Jeanne Theoharis and Komozi Woodward, 41–64. New York: Palgrave, 2003.
Roberts, Gene, and Hank Klibanoff. *The Race Beat: The Press, the Civil Rights Struggle, and the Awakening of a Nation*. New York: Knopf, 2006.
Robertson, Nancy Marie. *Christian Sisterhood, Race Relations, and the YWCA, 1906–1946*. Chicago: University of Illinois Press, 2007.
Robinson, Charles Frank, II. *Dangerous Liaisons: Sex and Love in the Segregated South*. Fayetteville: University of Arkansas Press, 2003.
Robnett, Belinda. *How Long? How Long? African-American Women in the Struggle for Civil Rights*. Oxford: Oxford University Press, 1997.
Sandweiss, Martha. *Passing Strange: A Gilded Age Tale of Love and Deception across the Color Line*. New York: Penguin Books, 2010.
Scranton, Philip. *Beauty and Business: Commerce, Gender, and Culture in Modern America*. New York: Routledge, 2001.
Self, Robert O. *American Babylon: Race and the Struggle for Postwar Oakland*. Princeton: Princeton University Press, 2003.
Senna, Carl. *The Black Press and the Struggle for Civil Rights*. New York: Watts, 1993.
Shaw, Stephanie. *What a Woman Ought to Be and Do: Black Professional Women Workers during the Jim Crow Era*. Chicago: University of Chicago Press, 1996.
Simmons, Charles A. *The African American Press with Special Reference to Four Newspapers, 1827–1965*. Jefferson NC: McFarland, 1998.

Sitkoff, Harvard. *A New Deal for Blacks: The Emergence of Civil Rights as a National Issue; The Depression Decade.* New York: Oxford University Press, 1978.
———. *Struggle for Black Equality.* New York: Hill and Wang, 2008.
Smith, Alonzo. *Black Nebraskans: The Nebraska Black Oral History Project.* Omaha NE: Black Studies Department, 1984.
Smith, Hattie Matlock. "The Good, the Bad and the Ugly Were All on 24th Street!" *Dreamland: The Rich Legacy of African Americans in Omaha* 1, no. 1 (2006).
Smith, Jeffrey. *From Corps to Core: The Life of John P. Markoe; Soldier, Priest and Pioneer Activist.* Florissant MO: Saint Stanislaus, 1977.
———. "The Omaha De Porres Club." Master's thesis, University of Nebraska at Omaha, 1967.
———. "The Omaha De Porres Club." *Negro History Bulletin* 33, no. 8 (1970): 194–99.
Smithson, Joyce E. "The *Omaha Star*: Its Main Concerns." Master's thesis, Kansas State University, 1972.
Spencer, Jeffrey. *Historic Photos of Omaha.* Nashville: Turner, 2007.
Stalvey, Lois Mark. *The Education of a WASP.* New York: Morrow, 1970.
Staples, Robert, ed. *The Black Family: Essays and Studies.* Belmont CA: Wadsworth, 1999.
State of Alabama Center for Health Statistics. *Index of Vital Records for the State of Alabama: Deaths, 1908–1959.* Montgomery AL: State of Alabama Center for Health Statistics, Record Services Division.
Stevens, John. "World War II and the Black Press." In *Perspectives of the Black Press: 1974*, edited by Henry La Brie III. Kennebunkport ME: Mercer House, 1974.
Stewart, Maria W. "Throw Off Your Fearfulness and Come Forth." In Lerner, *Black Women*, 526–30.
Strain, Christopher. *Pure Fire: Self-Defense as Activism in the Civil Rights Era.* Athens: University of Georgia Press, 2005.
Streitmatter, Rodger. *Raising Her Voice: African-American Women Journalists Who Changed History.* Lexington: University Press of Kentucky, 1994.
Suggs, Henry Lewis, ed. *The Black Press in the Middle West, 1865–1985.* Westport CT: Greenwood, 1996.
Sugrue, Thomas. *The Origins of the Urban Crisis: Race and Inequality in Postwar Detroit.* Princeton: Princeton University Press, 1996.
———. *Sweet Land of Liberty: The Forgotten Struggle for Civil Rights in the North.* New York: Random House, 2008.
Sullivan, Patricia. *Days of Hope: Race and Democracy in the New Deal Era.* Chapel Hill: University of North Carolina Press, 1996.

Szmrecsanyi, Stephen E. *History of the Catholic Church in Northeast Nebraska: Phenomenal Growth from Scannell to Bergan (1891–1969)*. Omaha NE: Interstate, 1983.

Taeuber, Karl, and Alma Taeuber. *Residential Segregation and Neighborhood Change*. New Brunswick NJ: Aldine Transaction, 2009.

Taylor, Marion M. "A Survey of Employer Attitudes toward the Employment of Qualified Negroes in White Collar Positions in Omaha." Master's thesis, University of Nebraska at Omaha, 1954.

Thailing, Dick. *1979 Consumer Preference Study: September 1978 Survey Results*. Omaha NE: Omaha World-Herald, 1979.

Theoharis, Jeanne, and Komozi Woodward, eds. *Freedom North: Black Freedom Struggles Outside the South, 1940–1980*. New York: Palgrave, 2003.

———. eds. *Groundwork: Local Black Freedom Movements in America*. New York: New York University Press, 2005.

Thompson, Liddie M. "Blocks and Robbers: An Analysis of the Frequency of Robbery on Public Housing Blocks and on Blocks Adjacent to Public Housing Blocks in Omaha, Nebraska." Master's thesis, University of Nebraska at Omaha, 2007.

Trotter, Joe William, Jr. *Black Milwaukee: The Making of an Industrial Proletariat, 1915–45*. Chicago: University of Illinois Press, 1985.

Tyson, Timothy. *Radio Free Dixie: Robert F. Williams and the Roots of Black Power*. Chapel Hill: University of North Carolina Press, 1999.

Urban League of Nebraska. *State of Black Omaha, 1984*. Omaha NE: Urban League of Nebraska.

———. *The State of Black Omaha: 1989, Economic Development and Employment, Education*. Omaha NE: Center for Applied Urban Research, 1989.

U.S. Department of Commerce, Bureau of the Census. *Eleventh Census of the United States, 1890*. Washington DC: GPO, 1891.

———. *Fifteenth Census of the United States*. Vol. 3, *Population*. Part 1, *Composition of Population for Cities over 10,000 and More, 1930*. Washington DC: GPO, 1931.

———. *Fifteenth Census of the United States*. Vol. 3, *Population*. Part 2, *Reports by States, Showing the Composition and Characteristics of the Population for Counties, Cities, and Townships or Other Minor Civil Divisions, Montana-Wyoming, 1930*. Washington DC: GPO, 1932.

———. *Fourteenth Census of the United States, 1920*. Washington DC: GPO, 1921.

———. *Negroes in the United States, 1920–1932*. Washington DC: GPO, 1935.

———. *Sixteenth Census of the United States, 1940*. Vol. 2, *Population*. Part 4, *Minnesota–New Mexico*. Washington DC: GPO, 1943.

———. *Sixteenth Census of the United States, 1940*. Vol. 3, *The Labor Force*. Washington DC: GPO, 1943.

———. *Tenth Census of the United States, 1881*. Washington DC: GPO, 1881.
———. *Thirteenth Census of the United States, 1910*. Washington DC: GPO, 1911.
———. *Twelfth Census of the United States, 1900*. Washington DC: GPO, 1901.
———. *Twentieth Census of the United States, 1980*. Vol. 2, *Population and Housing*. Washington DC: GPO, 1981.
U.S. National Advisory Commission on Civil Disorders. *Kerner Report*. New York: Pantheon Books, 1988.
Walker, Susannah. "Black Is Profitable: The Commodification of the Afro, 1960–1975." In Scranton, *Beauty and Business*, 254–77.
———. *Style and Status: Selling Beauty to African American Women, 1920–1975*. Lexington: University Press of Kentucky, 2007.
Wallace, Michelle. *Black Macho and the Myth of Superwoman*. New York: Verso, 1990.
Washburn, Patrick. *The African American Newspaper: Voice of Freedom*. Evanston IL: Northwestern University Press, 2006.
Washington, Booker T. *Up from Slavery*. 1901. Oxford: Oxford University Press, 1995.
Webb, Samuel L. *Two-Party Politics in the One-Party South: Alabama's Hill Country, 1874–1920*. Tuscaloosa: University of Alabama Press, 1997.
Weston, Jeanette. "In Search of Parity: Coverage of News Events Portraying Blacks in the *Omaha World-Herald*, from 1953–1988." Master's thesis, University of Nebraska at Omaha, 1993.
Wexler, Laura. *Tender Violence: Domestic Visions in an Age of U.S. Imperialism*. Chapel Hill: University of North Carolina Press, 2000.
White, Deborah Gray. *Ar'n't I a Woman? Female Slaves in the Plantation South*. New York: Norton, 1985.
———. *Too Heavy a Load: Black Women in Defense of Themselves, 1894–1994*. New York: Norton, 1999.
Wiese, Andrew. *Places of Their Own: African American Suburbanization in the Twentieth Century*. Chicago: University of Chicago Press, 2004.
Wilkerson, Frank. "The Impact of the Urban League on a Community." Master's thesis, Municipal University of Omaha, 1953.
Wilkins, Roy. *Standing Fast: The Autobiography of Roy Wilkins*. New York: Da Capo, 1982.
Wisch, Robyn. "Unnecessary Violence." *Reader*, June 25, 2009.
Wolcott, Victoria. *Remaking Respectability: African American Women in Interwar Detroit*. Chapel Hill: University of North Carolina Press, 2001.
Wolseley, Roland E. *The Black Press, USA*. 1971. Ames: Iowa State University Press, 1990.

Woodward, C. Vann. *The Strange Career of Jim Crow*. New York: Oxford University Press, 1974.
Wormser, Richard. *The Rise and Fall of Jim Crow*. New York: St. Martin's Press, 2003.
Wright, Richard. *12 Million Black Voices*. New York: Thunder's Mouth, 1941.
Zinn, Maxine Baca, and Bonnie Thornton Dill, eds. *Women of Color in U.S. Society*. Philadelphia: Temple University Press, 1994.

INTERVIEWS BY AUTHOR

Adams, Michael. Director of Affirmative Action and Equal Opportunity and Diversity, University of California, San Francisco. San Francisco CA. February 10, 2009.
Armstrong, Robert. Former Omaha Housing Authority director. Omaha NE. September 25, 2008; October 6, 2008; October 20, 2008.
Artison, Richard. Retired FBI agent. Omaha NE. September 28, 2008.
Baker, Gail. Dean of the School of Communication, University of Nebraska at Omaha. Omaha NE. March 2, 2009.
Banks, La Veeda. Former Malone AME Church member. Pinole CA. November 25, 2008; February 8, 2009.
Battiste, Andre. Great-nephew of Mildred Brown. Stuttgart, Germany. September 25, 2008; September 30, 2008; October 5, 2008; January 22, 2009.
Battiste, Kathryn. Niece of Mildred Brown. Munster IN. October 1, 2008; October 11, 2008; October 22, 2008.
Beermann, Allen. Former Nebraska secretary of state. Lincoln NE. December 18, 2008.
Bell, J. C. Elderly resident. Northern Omaha NE. May 2, 2009.
Benning, Don. First black head coach at a predominantly white university in the United States. Omaha NE. February 20, 2006.
Blumkin, Louis. Chairman of Nebraska Furniture Mart. Omaha NE. September 20, 2008; April 13, 2009.
Blumkin, Ronald. President of Nebraska Furniture Mart. Omaha NE. September 20, 2008; April 13, 2009.
Bodnar, Robert. Former Durham Western Heritage curator. Omaha NE. June 12, 2007.
Bonner, Della. Former northern Omaha activist. Omaha NE. December 7, 2008.
Borders, Druella Windham. Second cousin of Mildred Brown. Fairfield AL. December 12, 2008; May 25, 2009; June 10, 2009.
Boyle, Mike. Former Omaha mayor (1981–87). Omaha NE. October 16, 2008.
Breeding, William Taylor, III. Second cousin of Mildred Brown. Nashville TN. September 26, 2008; October 5, 2008; May 25, 2009; June 6, 2009.

Brockman, Deborah. Family Housing Advisor Services employee. Omaha NE. November 11, 2008.
Brooks, Walter. Former *Omaha Star* writer. Omaha NE. September 29, 2007.
Brown, Bennie Drew, Jr. Nephew of Mildred Brown. Chicago IL. August 6, 2008; September 1, 2008; September 19, 2008; September 25, 2008; September 27, 2008; October 30, 2008; November 29, 2008; January 29, 2009; July 5, 2012.
Brown, Pat. Northern Omaha resident. Omaha NE. July 21, 2006.
Brown, William Andrew, Jr. Attorney and nephew of Mildred Brown. Los Angeles CA. October 14, 2008.
Bryant, Paul. Wesley House executive director. Omaha NE. October 31, 2008; November 7, 2008; December 5, 2008.
Buglewicz, Bob. Douglas County engineer. Omaha NE. March 24, 2009.
Bunting, Deborah. Nebraska Arts Council Heritage Arts manager. Omaha NE. July 21, 2008.
Burkhalter, Lillian. Owner of JB's Beauty Salon. Omaha NE. May 21, 2009.
Cain, Don. Former northern Omaha resident. Los Angeles CA. September 11, 2008; May 3, 2009.
Calloway, Bertha. Former *Omaha Star* employee and founder of the Great Plains Black History Museum. Omaha NE. March 9, 2009; May 4, 2009; June 17, 2009.
Calloway, Earl. Retired *Chicago Defender* newspaper Fine Arts editor. Chicago IL. December 2, 2008.
Carter, Ernest. Former *Omaha Star* newspaper carrier. Omaha NE. August 3, 2008.
Carter, Naomi. Former *Omaha Star* secretary. Omaha NE. August 25, 2007.
Chandler, Virgil. Near North Side resident. Omaha NE. February 8, 2009.
Chapman, Clinton. Retired Washington attorney. He and his late wife were close friends of Mildred Brown. Silver Springs MD. November 12, 2008.
Christian, Evie. Former *Omaha World-Herald* journalist. Omaha NE. July 21, 2009.
Clare, Truman. Mildred Brown's lawyer. Saint Petersburg FL. February 21, 2009; May 2, 2009; May 5, 2009.
Conley, Fred. Former Omaha city council member. Currently on Metropolitan Community College Board of Governors. Omaha NE. August 15, 2007.
Cornelius, Samuel. Former vice president of the NAACP. Currently United Black Fund director. Washington DC. December 2, 2008.
Crittendon, Imogene. Director of Academic Records, Miles (Memorial) College. Fairfield AL. May 28, 2009.
Daniels, Peggy Wright. Daughter of Margaret Wright, Mildred Brown's dressmaker. Phoenix AZ. February 25, 2009.
Daub, Harold "Hal." Former U.S. House representative (1981–89) and Omaha mayor (1995–2001). Currently an attorney. Omaha NE. January 16, 2009.

Davis, Joan Adams. Granddaughter of Senator John Adams. Los Angeles CA. February 10, 2009.

Davis, Rosalyn Gilbert. Daughter of Shirley Edward Gilbert, first husband of Mildred Brown. Florence MO. October 28, 2008.

Davis, Tommie. Son of Anna Ruth Davis, one of Mildred Brown's close friends. Diamond Head MS. March 10, 2009.

Dennis, Emmett. Former activist and northern Omaha resident. Willingboro NJ. August 1, 2008.

De Sousa, Juanita King. Former *Omaha Star* employee. Pacoima CA. March 27, 2009.

Dow, Harold. CBS News correspondent. New York. August 6, 2009.

ElBashir, Joellen. Curator of the Manuscript Division of the Moorland-Spingarn Research Center, Howard University. Washington DC. May 26, 2010.

Eure, Darryl. Son of De Porres Club member Dorothy Eure. Director of Youth to Build. Omaha NE. October 30, 2008; February 12, 2009.

Eure, Harry. Son of De Porres Club member Dorothy Eure. Omaha NE. May 14, 2009.

Fletcher, Katherine. Retired principal of Omaha's Kellom Elementary School. Omaha NE. June 10, 2007.

Fowalkes, Katie. Retired secretary at Birmingham's Carrie Tuggle Elementary School. Birmingham AL. February 27, 2009.

Foxall, Gwendolyn. Daughter of Pitmon Foxall, Omaha's first black police officer. Arlington VA. August 30, 2008.

Foxall, Pitmon. Great-nephew of Pitmon Foxall and deputy police chief of the Omaha Police Department. Omaha NE. August 26, 2008.

Franke, Warren. University of Nebraska at Omaha professor. Omaha NE. February 6, 2009.

Frazier, Beverly. First black cashier at Skaggs Drugstore on the Near North Side. Omaha NE. August 31, 2009.

Galloway, Julia Sanford. Former *Omaha Guide* secretary. Omaha NE. December 19, 2008; December 29, 2008.

Gilbert, Shirl Edward. Son of Shirley Edward Gilbert. Currently superintendent of Recovery Schools. Baton Rouge LA. October 9, 2008; October 19, 2008; October 26, 2008.

Glen, Jesse. Wife of first black disc jockey in Omaha. Las Vegas NV. March 26, 2009.

Glenn, Dorothy. Former owner of *American Record* newspaper. Plattsmouth NE. October 11, 2008.

Godfrey, Archie. Retired business consultant. Omaha NE. November 20, 2008; November 24, 2008.

Goodwin, Alvin. President of Omaha Economic Development Corporation. Omaha NE. September 16, 2008.

Gottschalk, John. Retired chief executive officer and publisher of the *Omaha World-Herald*. Omaha NE. November 20, 2007; December 20, 2007.

Gray, Ben. Omaha city council member, District 2. Omaha NE. May 2, 2009; August 6, 2009.

Grice, Carolyn. Daughter of Alfred Grice, second black real estate agent in Nebraska. Currently Omaha Public Schools teacher. Omaha NE. December 11, 2009; December 18, 2009.

Gross, Robert. Retired Brandeis manager. Omaha NE. December 7, 2008.

Hall, Charles. Near North Side businessperson. Omaha NE. June 19, 2009.

Hannah, Harriet. Mother of William Brown Jr., nephew of Mildred Brown. Tuskegee AL. October 5, 2008.

Harrison, Shirley. Former *Omaha Star* employee. Omaha NE. July 29, 2008.

Harrold, Madeline. Daughter of eyewitness at the Omaha Riot of 1919. Currently retired Brandeis employee. Omaha NE. November 14, 2008.

Hart, Jim. Near North Side attorney. Omaha NE. February 19, 2009.

Hewins-Maroney, Barbara. University of Nebraska at Omaha professor. Omaha NE. July 11, 2008.

Hicks, Edgar. FC stone broker. Omaha NE. August 9, 2007; August 12, 2007.

Hicks, Phyllis. *Omaha Star* marketing director. Omaha NE. August 3, 2008.

Hogan, Buddy. Former Omaha City Relations director. Los Angeles CA. March 8, 2009; March 18, 2009.

Hogan, Wilma. Former Near North Side resident. Los Angeles CA. March 18, 2009.

Holland, Matt. Son of Denny Holland, president of the De Porres Club. Omaha NE. July 18, 2008.

Hughes, Cathy. Former *Omaha Star* employee. Currently owner of Radio One. Washington DC. August 3, 2007; August 7, 2007; December 3, 2008.

Humphrey, Hubert "Skip," III. Son of U.S. vice president Hubert Horatio Humphrey. Minneapolis MN. October 9, 2008.

Jack, Champer. Omaha Elks Lodge member. Omaha NE. May 5, 2009.

Johns, Karen. Daughter of Bernice Grice, Omaha Public Schools teacher. Currently an Omaha Public Schools teacher. Omaha NE. December 29, 2009.

Johnson, Annette Davis. Daughter of Anna Ruth Davis, close friend of Mildred Brown. Retired school nurse. Omaha NE. April 25, 2009.

Keller, Royce. Former *Omaha Star* salesperson and air force colonel. Baltimore MD. November 8, 2008; November 9, 2008; November 11, 2008; November 16, 2008.

Kellogg, Kenneth. Informal grandson of Mildred Brown. Atlanta GA. August 8, 2009; August 19, 2009.

Kellogg, Marvin, Jr. Informal grandson of Mildred Brown. Omaha NE. April 22, 2009; August 26, 2009.
Kellogg, Marvin, Sr. Informal son-in-law of Mildred Brown. Omaha NE. November 11, 2008; November 25, 2008; December 2, 2008; December 12, 2008; March 15, 2009.
Kyle, J. Timothy. Attorney and great-grandson of Oceola Kyle, Millard Breeding's lawyer. Decatur AL. July 23, 2009.
Leavell, Dorothy. Publisher of the *Gary Crusader* newspaper and historian of the National Newspaper Publishers Association. Chicago IL. October 31, 2008.
Lincoln, Joan McCaw. Daughter of Arthur McCaw, Nebraska's first black treasurer. Los Angeles CA. April 13, 2009; April 19, 2009.
Loder, James L. Officer involved in the death of Vivian Strong, which started the Omaha riot of 1969. Omaha NE. October 16, 2010.
Love, Portia. Daughter of Preston Love Sr. Los Angeles CA. September 5, 2008.
Love, Preston, Jr. Son of Preston Love Sr. Omaha NE. May 23, 2007.
Mason, David. Son of Avoca "Scoop" Mason, *Omaha Star* writer. Columbia MD. November 20, 2008.
McCaslin, Jack. Former pastor of the Holy Ghost Church. Currently Omaha Archdiocese priest. Omaha NE. September 11, 2008.
McClarity, Marvin. Founder of the Midwest Guardians (black police officer division of the Omaha Police Department). Omaha NE. July 22, 2009.
McCullough, Dorsey. Retired pastor of Saint John AME (Mildred Brown's church). Stockton CA. July 20, 2009; July 21, 2009.
McMillan, Helen. Daughter of Aaron McMillan, Nebraska's first black legislator. Los Angeles CA. May 13, 2009.
McSwain, Erven. City of Omaha Human Rights and Relations investigator. Omaha NE. April 3, 2010.
Menyweather-Woods, Larry "L. C." Retired University of Nebraska at Omaha professor. Winston Salem NC. June 2, 2007.
Monahon, Mary Jo. Retired Omaha Public Schools teacher. Currently Boys Town head librarian. Omaha NE. July 11, 2008.
Mosley Morrow, Juanita. De Porres Club member. Omaha NE. September 5, 2008.
Mudd, Mary. Retired University of Nebraska at Omaha vice chancellor for Student Services and Enrollment. Omaha NE. August 25, 2008.
Myers, Laurence Kenneth. Co-owner of Myers Funeral Home. Omaha NE. November 8, 2008.
Newbill, Mary Beth. Reference librarian at Birmingham Public Library. Birmingham AL. June 11, 2009.
Parks, Charles. Northern Omaha activist. Omaha NE. September 16, 2008.
Parks, Mary Green. First *Omaha Star* secretary. Omaha NE. July 21, 2008; July 31,

2008; February 6, 2009.

Parr, Bill. Former *Omaha Star* newspaper carrier. Hollywood CA. March 27, 2009; March 29, 2009.

Partridge, Bob. Near North Side resident. Omaha NE. February 28, 2009.

Peak, Frank. Creighton Community Outreach Services administrator. Omaha NE. August 5, 2008.

Pearson, Herman. Metropolitan Community College instructor. Omaha NE. February 6, 2009.

Peterson, Garneth. Former city of Omaha planner. Currently Minnesota Department of Transportation historian. Saint Paul MN. April 18, 2009.

Pettey, Rick. Owner of the Breeding family homestead. Decatur AL. July 8, 2009.

Phillips, Catherine Algernon Pryor. Mildred Brown's sister-in-law. Walnut CA. October 12, 2008; March 4, 2010.

Pierce, John. Creighton Affirmative Action director. Omaha NE. July 22, 2008.

Pitts, Sally. Stepmother of William Brown, nephew of Mildred Brown. Louisville KY. October 22, 2008.

Reaves, William. Former Great Plains Black History Museum maintenance worker. Omaha NE. November 5, 2008.

Redden, Oscar. Former *Omaha Star* newspaper carrier. Omaha NE. September 18, 2008.

Reeve, Garth, Sr. Publisher of *Miami Times* newspaper. Miami FL. December 18, 2008; March 26, 2009.

Reinhardt Jeff. *New Horizons* magazine writer. Omaha NE. June 13, 2009.

Reynolds, Everett. Retired pastor of Lefler United Methodist Church. Omaha NE. November 20, 2008.

Rhodes, Herbert. President of American Harvest Company. Omaha NE. March 21, 2009; March 31, 2009.

Rigby, Elaine. Northern Omaha resident. Omaha NE. February 24, 2009.

Rodgers, Bob. Former *Omaha Star* sportswriter. Kansas City MO. July 23, 2008.

Rucker, Charles. Former Creighton University associate dean. Omaha NE. November 7, 2008.

Sales, Lorraine. Former member of the Urban League Guild. Omaha NE. November 6, 2008.

Samuels, Robert. Former *Omaha Star* photographer. Omaha NE. August 11, 2007; October 6, 2007.

Schuerman, Norbert. Retired Omaha Public Schools superintendent (1983–97). Omaha NE. June 16, 2009; June 19, 2009.

Shaw, Beverly. Daughter of Bertha Calloway. Omaha NE. August 31, 2009.

Shelton, Reba. First cousin of Mildred Brown. Everett WA. January 25, 2009; February 20, 2009; March 13, 2009; June 13, 2009; July 8, 2011.

Shores-Martin, Barbara. Close friend of the Breeding and Brown families. Birmingham AL. September 27, 2008.
Simpson, Bradley. Salesperson at Omaha's Forest Lawn Cemetery. Omaha NE. July 14, 2009.
Smith, Alonzo. Former University of Nebraska at Omaha professor. Washington DC. April 27, 2009.
Smith, Dorothy. Northern Omaha resident. Omaha NE. March 8, 2009.
Smith, Jeffrey Harrison. Bellevue University professor. Omaha NE. June 15, 2009.
Smith, John B., Sr. Chair of the National Newspaper Publishers Association. Atlanta GA. November 2, 2008.
Smith, Rudy. Retired *Omaha World-Herald* photographer. Omaha NE. August 27, 2005; October 24, 2007; October 23, 2008.
Spencer, Charlene. *Omaha Star* employee. Omaha NE. September 22, 2008; October 21, 2008.
Stark, Agnes. De Porres Club member. Omaha NE. February 1, 2009.
Stephenson, Wilda. Retired Omaha Public Schools teacher. Cincinnati OH. July 21, 2008.
Stowdarski, Korea. Sister of Katherine Fletcher. Washington DC. June 10, 2007.
Suttle, James. Former HDR engineer for the Martin Luther King Jr. Expressway. Current Omaha mayor. Omaha NE. August 29, 2009.
Taylor, Warren. Retired Lothrop Elementary School principal. Omaha NE. September 23, 2008; December 5, 2008.
Thomas, Ruth. Co-owner of Thomas Funeral Home. Omaha NE. December 4, 2008; February 24, 2009; February 25, 2009.
Turner, Rusty. Owner of Sherman Apartments (Trans-Mississippi Exposition building). Omaha NE. April 11, 2008; August 13, 2008.
Tyler, Carl. Northern Omaha resident. Omaha NE. August 9, 2007.
Vavrina, Kenneth. Pastor of Saint Benedict the Moor Church. Omaha NE. August 7, 2008.
Vogel, Robert. Retired publisher of the *Philadelphia Tribune* newspaper. Philadelphia PA. November 6, 2008; November 25, 2009.
Waites, Luigi. Northern Omaha musician. Omaha NE. January 15, 2009.
Walker-Webster, Linda. Historian of Saint Paul Church in Des Moines. Des Moines IA. July 2, 2009.
Washington, Marguerita. Owner of the *Omaha Star* newspaper. Omaha NE. June 15, 2005; September 26, 2006; September 29, 2006; August 7, 2009; May 24, 2009.
Wead, Rodney. Former *Omaha Star* newspaper carrier. Currently Forest Park Community College professor. Saint Louis MO. July 7, 2008.
Westbrook, Floyd. Near North Side Omaha businessperson. Omaha NE. August 6, 2008.

Wetzel, Bob. *Omaha Star* accountant. Omaha NE. August 20, 2009.
White, Corinne. Near North Side resident. Omaha NE. March 17, 2009.
Wilson, Tommie. Retired Omaha NAACP president. Omaha NE. August 1, 2008.
Winton, David. Sixth cousin of Mildred Brown. Nashville TN. August 13, 2008; January 8, 2009; January 22, 2009; January 27, 2009; May 25, 2009; May 28, 2009.
Wirth, Eileen. Creighton University dean of journalism. Omaha NE. June 22, 2009.
Wright, Willard. Son of Margaret Wright, Mildred Brown's dressmaker. Lincoln CA. February 21, 2009.
Young, Joyce. Former *Omaha Star* secretary. Charlotte NC. August 3, 2008.
Young, Sharon. Former *Omaha Star* secretary. Omaha NE. July 15, 2007.
Zacharia, Laurence. Mildred Brown's physician. Omaha NE. March 27, 2009.

Index

Abbott, Robert, 74, 84, 92
Adams, John, 55
Adams, Michael, 52, 65, 66
advertisements: activism's impact on, 121, 137, 150, 151; in black newspapers, 85, 89–90; for *Omaha Guide*, 50; for *Omaha Star*, 93–99
African Methodist Episcopalian Church (AME), 16, 35
Afro-American Sentinel, 86
Afro hairstyle, 71
Alabama Constitutional Convention (1901–2), 31–32
Alabama Hill Country, 24–25, 30–32
Althouse Beauty Salon, 71
Amos 'n' Andy radio show, 64
Andersen, Harold "Andy," 1, 93–94
appearance: of Mildred Brown, 91; and politics of respectability, 67–74
Armstrong, Robert, 96, 99, 129, 153
Artison, Richard, 48, 118
As Long as They Don't Move Next Door (Meyer), 109–10

Banks, Eloise, 98
Banks, La Veeda, 38–39
Barnett, Ferdinand L., 86, 192n6
Bass, Charlotta, 84–85, 192n3
Bass, Joseph, 84
Bates, Daisy, 137
Battiste, Kathy Brown, 70, 74, 171
Bell, Cyrus D., 86

Bergan, Gerald, 104
Bethune, Mary McLeod, 66–67
Biddle, Francis, 88
Black Belters, 32
black matriarch, 13, 64–65, 76–78; Brown as, 2, 17; and politics of respectability, 59–60
Black Panther Party for Self-Defense, 13, 144, 154–55
black power movement, 13, 144, 146–48
black press: advertising in, 85, 89–90; in civil rights struggle, 150; function and influence of, 85–88, 90; government surveillance of, 9–10, 88–89; Mildred Brown on future of, 177; Mildred Brown's contributions to, 92; negro press and, 90
black women: child rearing and, 64–65; empowerment of, 13, 68, 71, 75–76, 78; as journalists and publishers, 83, 84–85, 98–99; stereotypes of, 63–64; work for, 49, 73, 136
Blumkin, Louis, 98
Blumkin, Ronald, 153–54
Blumkin, Rose, 98, 153
Booker T. Washington Club, 39, 186n36
boycotting. *See* consumer campaigns
Breeding, Aggy, 23
Breeding, Annie. *See* Owens, Annie Breeding
Breeding, David, 23

233

Breeding, Gus Edward, 21, 25–26, 32
Breeding, Henry Drew, 33
Breeding, James, 21, 27–28, 31
Breeding, John, 27, 28, 178
Breeding, Maggie Dreweather, 33–37, 186n39
Breeding, Mary Elizabeth Curry Jackson, 32–33, 34
Breeding, Millard William: education of, 25–26; following *Breeding v. Breeding*, 32–33; segregation and, 3–4; as William Breeding's coexecutor, 27; as William Breeding's heir, 21, 22, 28, 31
Breeding, Samuel, 23–24, 178
Breeding, Sopharina, 3, 21–25, 178
Breeding, Telitha Winton, 23
Breeding, William: common-law marriage of, 3, 21–22, 24–25; educates children, 25–26; grave of, 178; inheritance of, 23–24; will and estate of, 21, 26–31
Breeding, William Taylor, 21, 25–26, 27
Breeding, Wilson Peter, 21, 25–26
Breeding v. Breeding, 3, 22–23, 32
Brooks, Walter, 120
Brown, Andrew Cato, 8, 35, 180n12
Brown, Benjamin Joshua, 33–35, 36
Brown, Bennie Drew, 34, 63, 73, 172–73, 208n15
Brown, Bennie Jr., 2
Brown, Lila, 70, 173, 208n17
Brown, Maggie Breeding. *See* Breeding, Maggie Dreweather
Brown, Mildred "Millie" Dee: accomplishments of, 1–3; ad sales and, 50, 89–90, 93–99, 121, 137, 150, 151; attends Miles Memorial College, 35; attends Municipal University of Omaha, 76; birth date of, 184n24; black matriarchy and, 64–65, 77–78; buys *Omaha Star* property, 62; and Carnation Ballroom, 78–79, 107; clothing of, 69; corsages and, 51, 69–70, 74, 78, 91, 119; death of, 168–69; divorce of, 61–62; and Douglas County Probate Court case, 172–73; early years of, 34–36; education of, 75–76; estate of, 172–73, 207n9, 208n17; family and ancestry of, 21–37; fashion of, 69–71; funeral of, 169–71; hair of, 70–71; husbands of, 36, 61–62, 63, 78, 84, 157, 167–68; journalism and, 43–44, 83, 92–93; legacy of, 165, 174–78; maternal responsibility of, 65–67, 75, 175–76; ministry of, 83; as *Omaha Star* owner, 51–54, 61, 62, 83–85, 99, 127–28; relocates to Midwest, 5, 37–41; in Sioux City, Iowa, 16, 38–40; successor to, 166–68; teaching career of, 36, 37
Brown, William Andrew (nephew), 74, 171, 173
Brown, William, lynching of, 6–7, 46, 180n7
Brown, Willie "Bill" Andrew (brother), 34, 51, 167
Brownell, Noel Maximilian "Max": death of, 207n13; and death of Mildred Brown, 169; as De Porres Club member, 118; duties of, 78; gambling and, 173–74; infidelity of, 157; meets Mildred Brown, 63; as successor to Mildred Brown, 167–68; works for *Omaha Star*, 65, 66, 171–72
Brown v. Board of Education (1954), 12
Bryant, Paul, 96, 120, 166, 167
Buffalo Chip, 146–47
Bunting, Debra, 66, 99
Burke, Harry, 136–37
Burkhalter, Lillian, 71

California Eagle, 84–85
Calloway, Bertha, 104, 108, 133, 150
Calloway, James, 104
Carmichael, Stokely, 77, 146
Carnation Ballroom, 78–79
Carter, Leonora, 98

Carter, Naomi, 76
Cary, Mary Ann Shadd, 83
Catholics, activism of, 11–12, 103–4, 106
Central High School, 45, 110–11
Chambers, Ernie, 129, 130, 156; and North Freeway petition, 161–62
Cheeks, Jim, 93
Cheeks, Virginia, 61, 62
children: as motivation in community involvement, 75; raising, 64–67; refreshments for church, 38–39. *See also* maternalism; youths
Citizens' Coordinating Committee for Civil Liberties (4CL), 121, 128–32
City of Omaha: acknowledges positive effects of *Omaha Star*, 56; politics of, 145–46; North Freeway construction and, 160–62
Civil Rights Act (1957), 12
civil rights movement: black power and, 147–48; Brown's activism in, 56–57, 85, 178; Congress on Racial Equality and, 114–15; as country-wide action, 12–14; De Porres Club and, 105–9, 121; 4CL and, 129; *Omaha Star*'s coverage of, 149–50; Student Nonviolent Coordinating Committee and, 77
Clare, Truman, 98, 172
class factionalism, 119–20
Coca-Cola bottling company, 111–12
Colored Merchant's Association, 8
Colored Methodist Episcopalian (CME) Church, 26, 182n9
color gradation, 72–74
communism: Charlotta Bass and, 192n3; civil rights activism and, 9–11, 108–9, 111, 115; restrictive housing covenants and, 123; Urban League's Rumor Control Center and, 89
Congress on Racial Equality, 114–15
consumer campaigns, 8–9, 55–56, 102–3, 110, 111–18

CORE (Congress on Racial Equality), 114–15
Corrigan v. Buckle (1926), 124, 125
Countryman, Matthew, 154
Creighton University, 103–4, 105–6, 175

Dalstrom, Harl, 148
Daniels, Peggy Wright, 69
Danner, Edward, 129, 132, 135
Davis, Angela, 147, 185n29
Davis, Charles, 51
Davis, Steve, 92
Davis, Tommie, 93
Decatur, Alabama, 21, 23, 24, 27, 177–78
Dennis, Emmett, 45
Dennison, Tom, 6–7, 50
De Porres Club: activism of, 12, 101–5, 107–8, 109–18; communism and, 108–9; end of, 120–21; Mildred Brown joins forces with, 105–7
discrimination: at Central High School, 110–11; as crime, 107–8; in hiring and employment, 101–4, 110, 111–18; in housing, 109–10, 123–28; Mildred Brown faces, 95, 105; unifying against, 54–55
Dodge, N. P. III, 126
Don't Buy Where You Can't Work campaign, 8–9, 55–56, 102–3, 110, 111–18
Doss, Peter C., 111–12
Double V campaign, 9–10, 88–89
Dragoun, Richard E., 171
Draper, William Ira, 184n27
Dreamland Ballroom, 47
Du Bois, W.E.B., 37
Dunn, George, 109
Dunnaway, S. M., 21, 36
Dworak, James, 130

Edholm-Sherman Laundry, 110
Edmund Pettus Bridge, 12–13
education, as key to empowerment, 75–76

Index 235

employment: activism for black, 7, 101–4, 110, 111–18; of black teachers, 136–38; politics and, 145; and job creation, 52; in mass-production industries, 15–16; in Omaha, 49; for Omaha youths, 65–67; protests against inequality in, 87–88, 149

Enterprise, 86

Eure, Darryl, 93

Eure, Dorothy, 104, 137

European immigrants, 4–5

Evers, Medgar, 12

Fair Housing Act (1968), 14, 135

Federal Bureau of Investigation (FBI), 9–10, 88–89, 109, 112, 114

Federal Housing Administration, 8, 14–15, 47, 48–49

Flanagan, Edward, 11

4CL (Citizens' Coordinating Committee for Civil Liberties), 121, 128–32

Franklin, Ada, 98

Franklin, John Hope, 77

Franklin, S. F., 86

Front-Page Women Journalists, 1920–1950 (Cairns), 84

Galloway, Charles Chapman (C. C.), 40–41, 49–50, 53, 55, 93, 112

Galloway, Julia Sanford, 50

Gamble, Lucinda, 136

Garrison, William Lloyd, 83

gender roles, 77–78

Gibson, Tommie, 184n22

Gilbert, Mildred "Millie" Dee Brown. *See* Brown, Mildred "Millie" Dee

Gilbert, Shirl Edward II, 62

Gilbert, Shirley Edward: An Echo from My Den column of, 50; C. C. Galloway's rivalry with, 53; on consumer boycotting, 56; death of, 167, 206n3; divorce of, 61–62; encourages youth involvement, 54; marries Millie Dee Brown, 36; political aspirations of, 57; as radical, 88; relocates to Midwest, 5, 37–38; in Sioux City, Iowa, 38–40; supports Logan Fontenelle Housing Project, 48

Gilkes, Cheryl Townsend, 75

Godfrey, Archie, 95, 132, 134, 152

Gothard, Mac L., 111, 112

Gottschalk, John, 94

Graham, Hugh Davis, 145

Gray, Ben, 1, 127

Great Migration, 4–6, 37–38, 41, 87, 124

Groppi, James, 103

Hamer, Fannie Lou, 75

Harkert Café, 105

Harrington, Michael, 15, 128

Harris, David Harvey, 39–40, 60

Harris, Ruth Lee. *See* Kellogg, Ruth Lee Harris

Harrison, Shirley, 155, 170

Height, Dorothy, 67, 75

Helms, Jesse Alexander Sr., 74–75

Herman's Grocery, 154

Hewins-Maroney, Barbara, 149–50

Hogan, Buddy, 97, 167

Holland, Denny, 106, 107, 109, 111, 120, 129

Holland, Matt, 165

Hoover, John Edgar, 9–10, 13, 88–89, 179n6

Hope in a Jar (Peiss), 71

horse races, 173–74

Horton, John B., 86

Housing Act (1937), 47

Housing and Urban Development Act (1968), 14

housing discrimination: activism against, 109–10, 123–28; 4CL and, 128–32; legislation concerning, 14–15, 134–36; as means of controlling black spatial mobility, 7–8; in Omaha, 47–49

housing projects, 14–15, 47–49, 143
Hughes, Cathy, 66, 175
Human Relations Committee, 115

Immigration Act (1917), 5
interracial marriage, 3, 21–25, 131–32, 179n2

Jack, Champer, 154
Jackson, Tommie, 183n20, 184n27
Jewell, Jimmy, 46
Jewell Building, 47, 171, 207n12
Jewish immigrants, 11, 46
Jewish storeowners, 46, 145, 154, 155
Jezebel, 63
Jim Crow laws, 3–4
Johnson, Benny, 155
Johnson, Lyndon Baines, 12–13, 14, 148, 152, 202n8
Jones, Catherine, 170
Jones, Kelsey A., 129, 131
journalism: advertising and, 94; black women in, 83, 84–85, 98–99; Brown's views on, 83; *Omaha Star* and, 51, 92–93, 116, 126

Keller, Royce, 94–95, 175, 209n20
Kellogg, Marvin, 45–46, 60–61, 105
Kellogg, Marvin Jr., 167
Kellogg, Ruth Lee Harris, 1, 39–40, 44–46, 60
Kennedy, Robert, 152, 203n15
Kerner Report, 14, 18, 152–53
King, Coretta Scott, 12
King, Martin Luther Jr.: assassination of, 152; Brown as follower of, 144, 148, 174; completes March Against Fear, 146; De Porres Club and, 114; rhetoric and style of, 12
Kountze Place, 123–24, 198n1
Ku Klux Klan, 11, 12
Kyle, J. Timothy, 31, 183nn17,18
Kyle, Oceola, 31, 183n17

La Brie, Henry G. III, 177
Lane, Edward, 51
Leahy, Gene, 155, 156–57
Leavell, Dorothy, 91–92
Lee, James P., 116
Legislative Bill 263, 88
Liberator newspaper, 83
Lincoln, Joan McCaw, 92
Loder, James L., 143, 153, 156, 201n1, 203–4n17
Loebeck, Agnes, 6
Logan Fontenelle Housing Project, 47–48, 143
Love, Preston Sr., 172, 207n13
lynching, 6. *See also* Brown, William, lynching of

Malcolm X, 13, 146
Malec, Joseph Jr., 132, 134
Malone AME Church, 38–39
Mammy, 63–64
March against Fear, 146
Markoe, John: as 4CL member, 129, 131–32; activism of, 12; advancing age of, 120–21; on communism, 108–9; as De Porres Club leader, 102–3, 104; as leader and mentor, 106; Mayor's Human Relations Committee and, 115
marriage, interracial. *See* interracial marriage
maternalism, 64–67, 75, 77–78, 175–76
Matthews, Francis P., 56
McCaslin, Jack, 150–51
McCaw, Arthur, 55, 103
McCullough, Dorsey, 170
McGuire, Peter, 180n7
McNair, Rudolph E., 129
McVoy, Laurence, 127
Melton, Martha, 47
Meredith, James, 146
Meyer, Stephen Grant, 109
Miles Memorial College, 35, 168, 184n28

Index 237

Miliken v. Bradley (1974), 15
Miller, Loren, 128
Miller, Paul, 137–38
Minard, Larry, 204n21
miscegenation laws, 3, 21–23, 131–32, 179n2
Mitchell, Ophelia, 98
Monahon, Mary Jo, 139
Moore, Charlie May, 71
Morgan County, 3, 23–24, 27, 30–32
Morgan, Woodrow, 109–10
Morrow, Samuel M., 26
Moynihan, Daniel, 76–77
Moynihan Report, 13, 77
Mr. C's, 54
Mudd, Mary, 155
Municipal University of Omaha, 75–76
Myrdal, Gunnar, 72, 179n2, 190n22

NAACP, 127, 132–34
National Advisory Commission on Civil Disorders, 14, 152
National Negro Business League, 14
National Newspaper Publishers Association, 90–91, 202n8
National Origins Act (1924), 5
National Youth Administration, 67, 88
Near North Side: boycotts in, 118–19; Brown's dedication to, 85; Brown's legacy in, 18, 66–67, 79, 165; civic and economic improvements for, 113; employment in, 49, 102, 110; housing in, 15, 47–49, 125–26, 128, 130, 134–35; leadership in, 119; North Freeway construction and, 162; *Omaha Star* and, 53, 119–20; reconstruction of, 158–59; riots in, 143–44, 152, 154–55; segregation of, 7–8, 11–12, 109–10; social and economic inequality in, 145; unifying residents of, 57
Nebraska black newspapers, 85–87
Nebraska Furniture Mart, 98

The Negro Family (Moynihan), 13, 77
New Era, 87
Newsom, Horace, 85
1969 Omaha Race Riot, 13–14
NNPA (National Newspaper Publishers Association), 90–91, 202n8
nonviolence: honoring Martin Luther King Jr. through, 152; Mildred Brown endorses, 144, 146, 148
North Freeway, 159–62
North Omaha. *See* Near North Side

Omaha: civic center in, 150–51, 166; employment opportunities in, 49; freeway construction in, 159–62; Gilbert family moves to, 41, 44–45; housing and segregation in, 46–49; reconstruction of, following race riots, 158–59
Omaha city commissioners, 113, 116
Omaha city council, 115
Omaha & Council Bluffs Streetcar Company, 101, 113–17
Omaha Chronicle, 86
Omaha Guide: Brown's employment with, 49–51, 119–20, 188n15; content of, 57; Double Victory campaign and, 9; failure of, 93, 193n17; FBI investigation of, 10; job offer with, 40–41; rivalry with, 43, 52, 53–54, 84, 87
Omaha Housing Authority (OHA), 48, 136
Omaha Monitor, 87
Omaha Police, 105, 133, 148–49, 203n17
Omaha Public School Board, 136–37
Omaha Public Schools, 136–39
Omaha Real Estate Board, 126–27
Omaha Star: as activist tool, 2, 55–57; carriers of, 52, 65–66, 155, 175; content of, 149–52, 156–57; distribution of, 52, 65–66; Family of the Week column in, 53; financial troubles of, 157; function of, 52–55, 57; government surveillance

of, 88; impact of, 176–77; launching of, 43–44, 50–52; Mildred Brown as sole owner of, 61–62; Mildred Brown's successor in, 166–68, 171–72; on National Register of Historic Places, 165; *Omaha Guide*'s rivalry with, 53–54, 87; as *Omaha Star, Inc.*, 171; protected during race riots, 154–55; securing ads for, 93–99; Starite Club and, 54; unpaid youth positions at, 92–93; as voice of black community, 2, 43–44, 88, 139, 161, 165, 176, 178

Omaha World-Herald: Brown challenges stereotypical imagery in, 18; content of, 99, 147, 148, 151, 153, 154–56, 176–77; editorials for, 113; 4CL pickets, 131–32; interviews N. P. Dodge III, 126; and *1979 Consumer Preference Study*, 162; shuts down *South Omaha Sun*, 150, 202–3n11

open housing, 126–31, 134–36

Open Housing Legislative Bill 718, 135

Orr, Kay, 170

othermothering, 64–67, 75, 77–78, 175–76

Overall, Eulalia, 136

Owens, Annie Breeding, 186n39

Parker, George W., 87
Parks, Mary Green, 51, 54–55
Parr, Bill, 65
Partridge, Bob, 66
Pascoe, Peggy, 21–22
passing, 55, 72–73
Peak, Frank, 147–48
Pearson, Herman, 162
Peony Park, 132–34
perfume, 74
Peterson, Harold, 126
Pettey, Christopher, 208n17
Pettey, Richard, 208n17
Phillips, Catherine, 74, 96

Phillips, Wilbur, 149
Pignotti's Donut Shop, 108
Pittsburgh Courier, 4, 9–10, 57, 87
Plessy v. Ferguson (1896), 4
Poindexter, Edward, 154–55, 204n21
politics of respectability: appearance and, 67–71, 74; education and, 75–76; maternalism and, 64–67; Mildred Brown as model for, 60–61, 79; Mildred Brown teaches, 95; origination of, 59–60; skin color gradation and, 72–74

Progress, 86

race riots: during 1960s, 13–14; following assassination of Martin Luther King Jr., 152; following shooting of Vivian Strong, 143–44; during Great Migration, 5–7; Kerner Report on, 152–53; 1969 Omaha Race Riot, 13–14; in Omaha, 148–51, 153–56; politics and, 144–45; reconstruction following, 158–59

racism: activism against, 8–9, 174–75, 176; black matriarchy and, 64, 77–78; at Central High School, 45; De Porres Club's activism against, 103–9, 114–15; division caused by, 14; employment and, 137; estate laws and, 27–31; housing discrimination and, 123–27, 131; Jim Crow laws and, 3–4, 31–32; Omaha race riots and, 148–54; Peony Park segregation and, 132–34; politics of respectability and, 74–75

Randolph, A. Philip, 11
Reconstruction, 2–3, 4, 16, 26–27
red-baiting, 108, 115
redlining, 8, 135–36
Red Scare, 10–11, 108–9
Red Summer (1919), 5–7, 179n6
Reed's Ice Cream Company, 117–18
Reese, Russell, 51

Reeve, Garth Sr., 91
Reinhardt, Jeff, 165–66
Remaking Respectability (Wolcott), 69
A Report on Discrimination in House for Minorities in Omaha, Nebraska, 1965, 134–35
restrictive housing covenants, 123–28
Reynolds, Clemmie, 51
Reynolds, Everett, 65
Rice, David, 146–47, 155, 204n21
Richardson, Gloria, 13
Rigley, Elaine, 53
Robinson, Jackie, 92
Rodgers, Bob, 92, 97, 193n16
Roosevelt, Franklin Delano: assists black newspapers, 89, 90; housing reforms under, 47, 48, 187n11; support for, 86
Rosenblatt, Johnny, 116
Rosewater, Victor, 6
Rucker, Charles, 52, 175–76
Rumor Control Center, 89

Safeway, 148
Saint Benedict Church, 11, 104, 106
Saint John AME Church, 44, 119
Saint Philip Church, 119
Sapphire, 64, 77, 78
schools: desegregation of, 15, 138–39; employment discrimination in, 136–38
Schuerman, Norbert, 15, 138
segregation: in churches, 104; fight against, 10–12; under Jim Crow laws, 4; in Omaha, 46–49, 160; residential, 7–8; in schools, 15, 138–39; of swimming pools, 132–34
Self, Robert, 128
Shelley v. Kraemer (1948), 15, 125
Shelton, Reba, 32, 168, 184n27
Silent Messenger, 16, 40
Skeggs, William E., 21, 30, 34
Skinner, Eugene, 138
Smiley, Glenn, 12

Smith, Hattie Matlock, 46–47
Smith, John B. Sr., 91
Smith, Mercia, 137
Smith, Rudy, 65, 66, 97, 146, 155–56, 167
SNCC (Student Nonviolent Coordinating Committee), 77
social mobility: through passing, 73; through politics of respectability, 68–69
Somerville courthouse, 27, 182n11
Sorensen, Axel Vergman, 145–46, 149, 151
Stalvey, Lois, 125–26
Stephenson, Wilda, 45
stereotypes, of black women, 63–64
Stewart, Maria W., 83
Strong, Carol, 143
Strong, Vivian, 143, 153, 156
Student Nonviolent Coordinating Committee, 77
Sun, 202–3n11
Suttle, James, 161
Swiggart, Warren, 116
Szmrecsanyi, Stephen, 104

Talmadge, Herman, 109
Taylor, Warren, 131, 136
Terry, Lee Sr., 162
Thomas, Ruth, 95–96
Thompson, James G., 9
Trial by Fire (Dunn), 109
Trotter, Joe William, 44
Tuggle, Carrie, 36
Twenty-Fourth Street: businesses on, 46–47; demonstrations on, 106; and Lake Street, 7, 56, 57, 144–46, 165; North Freeway's impact on, 161–62; revitalization of, 158–59; riots on, 154–56
Tyler, Carl, 161

Urban League: Brown's involvement in, 85; challenges O&CB's hiring practices, 113; denounces shooting of Vivian Strong, 156; establishes Rumor Control Center, 89; founding of, 197; politics of respectability and, 59; as Public Mass Meeting sponsor, 149

Vann, Robert, 84, 94, 193n19
Vavrina, Kenneth, 106, 153
Vogel, Robert, 91
voting rights, 12–13, 174

Wagner Housing Act (1937), 47, 188n13
Waite, Jean, 107
Walker, C. J., 70
Wallace, George, 150–52
Walls, Cecile, 51
Washington, Annie "Anna" Lee Brown, 34, 77, 166, 184n27
Washington, Booker T., 86
Washington, Charles, 206n4
Washington, Frederick, 173
Washington, Margaret Murray, 67
Washington, Marguerita, 67, 137, 157, 171–73, 207n13, 208–9n17

Wead, Rodney, 65, 171
Wells, Ida Baker, 191–92n1
Westbrook, Floyd, 97–98
Western Post, 85
White, Corrine, 92–93
White, Deborah Gray, 63
Williams, John Albert, 87
Windham, Annie Breeding Owens, 183n20
Winton, David, 24, 172, 177
Wolcott, Victoria, 69
Wood, Leonard, 6, 7
Woods, Millard T., 56–57
World War I, 5, 7–8, 10
Wright, Margaret, 69

Young, Joyce, 95, 176
youths: activism of, 133–34; unpaid positions for, 92. *See also* children
YWCA (Young Women's Christian Association), 102

Zacharia, Laurence, 63, 168, 184n24
Ziff, W. B. Company, 89, 190n20

In the Women in the West series

When Montana and I Were Young: A Frontier Childhood
By Margaret Bell
Edited by Mary Clearman Blew

Martha Maxwell, Rocky Mountain Naturalist
By Maxine Benson

The Enigma Woman: The Death Sentence of Nellie May Madison
By Kathleen A. Cairns

Front-Page Women Journalists, 1920–1950
By Kathleen A. Cairns

The Cowboy Girl: The Life of Caroline Lockhart
By John Clayton

The Art of the Woman: The Life and Work of Elisabet Ney
By Emily Fourmy Cutrer

Black Print with a White Carnation: Mildred Brown and the "Omaha Star" Newspaper, 1938–1989
By Amy Helene Forss

Emily: The Diary of a Hard-Worked Woman
By Emily French
Edited by Janet Lecompte

The Important Things of Life: Women, Work, and Family in Sweetwater County, Wyoming, 1880–1929
By Dee Garceau

The Adventures of The Woman Homesteader: The Life and Letters of Elinore Pruitt Stewart
By Susanne K. George

Flowers in the Snow: The Life of Isobel Wylie Hutchison, 1889–1982
By Gwyneth Hoyle

Domesticating the West: The Re-creation of the Nineteenth-Century American Middle Class
By Brenda K. Jackson

Engendered Encounters: Feminism and Pueblo Cultures, 1879–1934
By Margaret D. Jacobs

Riding Pretty: Rodeo Royalty in the American West
By Renée Laegreid

The Colonel's Lady on the Western Frontier: The Correspondence of Alice Kirk Grierson
Edited by Shirley A. Leckie

Their Own Frontier: Women Intellectuals Re-Visioning the American West
Edited and with an introduction by Shirley A. Leckie and Nancy J. Parezo

A Stranger in Her Native Land: Alice Fletcher and the American Indians
By Joan Mark

The Blue Tattoo: The Life of Olive Oatman
By Margot Mifflin

So Much to Be Done: Women Settlers on the Mining and Ranching Frontier, second edition
Edited by Ruth B. Moynihan, Susan Armitage, and Christiane Fischer Dichamp

Women and Nature: Saving the "Wild" West
By Glenda Riley

The Life of Elaine Goodale Eastman
By Theodore D. Sargent

Give Me Eighty Men: Women and the Myth of the Fetterman Fight
By Shannon D. Smith

Bright Epoch: Women and Coeducation in the American West
By Andrea G. Radke-Moss

Moving Out: A Nebraska Woman's Life
By Polly Spence
Edited by Karl Spence Richardson

Eight Women, Two Model Ts, and the American West
By Joanne Wilke

To order or obtain more information on these or other University of Nebraska Press titles, visit www.nebraskapress.unl.edu.

www.ingramcontent.com/pod-product-compliance
Lightning Source LLC
Chambersburg PA
CBHW021822300426
44114CB00009BA/285